WILLIAM S. NIXON, ARIBA, AIA.
1985.

THE ARCHITECT'S HANDBOOK

THE ARCHITECT'S HANDBOOK

David Kent Ballast

PRENTICE-HALL, INC. • ENGLEWOOD CLIFFS, NEW JERSEY

Prentice-Hall International, Inc., *London*
Prentice-Hall of Australia, Pty, Ltd., *Sydney*
Prentice-Hall Canada, Inc., *Toronto*
Prentice-Hall of India Private, Ltd., *New Delhi*
Prentice-Hall of Japan, Inc., *Tokyo*
Prentice-Hall of Southeast Asia Pte, Ltd., *Singapore*
Whitehall Books, Ltd., *Wellington, New Zealand*
Editora Prentice-Hall do Brasil Ltda., *Rio de Janeiro*

© 1984 *by*
PRENTICE-HALL, INC.
Englewood Cliffs, N.J.

"This publication is designed to provide accurate and authoritative information in regard to the subject matter covered. It is sold with the understanding that the publisher is not engaged in rendering legal, accounting, or other professional service. If legal advice or other expert assistance is required, the services of a competent professional person should be sought."

—*From the Declaration of Principles jointly adopted by a Committee of the American Bar Association and a Committee of Publishers and Associations.*

Library of Congress Cataloging in Publication Data

Ballast, David Kent.
    The architect's handbook.

    Includes bibliographics and index.
    1. Architectural practice—Handbooks, manuals, etc.
2. Architectural services marketing—Handbooks, manuals,
etc. I. Title.
NA1996.B34   1984   720′.68   83-13795

ISBN 0-13-044677-7

Printed in the United States of America

The Author

David Ballast is a consultant and owner of Architectural Research Consulting, Denver, a firm offering applied research and information services to architects, interior designers, and others in the building industry. In addition to consulting, he teaches part time in the graduate interior design program of the College of Design and Planning at the University of Colorado at Denver.

As a licensed architect, Mr. Ballast has worked in all phases of practice, including interior architecture. Before starting his own firm, he worked for Gensler and Associates, Architects, as a project manager.

The author received a Bachelor of Architecture degree with special honors from the University of Colorado. He is a member of the American Institute of Architects, the Construction Specifications Institute and the Society for Marketing Professional Services.

What This Handbook Will Do For You and Your Architectural Practice

This book offers architects and interior designers practical information on the wide range of business, financial, and management knowledge needed for a profitable and successful practice. Dozens of topics are brought together in a concise, up-to-date reference work giving useful, money-making ideas and solutions to problems facing design professionals. New subjects are also included to provide additional resources to keep you ahead of the competition.

Success requires a balance between good design and sound business administration. Architects and designers often have little training or experience in management. This book fills that gap by summarizing the essential elements of effective business practice. It provides a means for small and large firms alike to evaluate their operational methods, improve efficiency, and increase profits. Hundreds of ideas are assembled in one convenient place to help you realize your full potential. Among other benefits, you will find this book. . .

- Outlines a seven-step strategy for developing a business plan—your custom road map to a better practice immediately as well as over the long term. See Chapter 1.
- Shows how to establish a marketing plan for continued success. Included is a Firm Analysis Checklist, vital for self-evaluation. See Chapter 2.
- Reveals sources for finding leads and researching contacts during your initial marketing efforts. See Chapter 2.
- Explains a simple method for tracking your marketing prospects from initial contact through follow-up. See Chapter 2.
- Explores the rapidly changing field of professional services marketing and presents little-used promotional techniques that can bring in new clients. See Chapter 3.
- Gives practical suggestions on how you can improve your marketing presentations and slide shows. A Pre-Slide Show Checklist accompanies the discussion. See Chapter 3.
- Offers dozens of ideas on how to foster a more creative and productive environment in the office along with ways to eliminate the biggest time-wasters. See Chapter 4.

- Describes methods of encouraging improved design processes and sets forth a graduated program for streamlining construction document production. See Chapter 5.
- Identifies valuable techniques of quality control as a basis for avoiding legal problems *before* they happen. See Chapter 6.
- Provides tips on how to get more from your employees while improving their morale and the work environment. See Chapter 7.
- Lists ways to get the most out of a limited salary and benefits budget. See Chapter 7.
- Clears up the mystery of financial management and shows how to establish a workable program for your office regardless of size. See Chapter 8.
- Puts the subject of overhead in the proper perspective and sets forth a sensible program for reducing unnecessary overhead costs. See Chapter 8.
- Presents straightforward techniques for effective, profit-building project management. See Chapter 9.
- Provides a comprehensive Project Management Task Checklist to guide you through each job. See Chapter 9.
- Demonstrates the power a well-designed graphic system can have on your marketing program. See Chapter 10.
- Shows how to vastly improve your in-house work flow and efficiency with the help of graphic design. See Chapter 10.
- Illustrates the essential elements of setting up an information management system in the office to give you quick access to your resources. See Chapter 11.
- Examines for the first time the untapped potential of commercial computer data bases for use in architectural and design practice. Dozens of available data bases are sorted out to quickly show which are most useful in any phase of professional practice. See Chapter 11.
- Simplifies the confusion surrounding the use of computers and shows how any office, regardless of size, can benefit from these new working tools. See Chapter 12.

In addition to the valuable ideas contained in each chapter, there are dozens of forms, checklists, illustrations, and charts that you can use immediately to begin managing a more organized, efficient, and profitable practice. The book is supplemented with examples of how other firms have benefited from the guidelines presented. You will also find listings of valuable sources of information if you want to pursue any of the topics in more detail.

You may want to read the book from cover-to-cover or simply choose those subjects that are of most interest to you. In either case, keep the book close by your work area for ready reference. It was designed to be your handbook—a fingertip reference to guide you in your planning, to offer suggested ways of dealing with everyday problems, to expedite workflow, to stimulate thinking with practical ideas, and most of all, to show you that success, profit, and quality design are all definitely possible in professional design practice.

ACKNOWLEDGMENTS

I wish to thank all those who contributed to the creation of this book. Your willingness to share knowledge, thoughts and experiences was invaluable. Specifically, contributions from the following people were of great help: John Coyne, Coyne Associates; William Downs, SHWC, Inc.; Gerald Treaster, Miles Treaster and Associates; Janet Goodman, Morris-Aubry Architects; Edgar Powers Jr., Gresham, Smith and Partners; Ken Schmohe, Design Network, Inc.; Richard Hannum, Ebert, Hannum & Volz; Jim Reinhart, HDR; Bill van Erp, Environmental Planning & Research, Inc.; Walter F. Geisinger, The Construction Specifications Institute; Frances C. Gretes, Skidmore, Owings & Merrill; John Carrigy, Engineering Information, Inc.; Stephanie Byrnes, Douglas DuCharme and William Hooper with the American Institute of Architects; and Kenneth D. Camp and Rolland Grote with KDC Architects, psc.

For financial information and assistance with portions of Chapter 8, my thanks to Howard Birnberg, Birnberg & Associates; Susan Kelsay, Robert Morris Associates; Sean Tierney and G. Neil Harper, Harper and Shuman, Inc.; and Michael Hough, Professional Services Management Journal.

Special appreciation is due to Milo Gonser, attorney, for collaboration on Chapter 6, William B. Tracy for his review of Chapter 8, and Gwen Amos for her assistance with Chapter 10.

Table of Contents

List of Illustrations

CHAPTER 1

Seven Planning Strategies for Improved Practice

ARCHITECTS AND DESIGNERS ARE EXCELLENT PLANNERS of the built environment, organizing resources to solve problems and meet goals. Planning their own professional destiny is often another matter. Poor business knowledge coupled with economic conditions, competition, and vicissitudes of markets, are often the guiding forces shaping their design practice. Successful firms have recognized that sound management must be on a level equal to design excellence. They use good business practices to guide their office in the direction they want rather than being completely at the mercy of outside forces. Although general business cycle variations may occur these offices maintain long-term health and profitability.

Improved management practices are crucial if professionals are to keep pace with the changes occurring in society, the building industry, and within the profession itself. Economic conditions will require that architects and designers deliver services in the most cost-effective way possible. Energy will continue to be a concern. National attention on productivity will question the effect of workplace design on output.

In the building industry changes will also affect how architects and designers practice. Increased collaboration among many people on the building team, including design-build, will require better coordination efforts. Building failures and litigation will force a more comprehensive view of quality control in the design office. The "explosion" of information in all areas of construction will mandate better research and information management.

The methods of design services delivery likewise are in transition. Revised laws and professional ethics are opening up new territories for marketing. Computer use will transform what services are offered and how they are provided to the client.

The increasing cost of labor will require firms to reassess their management of human resources. Larger and more complex projects will demand better project management. Finally, the state of the economy will absolutely force the designer to adopt better controls over financial matters.

Keeping up with these changes, the likely ones as well as the unlikely ones, requires continuous planning, much like the planning an architect would do for any growing organization with changing needs. This chapter outlines the seven basic issues a firm of any size must consider in order to prosper. It describes the planning strategies needed to help you direct your firm toward success. Following chapters explore specific ideas for improving particular areas of business practice.

STRATEGY ONE—ESTABLISH GOALS AND OBJECTIVES

Setting goals and objectives may be one of the most overworked phrases in the design profession, but it is critical to successful practice. Without a destination it is impossible to set any direction. Establishing these guidelines involves more than just "blue-sky" dreams like "to be the best design firm in the state," although these dreams are important as starting points. Goals must be specifically stated in such a way that you can monitor your progress against them. At any time you should be able to ask, "have we or have we not reached this goal?" or "how close are we to reaching this goal?"

Goals and objectives should cover all areas of practice. Some of the more common business aspects for which goals should be set include:

- Type of work the office wants to do
- Financial
- Markets to be tapped
- Human resources
- Geographical areas to work in
- Size of the firm and growth patterns
- Office organization and physical setup

When dreams have been translated into defined goals, specific objectives and steps to achieve those objectives can be clearly stated. Next to each step can be an assignment of *who* is to work on that objective and *when* the target date is for completion. Specifying goals and objectives this way is a procedural tool and ongoing monitoring device rather than just a one-time wish, forgotten when the pressures of practice take hold. All of these ideas need to be formalized in writing. This does not mean that they should never change, simply that you are taking this business strategy seriously and establishing it in such a way that it can be reviewed periodically. (Figure 1-1.)

Item	Goals	Specific Objectives	Responsibility for Meeting Objectives	When
Type of work				
Financial				
Markets				
Human resources				
Size and growth				
Office organization				
Geographical				

Figure 1-1
Goals and Objectives Worksheet

3

Both short-term and long-term goals need to be set, ranging anywhere from six months to five years. During reviews at the various milestones, new goals can be set based on changing circumstances and the success or failure of meeting original objectives.

STRATEGY TWO—THE POWER OF MARKETING

Marketing has traditionally been one of the design professional's weakest skills. Usually dependent on the cold call, personal contacts, or sheer luck, architects and interior designers have seldom developed their expertise in aggressively setting up a comprehensive marketing program pinpointed to the markets they want in order to achieve specific goals. As competition becomes more intense and more firms begin to specialize in expanded areas of service, marketing will have to take up an increasing amount of the professional's time. It will no longer be sufficient to assume that your client knows that all architects do about the same thing. You will have to market specifically what services you offer and your uniqueness in those areas.

Marketing is discussed in more detail in Chapters 2 and 3, but generally the basic steps in starting and maintaining a marketing program include:

- Setting your marketing goals
- Defining your marketing approach and image desired
- Specifying your target markets and geographical areas
- Deciding who will do the marketing
- Setting a budget
- Developing a specific plan
- Monitoring progress of the plan

STRATEGY THREE—PLAN FOR ORGANIZATION

Part of the decision about how an office is legally organized is based on financial concerns, liability questions, size, and other factors. These will suggest whether you want to be a sole proprietorship, general or limited partnership, or corporation. Other aspects of how you organize to get work accomplished and the general office "atmosphere" desired will depend on the personality of the principals, the types of services offered, the attitude toward employees, the size of the office, and the day-to-day work style you want.

There are dozens of possibilities, many of which are not explored by design firms. Of course, there are the traditional forms of the vertical and horizontal organizational structure with projects being assigned to teams that take the job from design through construction (vertical) or where a different department of specialists each works on one particular phase (horizontal). Association and joint ventures are additional methods of working.

Modifications of these organizations and new styles of working have also been tried. Many offices prefer to operate with a minimal number of personnel, farming out work to consultants as needed. This keeps the size of the firm small while being able to handle larger jobs. Some small organizations, one to five people, have shared-office arrangements with other small firms sharing a secretary, office machines, library and other common services. As long as there is no impression given to the public that it is one office (for legal reasons) this works well for many professionals.

Take a hard look at how you really want to practice and explore the possible ways of organizing to do it—don't assume that the traditional ways provide the only methods. Talk to your attorney and accountant to understand the legal and economic ramifications and then set up a plan to reorganize.

STRATEGY FOUR—CHOOSE YOUR CLIENTS AND THEIR WORK

An inevitable consequence of some of the traditional ways of marketing, that is, cold calls and personal contacts, is that the kinds of clients a design firm gets is very unpredictable. Most designers would agree with the old adage that "good clients make good architecture." On many jobs, a "bad" client means nothing but an unhappy, unsatisfying, and unprofitable working relationship.

Instead of this pot-luck approach, pursue the kinds of clients you feel best working with. Start with the type of services you want to offer (clarified in your goals and objectives statement) and work at finding the kinds of clients that can make it possible. This will help define part of your marketing program and give you at least a little more control over your destiny. Do you want to work for government clients? Real estate developers? Business people? Social and charitable organizations? You may find that what you really need to meet you goals is a new service type or some way of expanding your market.

More detail is given in Chapter 2 on marketing and finding information on potential clients. Your first step, however, should be to reassess your client base. Design is a service business and the personal relationships you have with your clients are important to your profit as well as your work satisfaction.

STRATEGY FIVE—PROFIT AS YOU PLAN TO PROFIT

With marketing, financial management is usually the weakest area of most design professionals' business skills. This is the area where all of a firm's problems concentrate if they are not solved as they occur. Many financial problems develop simply because of the central attitude of the firm's principals—that their business is design-oriented, they are designers, and competition makes it impossible to make much money at the business of architecture. These kinds of attitudes and their variations doom anyone to failure. Instead, firm management must believe that they are in business to make a profit and that this belief must operate on a level equal to or superior to being in business to "design." After all, without a profit and the business it creates, there can be no design.

The key elements to financial success are setting fees equitably for the amount of work the project requires and having a reporting and monitoring system to track the financial health of the firm. Nearly all designers' clients are business people of one kind or another and they generally appreciate an architect's or interior designer's negotiating a fee commensurate with the efforts expended. Designers need to stop being so thankful for the opportunity to do a job that they will take it at any cost. Clients that try to negotiate from this position are probably clients you can do without.

A good system of record keeping and financial analysis is the second key to financial success. You must know where you are at any given moment, whether your position is consistent with original goals, and what action to take if problems arise. A comprehensive financial management system is crucial. Fortunately, systems developed specifically for design professionals and the increased availability of microcomputers are making this easier than ever before, but these tools are of little use if firm management doesn't commit to use them.

Financial management is a complex subject. More detailed information is given in Chapter 8. The first step, however, is to question your beliefs concerning the role of profit in your business and how you want to integrate that with your practice. Next, make the commitment to devote the time and energy to improving your financial management knowledge and the processes needed to realize a fair return on your investment.

STRATEGY SIX—PROSPER AS YOU GROW

Design firms must grow in some way if they are to avoid stagnation. This growth does not necessarily have to be in size, but can be in profit, volume of work, types of services offered, new expertise, or geographical range. One or several of these ways of growth are critical to maintaining the vitality of any business.

Maintaining control over growth (or reverse growth) is difficult for professional design firms since much of their business is dependent on an industry and economy that fluctuate greatly. Architects and designers, though, can have more control over growth than they think by spreading their market base and organizing to adapt to variations in workload. For example, offering several services allows you to grow into more areas or shift personnel if one market area softens. Maintaining a list of qualified consultants and part-time help can assist in smoothing out the peak workloads without the necessity of staffing up then laying off when the jobs are finished.

Most design firms grow too fast too soon. A large job or a series of good fortunes may cause rapid increases in staff, capital expenditures and other major financial commitments. Usually, the management adjustments and operating systems necessary to support this kind of growth cannot keep pace with the actual numbers of people and money outlay. An even greater danger exists if the growth is due to only one or a few jobs that require more personnel. Once the job is over, these people may not be needed. If the marketing effort has not anticipated this and brought in new work, the results are layoffs, low morale, and most important, the lost *opportunity* for expansion and improvement that additional revenue provides. Having a well-thought-out master plan allows you to be prepared for unforseen growth and make the best of it.

STRATEGY SEVEN—THE ACTION PLAN FOR YOUR GOALS

All of the preceeding strategies should be formalized into a written business plan. This gives your business documentation of the goals, objectives, philosophies, and directions required to set yourself into a "success mode." It outlines a specific plan to follow, a schedule, and gives you a tool to use in evaluating all of your office's efforts. If you like, you can include a pessimistic scenario, an optimistic one, and a realistic idea of how you would like to grow. Having all three makes you pre-think what actions may be necessary if business gets significantly better or worse.

A business plan might include the following:

- A summary of the business as it now exists
- A philosophical statement concerning the business
- General goals of the practice
- Financial status and financial goals
- Specific objectives to reach the stated goals broken down into distinct categories—marketing, profit, etc.
- A specific plan and schedule for meeting those objectives along with who is responsible for doing what

The business plan need not be long; it should primarily be a thought process and a commitment to set yourself on a course to a more profitable, efficient, and enjoyable practice.

CHAPTER 2
Marketing Your Talents for Increased Volume and Profit

DESIGN PROFESSIONS ARE ENTERING AN EXCITING PERIOD of marketing their services. The days of corporate and political patronage, deals made on a handshake, and cold calls are fading as fast as the T-square in architectural offices. Buyers of architectural and design services are becoming more sophisticated and demanding the best possible service for their money. The architect is viewed as part of a team formed to create physical facilities—not as a design luxury. As such, businesses, school boards, industry, or whoever is purchasing the architects' services demand that their problems be solved on time and on budget. They look for the firm that can deliver.

In response to this client need for economic survival, more and more architects are making marketing a significant and *organized* part of their practice. As a result, many support groups and services have developed. There are dozens of seminars, correspondence courses, books, newsletters, and workshops dealing with the marketing of services. Marketing consultants for design professionals are becoming more prevalent. Most significantly, the Society for Marketing Professional Services (SMPS), formed as recently as 1973, continues to grow in membership every year.

This new era of marketing is also becoming recognized by the courts and the American Institute of Architects. Beginning with the prohibition of recommended fee schedules as violating antitrust laws, the courts have consistently made rulings that are bringing professional services into the realm of other "consumer" businesses. Most recently, in 1981, the AIA revised its traditional Code of Ethics and Professional Conduct to make it voluntary. These actions are both allowing and encouraging professionals to become more aggressive in their marketing. For example, some of the long-held prohibitions against involvement in contracting, advertising and the like are slowly dissolving.

In many offices, you are now seeing a separate position being created for the person who specializes in marketing, and this person is not always an architect. The titles are varied, but it is evidence that the marketing function cannot be effectively handled by the owner of the firm alone, or one of the partners on a personal contact or "shotgun" basis. Marketing efforts in these offices are becoming organized, aggressive, and more creative. The profession is beginning to see rigorous marketing research, new techniques (for architects) such as direct mail, newsletters, video presentations, and advertising, larger marketing budgets, and other ideas that would have been unheard of ten years ago.

In spite of this changing climate, however, it is estimated that only about 10 to 15 percent of architectural and engineering firms have an organized marketing effort. To many designers it is still an unknown area, one in which they feel uncomfortable, or a part of the practice that some may think "beneath" the traditional professional status of the architect.

This chapter will outline the status of marketing in today's professional practice, explain ways to develop a marketing plan suited to your individual needs, and get you started on the "game of leads." The following chapter will offer suggestions on how to improve the promotional tools you have at your disposal and provide a list of valuable sources of information if you want to pursue some topic in more detail.

MARKETING BASICS

Before getting into specifics, it is important to have a clear notion about fundamentals—what is essential to any marketing effort. Marketing is simply a set of activities related to facilitating an honest exchange of something you have for something someone else needs. As such, marketing (often read "selling" which it is, too) should not be viewed as the unprofessional thing many architects still believe it to be.

The following list includes some of the basic precepts of marketing. You may want to add to the list from your experience or rearrange the order. Simple as these precepts may seem, it is surprising how many architects forget some of them.

1. Know what you are marketing. Understand your service, the people providing it, what problems it solves. Know, also, your strengths and weaknesses.
2. Know your buyer's needs and wants. This is simply market research in whatever way it is conducted.
3. Offer something unique. Give them something unexpected. Why should a client come to you instead of another firm? What is your competitive edge?

4. Show the benefits of what you are marketing. Quite often, the value of what you have to offer is perceived differently by clients and potential clients from the way you perceive it. What may seem great to you may look useless to a potential client.
5. Let your presence be known. Communicate your service to your desired market in the most effective, cost-efficient way.
6. Repeat the message. People often have short memories or do not hear or understand the first time. Keep reminding them.
7. Play the percentages. You cannot get every job you try for—expect only a certain number of contacts to develop into contracts.
8. Know what the buyer is willing to pay. The right balance between the cost of services, profit, and competitive price must be achieved.
9. Give the buyer a choice.
10. Deliver on time and on budget.

THE MARKETING PLAN

A marketing plan is absolutely essential for your long-term survival and growth. Even those few firms that are fortunate enough to know the right people at the right time in the right situation that leads to an enviable backlog of work and healthy profits cannot exist like that forever. In today's economic and business climate it is unlikely that personal contacts of the firm's principal can sustain the workload necessary for a successful practice. Regardless of size, every firm needs a marketing plan to 1) organize the efforts of the firm for the most efficient use of the available marketing dollar, 2) provide a set of specific, attainable goals, and 3) establish a base by which to evaluate progress.

Generally speaking, there are six basic elements in a marketing plan. If your firm does not already have one, use these as a starting point for outlining your plan. If you have a plan, check it against this list and the discussion that follows.

1. Set goals.
2. Analyze your firm.
3. Analyze the market.
4. Develop objectives and strategies.
5. Establish a budget.
6. Define a schedule and responsibilities.

Set Goals

Marketing goals should spring from some of the basic elements of the business plan discussed in Chapter 1. In setting marketing goals you should consider your philosophical goals of practice, profit targets, the type of work and clients you want to have, the geographical area in which you want to practice, growth goals, and the image you want to project.

Marketing goals should also include more measurable objectives that give you clear objectives: for instance, a set increase in gross fees, jobs to support the addition of a certain number of staff members, a given number of new project types within a certain size range, or whatever is most appropriate for your circumstances. One large firm, for example, had as one of their marketing goals to have a specific number of the "Fortune 500" on their client list.

Keep the number of short-term goals and objectives to a reasonable number. You can only concentrate on a few at a time. Too many will overburden your firm's resources and make it difficult, if not impossible, to reach any of them.

Analyze Your Firm

A thorough analysis of your firm is the most important part of the marketing plan. It will tell you what kinds of markets you can successfully sell to or what additions or modifications you may need to make to reach the markets you want. Use the following checklist to outline the present status of your firm.

Firm Analysis Checklist

1. What is your mix of practice now? Consider building types, building cost ranges, size of jobs in square footage, geographical location, and fees.
2. What are your strengths as you see them? What are you offering to clients? How will you capitalize on your strengths?
3. What is your track record for fees, meeting schedules, and maintaining project cost control?
4. Why have you been awarded jobs in the past?
5. Why have you lost jobs in the past?
6. What do you think your weaknesses are? How can they be eliminated?
7. What is your recognition factor in the marketplace? Highly visible, unknown, known for only one building type, or what?
8. Is your reputation based on one or two strong people, total capabilities of the firm, or work people have done with other firms?
9. How do you market now? Referrals, cold calls, follow-up on published leads? What percentage of each do you use?
10. What is your public relations program, if any?
11. How do you do proposals now? Are they effective, easy to put together, targeted to the client?
12. What presentation techniques do you use? How do they differ throughout the duration of the job with different phases? Are they effective, do they tell your story?

13. Who is your competition? Is the competition for the same clients, the same building types, similar services? Are firm size and capabilities of other offices the competition?

14. What kind of work is your competition doing? Are they doing it competently, faster, cheaper, more dramatic, winning awards, or expanding geographically?

15. What is your competitive edge? What do you offer that the competition does not?

16. How does your competition market *their* services?

Finally, analyze your existing staff capabilities. There may be more experience there than you may think. Set up a matrix and list each staff member on one axis and areas of expertise on the other. Add to this list as you go along. Do more than just look at resumes; interview each person in your office individually. You may find that your firm has more experience than just the building types you have completed. Although this kind of experience is more difficult to market than actual buildings done by the firm, it is a starting point, and a valuable one for young firms or practices trying to expand into new building types.

Analyze the Market

Traditionally, market research in any organized form has been ignored by architects although it is one of the most valuable tools that can be used to maintain at least a steady flow or work if not an increase in jobs. The situation has probably been perpetuated by the belief that market research is very expensive and more appropriate for high-volume, product-oriented businesses instead of service firms. You can pay a marketing research firm large fees for very detailed and extensive research if that is appropriate, but there is a lot you can do yourself.

Adopt the attitude that some form of research is vital to the continuation and growth of your practice. Marketing research should help pinpoint the kinds of projects and business activity needing the services you offer so that you can plan the most apropriate strategies. Keep in mind that this type of investigation is for general building/project/client information and not "intelligence gathering" for a specific project. As such, it is geared to developing action plans to be put into effect anywhere from six months to five years in the future.

To begin, decide whether you want to find out more about the potential of project types you have done in the past or whether you want to explore new territory. Investigating the future market of work you are doing now will help you decide on people to contact, what to emphasize in your promotional tools, and ultimately what adjustments you may need to make in your staff. Researching new markets will help you weed out those project types that hold little promise, so you can concentrate your resources where they are likely to do the most good.

Next, determine whether to study markets by building type or by geographical location. These are the two broad divisions that make the most sense for architectural firms, although there are others. One alternative, for example, might be to inquire into the market for expanded services such as programming, master planning, interior architecture, energy audits, or renovation. Or you may want to know more about certain client groups that are responsible for a variety of building types such as state or federal government agencies or real estate developers.

Making decisions about both of these questions will allow you to narrow your research efforts to manageable and productive limits. What areas you decide to explore will depend on your firm's goals, the capability of your staff, and general knowledge you glean from staying current with economic and business activity through reading and personal contacts.

CASE IN POINT

John Coyne, a national marketing consultant serving A/E's out of St. Paul, Minnesota, suggests that firms starting to put together their first organized marketing program conduct what he terms "50 cent marketing research." After you have decided on what project types you want to investigate, Coyne suggests, first make a list of people to contact who are knowledgeable in the field you want to explore. This list might include past clients, building owners, real estate people, bankers, and other sources who might share their knowledge with you.

Next, he suggests, outline what you want to ask them and begin to telephone. By your using good telephone techniques, identifying exactly what you are trying to do, and asking open-ended questions, Coyne maintains, a majority of people will be happy to share their thoughts with you if they see your efforts as research, not a ploy for obtaining leads.

Listen carefully to the feedback you receive and take good notes. By analyzing the responses, you should be able to get a pretty good idea of what the market potential will be for a particular building type in a certain part of the country. Coyne maintains that as simple as this technique is, it is valuable for firms that want to understand project potential and improve their planned marketing efforts.

Whether you rely on your own knowledge, conduct do-it-yourself market research, or hire a consultant, the analysis of your market should answer the following questions.

1. Who is the primary market? Who are the secondary markets?
2. What are the geographical boundaries of the markets you are studying?
3. How many projects of the type you are interested in have been built in the past several years? What is the projection for the next three years? What is the dollar value of these projects?
4. What are the current market trends in general? Where is the market likely to go in one year? Three years?

5. What is your estimate of what the market needs and/or wants? What are the unique characteristics of the market?
6. Are there some market needs not being filled?
7. How can your firm capitalize on unfilled needs? What must be offered to compete in the market?
8. How are jobs typically awarded? What is the selection process used by those clients you want?
9. What events outside your profession are happening that might affect the market?
10. How well do you know the market? What are current attitudes, business activity, profitability, etc.?
11. Who are your market information contacts? Manufacturers' representatives, trade associations, real estate agents? Which one is the most regular, reliable source?
12. Who is the competition?
13. What part of the market does the competition have?

For more information on conducting and using market research, see the list of sources at the end of this chapter.

Develop Objectives and Strategies

Based on your overall goals, a clear understanding of your firm, and an analysis of the market, establish specific methods of achieving the workload your office needs. Not only will a detailed plan make it easier to target your efforts, it will also provide you with a way to evaluate the success of those efforts.

Figure 2-1 shows one way of organizing this information. I would suggest you first divide your potential market into three categories: past clients, present clients, and future (potential) clients. Since it is easiest to sell your existing services to past and present clients, these categories should be given careful attention. What percentage of effort you devote to these clients as opposed to new contacts depends on your desires, age of your firm, size of firm, size and potential of any one market, and other considerations. Generally, however, one rule of thumb is that a comfortable mix is to have 80 percent of your work based on past clients and 20 percent on new clients. It usually takes about 80 percent of your marketing effort to secure that 20 percent while only 20 percent of the effort is required to sell the other 80 percent. This chart can be as general or detailed as you need. You can first list your markets generally by project type or service offered, and later list each job if you need to be that specific. Separate charts can also be used for different planning periods—three months, one year, three years.

Next, summarize the status of current projects and recent past jobs. Knowing the percentage of fees each client or project type is responsible for will help you understand whom you are dependent on and where adjustments may need to be made.

Planning Period	Current Status			Objectives			Strategies		
Page _____ Clients ☐ Past ☐ Present ☐ Potential	Gross Fees	% of total	Past and Present clients / How we got the job	Desired % of total	Fee Goal	Services offered to the market	Methods of contact and sales tools	No. of contacts req'd.	Time/Money Budgeted / Person Assigned
Totals									

Figure 2-1
Marketing Objectives and Strategies

Outline your objectives by the percentage of the total you would like to have each project type or client type contribute to your workload, and the fee goal that is necessary to support your office for the time period you are studying or to allow for the kind of growth you want. The exact fee goal necessary will, of course, depend on your particular financial picture, profit goals, overhead, productivity, number of technical staff to total staff and so forth. One way to estimate needs and build up a historical data file is to evaluate fees per employee and fees per technical employee you need to remain profitable.

Finally, complete your outline of objectives by specifying exactly what services you are proposing to offer to your various markets. Is it a traditional, established service of your firm or something new you want to offer? Is it identical to your competition? Is it unique? These kinds of questions will help you select the most appropriate strategies.

Based on the objectives, you can now determine the most appropriate method of contact and sales tools to be used in pursuing your market. For example, you may think that an informal lunch and updated brochure are appropriate for some of your past clients while an entirely new slide presentation may be needed to communicate a new service you are offering to a new list of possibilities. You should tailor your approach to the unique needs of each client prospect.

Finally, estimate the number of contacts you need to make within a given time period to realize your objectives and define how much time and money you can budget for this.

There are several rules of thumb for "guestimating" these. One used is that of 100 contacts you may find ten good leads and/or interviews which may result in one or two jobs. With good market research you may be able to increase this ratio to about six to one. Keep track of your own experience to establish an in-house percentage.

Set a Budget

Marketing should be budgeted for like any other expense of running your business—it should not receive the "left-over" money (if any) after other bills have been paid. Several factors will affect how much you allow for this function and how it is distributed, such as the size of your firm, your marketing techniques, type of work you do and so forth.

Generally, marketing expenses can range from about 5 percent to 15 percent of your total annual revenue (including fees, consultants and reimbursables). One of the generally accepted averages is 7 percent. Smaller firms spend a higher percentage, however. Of this amount, about 50 percent is spent on salaries of people who devote more than three-fourths of their time marketing, 25 percent for salaries of non-marketing staff, and the remaining 25 percent on non-salary expenses such as brochures, travel, direct mail, memberships, and similar items. Your figures may vary, so keep accurate records of time and money spent on getting work.

A good source for comparing what other firms are spending on marketing is the *Marketing Salary and Expense Survey* published by the Society for Marketing Professional Services and the *A/E Marketing Journal*. Write to SMPS at 1437 Powhatan Street, Alexandria, VA 22314, for a copy of the most current edition.

Define a Schedule and Responsibilities

There has been a dramatic increase in the past few years in the number of design firms that have one or more people whose primary responsibility it is to market. The selling of a firm has become organized, well-funded, and more competitive among design firms. Responding to this, a whole new set of job descriptions has sprung up. The names are different, but the intent is the same: let someone specialize in getting work. In small firms this may be one of the principals devoting a majority of his or her time to marketing. In large firms it may be a marketing director with a sales staff and administrative backup.

Regardless of who may do the work, you must assign specific duties, establish a time schedule for completing them and evaluate the results of effort. Scheduling should include both short-term objectives (one year or less) and long-term objectives (one to five years).

By far, the most popular and well-used specialist among those firms that have an organized marketing program has been the marketing coordinator. This person is often a former secretary who has been with the firm for a period of time and knows the operation, services offered, and the "personality" of the office. This person works under the direction of a principal or marketing director. While usually not making sales calls, presentations, or otherwise tracking potential clients, the marketing coordinator is responsible for managing a diverse range of activities. Some of these include:

- Maintaining contact files and data sheets on proposed or actual jobs
- Organizing and maintaining the promotional tools of the firm: brochures, slides, etc.
- Maintaining up-to-date resumes of all staff
- Helping to prepare proposals
- Developing and maintaining a mailing and contact list
- Coordinating publicity and public relations efforts
- Doing market research or coordinating with consultants
- Coordinating follow-up activities on all actual and potential clients

For more information on the role of the marketing coordinator, the Society for Marketing Professional Services puts out a publication titled *The Marketing Coordinator* that you may find useful.

HOW TO FIND AND FOLLOW LEADS

As clients become more sophisticated about selecting an architect or other designer and market conditions sharpen competition, professionals must hone their business development skills to pierce the markets they want. It is no longer possible to assume the reactive mode, waiting for a referral from a friend, a past client to call with more work, or an invitation to submit a proposal along with every other office in town. A critical part of every office's marketing effort is that of initiating contacts on a continuing basis, developing some of them into leads, interviews and, ultimately, signed contracts.

The difference between a contact and a lead is worth noting. A contact is simply a source of information about possible jobs or about other people who may know of likely building programs. A lead develops from a contact and relates to a specific building project for which there is a need for a designer. Typically, a lot of contacts have to be identified and explored to find a few leads that may result in the kinds of jobs that you want to do.

There are many sources of contacts and leads for the design professional. They can be broadly categorized into two groups: informal and systematic. The informal contacts are those that architects are the most familiar with, referrals, social acquaintances and so forth. They are usually unorganized and not directed at a specific market. Systematic contacts rely on published sources, deliberate planning and are usually more in line with what is considered "lead generation." Even though both originiate differently they must be used together. Systematic sources can pinpoint and round out information on informal contacts while the informal can verify and add depth to the cold statistics of published lists. There is no best source—each office must plan its own approach and use what sources produce the best results.

Informal Sources

1. *Past clients and referrals.* This group is probably your best sales force and the reason why you must have an organized procedure for project follow-up. Having no unsolicited referrals probably will not help your practice, but only one bad comment can nearly ruin it.

2. *Business organizations.* Try to stay away from professional design groups as much as possible for marketing purposes. There are few leads, and any useful marketing information will remain a secret with the person who has it. Rely, instead, on other groups that are related to your desired client or project type or represent varied business interests such as the local Chamber of Commerce.

3. *Clubs and community organizations.* Once again, athletic clubs, service clubs, and similar organizations appeal to a wide range of people who may need the services of an architect or who may know someone else who does.

4. *Consultants.* These people contact a wide range of professional situations and geographical areas and usually have a good feel for character of the market. While professional ethics will keep proprietary information off the grapevine, consultants can provide an objective look at the current state of the market and the services being offered it.

5. *Manufacturers' representatives.* Like consultants, these people are in constant touch with the market. They can often suggest areas of activity worth investigating and suggest people who need particular services. They are also very effective in spreading the word about what your office may offer.

6. *Newspapers and trade journals.* These are the obvious sources for general clues about what is happening in your area of interest. For the alert eye, they can also provide tips on pending building projects. News stories, advertisements, press releases—all of these can contain information of potential value such as new businesses in the making, people of importance, or economic and political events affecting construction. Once again, design trade journals are of little use; instead, subscribe to trade journals of the markets you are interested in and other publications that report on your desired type of work.

7. *Staff.* One of the most overlooked sources for informal contacts is the architect's own staff. They are in touch with their own circle of friends, business relations, and social contacts and often hear of possible sources of leads. Every office should encourage the kind of interoffice cooperation that could turn a casual remark to an employee into a profitable job.

Systematic Sources

Systematic sources of contacts are those generally available to everyone. Oddly enough, many of them are not used to their full potential. None of them, however, are complete and uniquely tailored to any one office's use. There is a lot of work that must go into refining and using them properly and they must always be used in conjunction with personal contacts and other promotion techniques. The list is potentially very long. Here are some of the better ones.

Directories

Guide to American Directories
B. Klein Publications, Inc.
P.O. Box 8503
Coral Springs, FL 33065

> Lists over 6000 directories by subject with an alphabetical index. Useful for pinpointing those directories related to your marketing interests.

Directory Information Service
Gale Research Company
Book Tower
Detroit, MI 48226
> Guide to over 1,800 directories indexed by subject and title.

State Industrial Directories
State Industrial Directories Corporation
2 Penn Plaza
New York, NY 10001
> This is one of several sources that publishes directories to businesses in individual states. The State Industrial Directories put out by this publisher provide listings of businesses in the manufacturing divisions of the SIC coding numbers 2000-3999. Information includes company name, address, telephone number, product description, number of employees, names and titles of company officers and is published annually. Check with your local library for those available in your state.

Standard and Poor's Register of Corporations, Directors and Executives
Standard and Poor's Corporation
345 Hudson Street
New York, NY 10014
> Lists over 37,000 public and private U.S. corporations with information on names of officers and directors, number of employees, annual sales and products produced with SIC (Standard Industrial Classification) codes. Also includes biographies of over 72,000 executives, and directors of those companies, and the titles and functions of approximately 390,000 officers. Published annually with supplements quarterly. By subscription, but is usually available in public or college libraries. Also includes company's accounting firm, primary bank, and primary law firm. This source is useful in starting a list of contacts in a particular business type, locating the right contacts, checking interlocking business connections, and investigating key personnel.

Dun & Bradstreet Million Dollar Directory and *Middle Market Directory*
Dun & Bradstreet, Inc.
99 Church Street
New York, NY 10007
> Two sources that include information on U.S. firms with a net worth of $1,000,000 or more, and between $500,000 and $1,000,000 respectively. Information includes name, address, telephone number, state of incorporation, annual sales, number of employees, names of officers and other executives and SIC codes. Several indexes list

information by SIC codes, geographically and alphabetically. Published annually. By subscription, but it is usually available in public libraries.

National Directory of Addresses and Telephone Numbers
Whitney Communications Corp., New York, NY
> Lists over 120,000 companies with sales of six million or more or with more than 300 employees, major banks and brokerage firms by state, leading law and accounting firms by state, advertising agencies, as well as other types of businesses.

World Wide Chamber of Commerce Directory
Johnson Publishing Company, Inc.
P. O. Box 455
Loveland, CO 80537
> Lists Chambers of Commerce in the United States, Canada and foreign countries. Contains name of president, address and telephone number. Published annually.

American Hospital Directory
American Hospital Association
840 N. Lake Shore Drive
Chicago, IL 60611

American Universities and Colleges
American Council on Education, Publications Division
One Dupont Circle N.W.
Washington, DC 20036
> Contains information on physical plant of all accredited colleges and universities along with size, curriculum and history of the institution.

College and University Administrators Directory
Gale Research Company
Book Tower
Detroit, MI 48226
> Lists more than 35,000 administrators at over 3,100 colleges and universities in the United States. Included are names and addresses arranged by job title, individual, and by state.

Polk's World Bank Directory
R. L. Polk & Co.
2001 Elm Hill Pike
P. O. Box 1340
Nashville, TN 37202
> Directory of banks listed by state and city giving name, address, officers and directory, as well as financial information such as assets, loans, deposits.

Commercial Lead Sources

Dodge Reports
F. W. Dodge Division
McGraw-Hill Information Systems
1221 Avenue of the Americas
New York, NY 10020
     Daily, local reports on the progress of various building projects. Unfortunately, most of the listings already have architects.

Contacts Influential
Weatherly Building, 10th Floor
516 S.E. Morrison
Portland, OR 97214
     Offers list of sales prospects for various regions of the country. Information is available in printed form, on custom-generated 3″ × 5″ cards, computer printouts and magnetic tape. Mailing labels are also available. Information in the printed volume is indexed by firm name, kinds of businesses, zip code, key people, and numerical telephone sequence. Cards or other output can be custom-generated to meet your specific needs. Some of the information available includes names and address, SIC codes, key people and their title, number of employees, and telephone number. Available in about thirty metropolitan areas in 1982. The printed version may be found in the business section of your library.

Corporate Buyers of Design Services/USA
BIDS, Inc.
P. O. Box 3344
Springfield, IL 62708
(217) 753-8080
     Directory of about 5,000 corporations responsible for approximately two-thirds of all U.S. private construction. Includes address, A/E selection, phone numbers and name of person to contact in the organization about building plans. Also included are non-proprietary construction plans, contact procedures preferred by the corporate contact, U.S. industrial outlook forecast through 1986, and rapid growth industries. Published biennially. BIDS, Inc. also publishes the "BIDS Jobletter."

Annual Analysis of Capital Spending
Economic Research Council
5213 Westbard Avenue
Bethesda, MD 20816
(301) 229-5954

The current edition lists 153 companies most likely to be budgeting for new plant construction in the next two years. The Economic Research Council also publishes *The Directory of Selected High Tech Companies,* listing over 250 companies producing high technological products that meet the Council's standards of financial stability and growth potential. An additional publication is *The Fastest Growing Divisions of the Largest Companies.*

Mailing Lists

Although purchased lists may seem too commercial and general at first, they can provide a starting point for identifying a wide range of possible contacts. Mailing list houses are very sophisticated in their manipulation of large data bases to provide their customers with lists as broad or specific as necessary. The biggest disadvantage is that they are not always as up-to-date as the design professional needs for marketing. For a relatively low cost, however, they can be used *in conjunction with* other sources. Check with local suppliers in your area or get a copy of *Directory of Mailing List Houses,* B. Klein Publications, P.O. Box 8503, Coral Springs, FL 33065. (305) 752-1708.

Government

Commerce Business Daily
Government Printing Office
Washington, DC 20402

> Published daily, this is the basic source for U.S. government procurement invitations, including those for professional services. If you want to do much work for the government, this is a must, but it gives the same information to everyone at once. Try to find out about future government projects by researching the process a project must go through to first be approved and then funded before invitations for proposals are published. This usually happens years before the project. One example of an available source is the *Military Construction Authorization* book. One is put out by each department of the military and includes, among other information, projects for the next fiscal year and future years including location, type of building project, estimated cost, and contact.

U.S. Government Purchasing and Sales Directory
U.S. Small Business Administration
U.S. Government Printing Office
Washington, DC 20402

> This publication provides basic information on the various aspects of selling to the government including military purchasing offices in a state-by-state listing. The various agencies that buy services are identified with requirements on preparing proposals.

Chambers of Commerce

Local chambers provide not only a source for personal, informal contacts, but they also know the local business scene and may be able to provide you with information on businesses moving to your area, or at least projections of areas likely to be developing, and types of enterprises moving to your region. In addition, most chambers publish a wide variety of pamphlets, reports and newsletters useful for staying on top of local developments. Most can provide you with access to their membership list, too. Certainly worth the cost of joining.

Other Sources

Sources of State Information and State Industrial Directories
Chamber of Commerce of the United States
1615 H Street N.W.
Washington, DC 20062
   Provides names and addresses of private and public agencies which publish information about their states.

Fortune Magazine
   If you are interested in going after the big ones, the May issue lists the top 750 U.S. companies.

Clipping services
   Clipping services provide a more comprehensive way to use newspapers as sources of contacts than just scanning a few yourself. The services can watch for specific items of interest to your office on as large a geographical scale as you want. For local services, consult the telephone book. A few of the national bureaus include Burelle's Press Clipping Service, 75 E. Northfield Avenue, Livingston, NJ 07039; Luce Press Clippings, 420 Lexington Avenue, New York, NY 10017; ATP Clipping Bureau, Inc., 5 Beekman Street, New York, NY 10038; and Bacon's Clipping Bureau, 14 E. Jackson Boulevard, Chicago, IL 60604.

Local banks and universities
   These sources often publish or make available information on the region in which they do business. It is usually fairly accurate and up to date.

All these sources are simply ways to begin to identify contacts that may need the kinds of services you offer. They are not leads and certainly not potential jobs at this point. To determine which ones are or may be, if you can make a presentation or proposal, requires investigation and the right kind of effort with your promotional tools.

Once you have a list of contacts, the key word is research; know the organization you are tracking, know about the people in the organization, and know the organization's building program needs. Your initial contact inquiries should begin to answer the following questions:

1. Is there an immediate building project being considered? If not, when might your contact need services?
2. What is the contact's process of facility planning?
3. What is the project type or kinds of design services that will be needed?
4. Who is the right person to be talking to if not the one you have contacted?
5. What is the anticipated scope of the project? Size, budget, schedule?
6. Has a site been selected?
7. What will be the selection process for design services?
8. What kind of firm is the contact looking for: specialist, general practice, nationally known, local?

Answers to these questions will tell you if your contact is worth pursuing. If so, additional information needs to be gathered during the "courting" process. This data is summarized on the forms shown in Figures 2-2, 2-3, 2-4 and 2-5.

Researching the Contact

There are many ways to research your contact. Generally, some combination of all is useful. Some of these methods include the cold call, discussion with business acquaintances of the contact, references to published information sources, trade associations your contact may belong to, competing organizations, and real estate people. There is no hard and fast rule since every research effort must be tailored to the job at hand. Be creative—valuable information can be gathered from the most unlikely sources as well as through the usual channels. The following list provides some useful published sources of information about companies.

Annual Reports

For public corporations these are readily available and will tell a lot about the company. Annual reports are usually all public relations, but do give an overall feeling for the company and potential growth.

Moody's Manuals

Moody's Investors Service, Inc.
99 Church Street
New York, NY 10007
Separate publications covering large industries, transportation companies, public utilities and banking and finance institutions. Contains information on thousands of companies in these categories.

Dun & Bradstreet Reference Book

Dun & Bradstreet, Inc.
99 Church Street
New York, NY 10007
> Provides information on almost three million businesses in the U.S. and Canada listed alphabetically by city and state. Information includes business name, principal officers, Standard Industrial Classification code, approximate holdings of banks in the city for the company, and a rating on the company's estimated financial strength. Published bimonthly.

Dun & Bradstreet Reference Book of Corporate Managements

Same address as above
> Gives biographical information on over 30,000 top-level executives in over 2,500 companies. Useful for targeting direct mail, sales calls, and for general background information for presentations and proposals.

Directory of Corporate Affiliations

National Register Publishing Co., Inc.
5201 Old Orchard Road
Skokie, IL 60077
> Published annually, this reference work can be used to sort out the relationship between parent companies and their domestic and foreign divisions, subsidiaries and affiliates. Includes companies listed on the New York Stock Exchange, American Stock Exchange and many other industrial companies.

Funk and Scotts Index of Corporations and Industries

Predicasts, Inc.
200 University Circle Research Center
11001 Cedar Avenue
Cleveland, OH 44106
> Index to over 750 business information sources such as trade journals, newspapers, and reports. Published weekly by subscription, but most large public libraries carry it. Also available in computer data base form.

Business Periodicals Index

H. W. Wilson Company
950 University Avenue
Bronx, NY 10452
> Index to articles found in business publications. Available in most libraries.

Who Owns Whom: North America

Dun & Bradstreet International, Ltd.
P. O. Box 3234
Church Street Station
New York, NY 10008

> Lists about 60,000 U.S. and Canadian parent companies with their
> foreign subsidiaries, and U.S. and Canadian subsidiaries of foreign
> companies. Published annually.

Who's Who in America

A. N. Marquis Co.
200 E. Ohio Street
Chicago, IL 60611

> One of the many basic reference works for learning more about
> prominent people. Also check *Who's Who in Commerce and Industry,*
> *. . . Finance and Industry, . . . Banking, . . . Government, . . . Insurance,*
> and the others published by this company.

Congressional Directory

Superintendent of Documents
U.S. Government Printing Office
Washington, DC 20402

> Contains information on members of the current Congress, govern-
> ment agency executives and staffs of both. Helpful if you do work
> for the federal government. Published for each session of Congress.

U.S. Government Organization Manual

Superintendent of Documents
U.S. Government Printing Office
Washington, DC 20402

> Useful for finding your way through the maze of agencies of the
> legislative, judicial and executive branches of the government. It lists
> functions, responsibilities and staff members. Published annually at
> a nominal cost, it is a basic reference if you do or plan to do work
> for the government. Be careful, though, some obscure offices and
> agencies are not listed.

How to Find Information about Companies

Second Edition, 1981
Washington Researchers
918 16th Street N.W.
Washington, DC 20006

Contains a gold mine of information on available sources in both the public and private sector on learning more about companies and individuals. Also includes tips on how to proceed with research using the sources listed.

Encyclopedia of Business Information Sources

Gale Research Co.
Book Tower
Detroit, MI 48226
Reference work to sources of information on approximately 1,200 business topics, directing the searcher to handbooks, professional associations, periodicals, abstract services and other specialized sources.

Where to Find Business Information

David M. Brownstone & Gorton Carruth
New York: John Wiley & Sons, 1982
Reference book of about 5,000 prime sources of business information indexed by subject heading, source name, and publisher's name.

Commercial Computer Data Bases

For a modest fee, several data bases can be searched to find additional information on companies, individuals and industries that may help in adding depth to your contact or lead list. See Chapter 11 for more details on computer data bases. Several of these have already been mentioned such as those used by Dun & Bradstreet and the F.W. Dodge Division. Another you might find useful is ABI/INFORM. This indexes about 500 periodicals in the area of business, management and administration, emphasizing general decision sciences information with secondary emphasis on specific industry information. It is available through Lockheed DIALOG, SDC ORBIT, and BRS.

Another useful data base is EIS Non-manufacturing Establishments. This provides data on over 240,000 non-manufacturing companies that employ 20 or more people including location, percent of industry sales, industry classification, etc. A companion data base, EIS Industrial Plants, provides similar information for over 130,000 industrial firms with annual sales of over $500,000. These account for over 90 percent of all U.S. Industrial activity.

No matter how you establish your leads, the idea is to make the contact well ahead of when a selection for designer is going to be made so you can have the necessary amount of time to cultivate the lead and secure a place on the "short list" for interviewing. The next chapter will discuss some considerations in making your presentation where you finally sell your firm over the competition.

Regardless of how you make contacts or find leads, you must have some method of tracking them. It is often months and sometimes years between the first contact and the time the agreement for architectural services is signed. Timing your actions and having the right information is crucial to the success of your marketing effort. Having an organized method of reminding you when to take the appropriate steps will increase your chances for success. The same system is also useful for follow-up; satisfied past clients are your best sources for more work or referrals.

Several methods can be used depending on the size of your firm, number and method of making contacts, and number of people involved in the marketing effort. Some people use file folders for each potential job, some use printed forms and others develop card files. I think whatever system you adopt should recognize the various stages a potential job goes through before it is actually a signed agreement: preliminary contact, a lead on an actual project, the proposal, and follow-up.

The preliminary contact is the result of your broad-based marketing and may contain nothing more than sketchy information from a newspaper article, someone met at a party, a name from a mailing list, a proposed project announced in a trade magazine, a referral, or any number of places where you might hear about the possibility of a job. Here, there is a large number of listings with very little information on each one.

A lead develops from a contact when there is an actual project being considered and when the person you are contacting shows an interest in knowing more about your firm. Here you need more information about the project, the potential client, and how to go about presenting your firm. The proposal stage confirms you are on the short list and requires you to target your marketing work to a specific job and specific people who are making the final decision. Follow-up is critical for understanding why you did or did not get a job and how it may be a springboard for more leads.

Figures 2-2, 2-3, 2-4, and 2-5 show the various marketing reports that can be used to record this information. They show what data are important for any type of rigorous marketing approach. They are broadly organized into four parts, each one corresponding to the four phases described above. Part One is shown in a card format since there will be a larger quantity of these than the other parts; the information is limited in quantity, and a card system allows them to be filed in any order that is most useful for your office. For example, some firms may want to file chronologically so follow-up can be made at the right time. Others may want to arrange according to project type or services required. If they are not filed by date of follow-up, a colored tab system can be used across the top to remind you of when action needs to be taken.

As soon as a preliminary contact develops into a lead, the card is pulled

Contact Information

Contact name _____ Follow-up date _____

Company _____

Address _____

Phone _____ Location (if known) _____

Project name _____

Service/Project type _____

Source of contact _____ Date _____

Type of contact _____ By _____

Result/Follow-up _____

_____

_____

_____

Figure 2-2
Contact Information Card

and attached to a lead information form. This part can be placed in a three-ring binder, again filed in any convenient order. Date lines at the far right side of the page make it easy to thumb through to quickly check critical dates. Copies can be made as needed for management review, other people on the marketing team, or for the project notebook if the lead turns into a job. The proposal information and follow-up report should be with the lead information so that a complete marketing history of any project can be viewed at one time. The different parts can also be color-coded to easily differentiate between the various phases.

If this kind of system is more involved than your firm needs, you may want to condense it to a card system and single sheet printed on both sides. For offices with a micro- or minicomputer, this type of information can easily be recorded using database management software. In addition to having an "electronic tickler file," you have a powerful tool for analyzing the results of your marketing efforts in any number of ways.

Lead Information

Project name _____ Number _____

Primary contact _____ Title _____ Date _____

Company _____

Address _____

Phone _____ Follow-up by _____ Date _____

Project Description

Type _____

Size _____ Rev. _____

Est. cost _____ Rev. _____

Design start _____ Const. start _____ Completion _____

Location _____

Services required _____

_____

_____

Estimated fees _____ Rev. _____

Project financing _____

Designer selection process _____

_____

_____

_____

Project Status _____ Date _____

_____

_____

_____

_____

_____

_____

_____

Figure 2-3
Lead Information Report

Proposal Information

Project name _____ Number _____

Location _____

Company _____

Address _____

Contact _____ Phone _____

Proposal Description

Type of proposal requested _____ Date rec. _____

_____ Date due _____

Proposal/Presentation requirements _____

_____

_____

_____

_____

_____

Qualifications for selection _____

_____

_____

_____

_____

_____

_____

Decision makers _____

_____

Other firms being considered _____

_____

_____

Proposal review schedule _____ Award date

_____ _____

Figure 2-4
Proposal Information

Follow-up

Project name _____ Number _____

Contact _____ Phone _____

Awarded contract?   Yes   No   Date _____

People making proposal/presentation _____

_____

_____

Who was selected? _____

Why was contract given/not given? _____

_____

_____

_____

_____

_____

How could marketing effort been improved? _____

_____

_____

_____

_____

_____

_____

_____

_____

_____

_____

_____

Possible follow-up? _____ Date _____

_____

_____

Figure 2-5
Marketing Follow-up Report

SOURCES FOR MORE INFORMATION

Books

Bachner, John Phillip, Khosla, Naresh Kumar. *Marketing and Promotion for Design Professionals.* New York: Van Nostrand Reinhold, 1977.

Coxe, Weld. *Marketing Architectural and Engineering Services,* 2nd Ed. New York: Van Nostrand Reinhold, 1982.

Jones, Gerre L. *How to Market Professional Design Services,* 2nd ed. New York: McGraw-Hill Book Company, 1983.

Jones, Gerre L. *Marketing for Design Professionals.* Washington: Glyph, 1977.

Newsletters and Magazines

A/E Marketing Journal. P.O. Box 11316, Newington, CT 06111.

Professional Marketing Report. Gerre Jones Associates, Inc., P.O. Box 32387, Washington, DC 20007.

Professional Services Management Journal. MRH Associates, Inc., P.O. Box 11316, Newington, CT 06111.

The Real Estate Intelligence Report. Phillips Publishing, Inc., 7313 Wisconsin Avenue, Bethesda, MD 20814.

SMPS News. Society for Marketing Professional Services, 1437 Powhatan Street, Alexandria, VA 22314. Available to SMPS members only.

Market Research

A Basic Bibliography on Marketing Research. American Marketing Association, 222 S. Riverside Plaza, Suite 606, Chicago, IL 60606.

Bradford's Directory of Marketing Research Agencies and Management Consultants in the United States and the World. Bradford's Directory, P.O. Box 276, Fairfax, VA 22030.

Directory of U.S. and Canadian Marketing Surveys and Services. Charles H. Kline & Co., Inc., 330 Passaic Avenue, Fairfield, NJ 07006.

FINDex: The Directory of Market Research Reports, Studies, and Surveys, 4th ed. Information Clearing House, Inc., 500 Fifth Avenue, New York, NY 10036.

Seminars, Workshops, Seminar Participants Contact each for current schedule and topics.

A/E Marketing Journal. P.O. Box 11316, Newington, CT 06111.

AIA Professional Development Programs. 1735 New York Avenue N.W., Washington, DC 20006. Also offers a home study course in "Marketing Architectural Services."

BIDS, Inc. P.O. Box 3344, Springfield, IL 62708.

Ernest Burden. 20 Waterside Plaza, New York, NY 10010. Visual marketing seminars.

The Coxe Group. 2 Girard Plaza, Philadelphia, PA 19101.

John Coyne, Coyne Associates, 1821 University Avenue, St. Paul, MN 55104.

Harvard University. Harvard Graduate School of Design, Gund Hall 503, Cambridge, MA 02138.

Infoscan, Inc. 32 Elmdale Avenue, Ottawa, Canada K1M IA2.

Gerre Jones. Gerre Jones Associates, Inc., P.O. Box 32387, Washington, DC 20007.

PSMJ Seminars. 126 Harvard Street, Brookline, MA 02146.

Stuart Rose. Professional Development Resources, Inc., 1000 Connecticut Avenue N.W., Suite 9, Washington, DC 20036.

Society for Marketing Professional Services. Contact SMPS address listed below.

Others

National Trade & Professional Organizations of the United States. Columbia Books, Inc., 777 14th Street N.W., Washington, DC 20005. Published annually, this directory lists 4,700 national trade associations indexed by industry, subject, geographical location and budget.

Professional Services Management Association. 1700 E. Dyer Road, Suite 165, Santa Ana, CA 92705.

The Society for Marketing Professional Services. 1437 Powhatan Street, Alexandria, VA 22314. Also maintains the SMPS Institute which offers an 8-day instruction program for people involved with marketing design services. It is the primary organization for professionals involved in marketing design services.

CHAPTER 3
How to Improve Your Promotional Tools

WITH CHANGING LEGAL AND ETHICAL ISSUES and the evolution of sophisticated architectural marketing programs, the number and variety of promotional tools available to the design professional continues to increase. In addition to traditional devices like brochures, more and more architects are making use of techniques that have long been a part of the marketing programs of other businesses: direct mail, newsletters, advertising, and more aggressive public relations. While some architects still eschew many of these practices they can be done professionally and greatly support a design firm's overall marketing plan.

Since many of these topics have been covered in detail in other books and publications, I will only highlight some of the more important considerations. A listing of sources for more information is given at the end of this chapter. Additionally, a more detailed discussion of a graphic program as part of the marketing effort is presented in Chapter 10.

BROCHURES

Probably one of the most common, but misused promotional tools is the brochure. Traditionally, the brochure was *the* main aid to selling professional services, supporting personal contact by the architect and showing what the firm had to offer. Many firms are developing innovative approaches to brochures, but still the majority of professionals are expecting their brochure to be all things to all people.

The most important decision in designing a brochure is to determine what function it is to serve. It can do one of three things, but never all three at once.

1. The brochure can be used as a *catalogue* to show all, or most of, the work experience the firm has. It tries to tell the client all you do. This has been one of

the typical uses and has resulted in the "gilded volumes" some of the large firms produce to impress potential clients. On a more modest scale, small to medium-size firms often try to cram as many of their completed projects and service descriptions as possible into one portfolio. Economics becomes the limiting factor.

2. The brochure can be used as a true *marketing item* that is directed toward one particular job or project type. This kind of printed piece tells the client if you can do his or her job.

3. The brochure can be used as a *leave-behind* to remind people your firm exists, generally what kind of services you have to offer, and your capabilities.

One of the more popular trends is to design a system of promotional items that can be combined in various ways to create any of the three kinds of brochures as the need arises. For example, project descriptions and photographs can be printed separately on loose sheets and combined by project type to form a *sales piece* for a job of that class. All of the project sheets can be collected to form a *catalogue*, or the best of each project type done by the firm can be combined to briefly illustrate the firm's diversity of experience. This can be a relatively inexpensive *leave-behind*. This approach is discussed in more detail in Chapter 10.

Here is a checklist of some of the critical points to keep in mind when you develop or revise your office brochure(s).

1. Keep the brochure concise. They typically are scanned and not read. If you cannot write succinctly, hire a copywriter. Having someone else write the copy is probably a good idea anyway since it provides an objective approach to the material. When you have condensed as much as you think is possible, go back and edit another 50 percent.

2. Avoid professional jargon. Use language the potential client understands. Nothing disinterests a reader more than confusing explanations of the architect's work. Using an outsider to write copy helps avoid this problem.

3. Make the brochure client-oriented. Show and tell what will interest your *audience*, how you can solve *their* problems, and how *they* can get the most value for their money. Avoid self-serving statements and explanations about how great your project designs are or how many times a project has been published. If it doesn't show you can meet the anticipated needs of the client, it will not look good no matter how many awards it has received.

4. Be specific about what services your firm offers. "Complete architectural services" does not tell people the wide diversity of work you may do. Some items in a detailed listing might catch the eye of a prospective client who might otherwise dismiss you as another architect knocking at his door.

5. Avoid calling yourself a "design-oriented office." This is probably one of the most overused and meaningless phrases in promotional material. *Every* office is design-oriented by definition whether they produce avant-garde, magazine-cover buildings or "out-of-the-drawer" identical units for retail chain stores. Explain what you mean, precisely, so your audience will understand. The word "design," like "beauty," means many things to many people.

6. Use the best graphic designer you can find. It is estimated that only 5 to 10 percent of architectural and engineering brochures are professional in content or appearance. A poorly designed and executed brochure is nothing but an unnecessary disadvantage.

7. Keep the listing of key personnel and their credentials to a minimum. Potential clients are interested first in the major project experience and knowledge of the project team, not every professional society or civic club they belong to. Detailed resumes can alway be given if requested. The personal interview is the place where the client really begins to know the people assigned to his job.

8. Use "people" photographs along with project photographs. In addition to reading resumes, clients like to actually see the people with whom they might be working. Pictures of staff in the office and on the job site reinforce the fact that architecture is a service business.

9. Vary the photography of projects with close-ups, aerials, and other ways of viewing to add interest.

10. If you use loose sheets as part of the system, have your firm's name and address printed on each sheet. They sometimes get separated from the cover or are given out separately.

11. As with a book, the cover is important. It must get the viewer's attention and get him or her to open it.

12. Provide some method of updating the brochure. Whether you use a system of loose sheets or a binder there should be some way of keeping up with new projects, personnel and services without reprinting the entire piece.

13. Always include a client list.

14. Be accurate in your credits for projects. Work done in association, joint venture or while employed by another firm should be clearly stated. Prospects get suspicious if they begin to see the same project in several brochures.

15. Use only the best quality photographs. Hire a professional photographer. Negative format should be 4″ x 5″ for both color and black and white. This is especially true of photographs that will be fairly large in the brochure. In some cases, 2¼″ square negative format may be acceptable, but try to limit them to photos that will be reproduced in a small size.

16. Consider using more than one brochure. Mini-brochures can be produced inexpensively for leave-behinds or mailings. If designed properly, they can have a great impact and outline the most important aspects of your firm. Double-folded 8½" x 11" single sheets, newsletter formats, and fold-out posters are some of the ideas that you might consider.

CASE IN POINT

SHWC Inc., for example, uses a four-leaf mini-brochure that folds to an 8½" x 11" size. The brochure shows examples of some of the major project types the Dallas-based architectural, engineering and planning firm does along with a very brief description of the office. Four-color pamphlets are then printed for individual projects with photographs, floor plans and brief project descriptions to use individually or in combination with other material. In this way, several different kinds of "packages" can be assembled to meet various needs.

NEWSLETTERS

Newsletters are becoming more popular with professional design firms as a way of keeping their name in front of a large audience on a regular basis. They are an accepted medium of business communication and provide an inexpensive way of keeping past, present, and potential clients and others current with a firm's activities. Properly designed, they can even fit into an overall brochure system to get double duty out of the same material.

There are basically two different types of newsletters for design business and they should be kept separate. There is the newsletter for in-house communication, oriented toward employees with news of new staff, promotions, company picnics, office policy changes and the like. The marketing newsletter is directed toward potential clients, consultants, the news media, and anyone else you want to keep informed about your current business activities.

Before starting a newsletter, talk to your graphic designer about format, coordination with other parts of your graphic system, and the relative costs of various printing processes. Keep the following points in mind when you start to plan your newsletter.

Checklist for Newsletter Design

1. Your newsletter should be concise, easy to read, and offer information that will interest your readers. Avoid lengthy descriptions and, as with brochures, avoid professional jargon.
2. Be consistent from one issue to the next. Maintain the same masthead design and placement, graphic layout, and overall feeling of the newsletter. You may even consider having "columns" in each issue, with

similar content in the same place. For example, new projects may always be featured on the second page while new employees and promotions will always be found on page four.

3. Consider what the frequency should be. As a marketing tool, your newsletter should be keeping your firm's name and activities in front of a large number of people. For this reason, you will want to publish at least quarterly. If you have the content available, and the financial resources, more frequent publication may be appropriate.

4. The graphic layout, logo, and title should be consistent with your overall graphic image. Does the appearance of the newsletter command attention? Once again, it pays to have the best graphic design talent available.

5. Use a type face that is easy to read and conveys the image of your company. Many people use typewriter typefaces to give the feeling of an up-to-the-minute publication while others use a more refined face with justified right margins to give a commercial quality look to the newsletter.

6. Use photographs, charts, drawings and other graphics to add interest and communicate your message more effectively.

7. Consider highlighting important parts of the text by using emphasis techniques such as boldface type, underlining, italics, or all caps.

8. Determine how you want to mail the piece. It can be mailed flat, double-folded and taped or stapled with the postage, address and return address on the front, or folded and mailed in a #10 envelope. Other techniques are also possible. All of them, however, have implications for postage rate, appearance and ease of processing. How you decide to handle your mailing will depend on the quantity, appearance you want, money available, whether you do the mailing in your office or contract it out to a mailing house, and the amount of time you have to devote to production.

9. Be sure you are mailing to the right people. Are they the ones who are in decision-making positions, likely to spread the work about your firm, likely to be in need of your services, or truly interested in your activities? Make sure your mailing list is up to date and is properly targeted. Refer to the section on direct mail for more discussion of mailing lists.

10. Try to include information your readers will find useful. In addition to news about your firm, consider including features such as checklists for planning a new office, how to select an architect, or anything that would appeal to the people you are mailing to and *their* business. The slant will always be toward the services you offer, of course, but including this type of material makes the newsletter appear to be less of a self-serving instrument and more of an information source that people will look forward to receiving *and* reading.

11. From time to time include an additional insert to announce a new service, opening of a new office or some other special event. This not only gives your readers an added bonus, but allows you to piggyback more information on the same postage.

12. Work on three issues at a time: be writing for the next publication, researching for the one after that, and planning and outlining the following one. This way you will not get caught in the last minute panic of trying to produce an issue.

13. Consider having a section for how the reader can get more information for follow-up. Give names and addresses and phone numbers of data sources, people to contact, and, of course, the person in your firm to contact if needed.

14. Briefly mention somewhere in the letter what is coming in the next issue. This keeps people interested and piques their curiosity.

15. Demand the best writing possible. If you don't think anyone in your office is capable of this, use an outside copywriter. Good writing is not as easy as it seems and most architects do not excel in this area. Generally, the style of a newsletter should be simple, direct, personal, and directed to the audience you are trying to reach. If your readers are developers and financiers, talk money and business. If your readers are engineers, be technical. If your readers are medical facility administrators, discuss management and how it relates to medical facilities. Any good stylebook will give you detailed pointers on writing style, but in general, use the active voice, and employ active verbs and concrete nouns. Talk to your readers as though you were in the same room with them in a normal conversational way.

Doing a good newsletter takes a major commitment. You *must* publish regularly, maintain a high quality and constantly review and update your mailing list. If you don't believe you can keep up the pace with in-house production, consider using a newsletter service. Provided with rough copy and photographs or with just an idea, they can handle the writing, production and mailing of your publication, often at a cost lower than you would incur if you had to stumble through the process time after time.

DIRECT MAIL

Direct mail is increasingly being used by design professionals as a way of directing a specific message to a specific audience. Although some architects may consider this marketing tool to be non-professional and nothing more than "junk mail," if well done it can provide a valuable service to clients and potential clients by informing them of services they might not have known existed. Direct mail has many advantages as a marketing tool.

1. It is very selective. You can reach just the people in just the geographical area you are interested in and concentrate on those prospects you think may be the most likely to use your services.
2. It is inexpensive. You can print and mail a sizable quantity for about the same price as a one-time advertisement in a trade magazine.
3. It is comprehensive. For a minimal effort in a given amount of time you can reach a greater number of prospects than your marketing staff could ever hope to contact.
4. It works. If the campaign is done properly with a refined mailing list, top-quality graphics, proper timing, and correct follow-up, direct mail can add to your success rate.

CASE IN POINT

For example, Miles Treaster and Associates, a Sacramento-based design and space planning firm and furniture representative, planned a four-stage direct mail campaign targeted to past clients and top executives of companies with more than ten employees. The company names were assembled with the aid of Dun & Bradstreet listings and lists from one of the major furniture manufacturers they represent. The mailings were spaced about three months apart and discussed key issues concerning interior design and business (Figure 3-1). The response rate of the first three mailings was about 5 percent. Of these, Treaster reports 60 percent to 70 percent became actual jobs. Overall, they were well-received, educated the business community and paid off in new design projects. A second series was planned based on the success of the first try.

You can use direct mail for many purposes. How your firm adds it to the group of other marketing tools depends on your overall marketing plan. Some of the more common uses include:

- Producing sales leads for personal follow-up
- Advertising
- Announcing a new service
- Gathering market research data
- Announcing new personnel and promotions
- Penetrating new, unfamiliar market areas

Direct mail is a specialty in itself. A quick glance through the yellow pages listings will give you an idea of the number of firms that provide this kind of service. If you would like detailed information, you should contact the Direct Mail/Marketing Association, Inc., 6 East 43rd Street, New York, NY 10017.

One of the most important tasks in a successful direct mail campaign is the mailing list. This is what gets your message to exactly the right person. Although building a quantity of names is important, it is equally critical to "narrow" it as

**Figure 3-1
Direct Mail**

much as possible. That is, include only those names who are the most likely to respond to the mailing. The best list is one you develop in-house. This can include past clients, business associates, dealers, and others you know you want to keep informed. To expand the list of potential contacts, however, you probably need to start with outside sources and refine the list to fit your needs. Some of the more common sources include:

Trade Directories

Check the *Guide to American Business Directories* to find the ones that will help you the most.

Membership Lists of Professional and Trade Associations

Many of these groups will give or sell you their lists. For some, like a Chamber of Commerce, you may have to be a member yourself to get the list.

Commercial List Houses

These businesses have very large lists of practically any grouping you could want. The cost per thousand names is usually inexpensive, but the biggest disadvantage is that they are not always current. List houses also go for quantity rather than quality since that is where their income is derived. For an unfamiliar market, however, they may be a good place to start.

Trade Magazine Publishers

You can sometimes buy the subscription list of a specialty magazine that reaches the market you also want to reach.

List Brokers

These are people paid by commission from list owners. They know the sources and can get you the kinds of lists most helpful for your use.

Telephone Books and Local Trade Directories

These are rather hit or miss sources, but can be a starting point for fairly comprehensive coverage of a local area.

Maintaining a mailing list is one of the most difficult jobs of direct mail. You should update it at least twice a year, deleting and adding names as required and verifying addresses and personnel in the companies you mail to. If your list is small, maintenance can be done by your staff or you can have a commercial mailing service do it for you. If you have or plan to purchase a microcomputer for your office, maintaining a mailing list is one of the extra chores it can do very easily, including printing labels or addressing envelopes and typing personalized letters to the names on your list.

After you have established a list and decided on the content of the mailing, the next step is to get it read by the person to whom it is mailed and to get some kind of response. Response is the name of the game: direct mail is of no use if it goes from the in-box to the wastebasket. Volumes of research have been produced on what factors increase response. If you are interested there are many books and articles on the subject, or you can contact the Direct Mail/Marketing Association, Inc. You should expect, however, about a 2 percent to 5 percent response rate.

In summary form, here are some of the most significant points to keep in mind when you are planning your direct mail campaign.

1. Use high-quality packaging. This means that the graphic design, choice of paper and quality of printing must be the best. The envelope should be consistent with the material the reader will find inside; for example, if the copy and graphics of the mailing are formal and conservative, the envelope should be similar. Tests have shown that color increases the likelihood the piece will be read and improves the response rate. A four-color reproduction is useful with "sight-appeal" services

such as architecture. Tests have also suggested that the use of colored and/or textured paper improves response.

2. Explain benefits to the reader immediately and concisely. Tell what the mailing will do for the reader. Use action headlines.

3. Talk the language of the reader. Know your audience and use language and style they will find most informative.

4. Be brief. Most people give direct mailing very little time so you must convey your thoughts quickly. Get to the point fast.

5. Include a cover letter or some other form of personal communication. Tests have shown that direct mail impact is often doubled when a personal letter is enclosed.

6. Use testimonials of similar businesses that you are mailing to. Where a recipient may be doubtful of your claims, he or she may believe the word of someone you have done work for previously.

7. Consider the idea of "involvement." Direct mail experts claim that if the reader can tear off, fold, punch out, or somehow participate in the mailing the response is likely to be greater.

8. Use postscripts. This is often the most remembered part of the letter or mailing.

9. Provide an easy means of response. This is probably one of the most important parts of the mailing since some kind of response is what you want. Include a postage-paid business reply envelope with a card already filled out with the addressee's name and address. Or you might give your phone number and suggest a collect call or set up a toll-free number.

10. Offer something in return for a response. The standard offers you see so often in direct mail, as a free poster, a quarter for your time, or a sample of the product may seem unprofessional, but the basic idea works. You might consider offering a more detailed brochure or a free copy of the survey you may be taking.

11. Have the correct spelling and title of the addressee. Mr. Williamsen certainly will not think much of your mailing if you address it to Mrs. Williamson.

12. Address the piece to the exact person you want to reach. If you cannot obtain a name, address it to a title.

13. For a personalized appearance and to take the mailing out of the junk mail category, type the address instead of using a label. This may take more time but is well worth the effort. If you are using automated equipment, envelopes can be adhered to a continuous roll of "tractor-feed" backing paper so that they can be fed through your letter-quality computer printer. When the addressing is done, they are peeled off and ready for inserts. Check with your mailing house or business forms printer for more detailed information on the mechanics of mailing.

14. Send the mailing first-class with a stamp or meter mark. Bulk rate is cheaper but for a small investment the first impression your letter will make is well

worth it. For the quantities most architects mail, the savings does not amount to much anyway.

15. Make sure the postage is accurate. A direct mail letter with "postage due" stamped on it will not be read or responded to, and is likely to damage any image you might have had with the recipient. If you have any doubts, have post office personnel weigh it.

Once you begin to get replies, respond to them promptly, within a day or two at the most. Also, consider sending out a second or third mailing; sometimes these are more effective than the first. Timing of mailings is important. Tests show that January and February are the best months for direct mail, followed by October, August and November.

Do not discount direct mail as a marketing tool because of any bad image you may have of it. If well done and properly targeted, it can be a valuable addition to your overall marketing plan.

PUBLIC RELATIONS

Every design firm has a public relations image whether it likes it or not. In the worst case it may be being known as the architect of a major public building whose roof collapsed, and in the best case, perhaps, it may involve being featured on the cover of a national news magazine. Most firms are somewhere in between, of course, and the degree to which the public has a positive image of them often determines continued success, profitability, and a steady rate of growth.

Public relations differs from marketing in that the former is not directly tied to a particular potential job. Rather, it establishes and communicates your presence to various groups of "publics" on many different levels. Of course, the most important audience group you are trying to communicate with are those people who may need your services or are in a position to recommend you to others.

Instead of placing the public relations effort on the back burner as many firms do, you should use it as a tool in support of your overall marketing effort. You should control the image you want to project instead of relying on chance events to be your public relations agent. A good public relations program doesn't necessarily require a separate PR director, retaining an expensive public relations firm, or a large cash outlay to be effective. What it does require is planning and consistent and repeated work on your part.

A public relations program must be part of a marketing plan that sets the direction of the PR effort. The first step is to identify who your publics are and what *their* needs are since you are ultimately trying to communicate that overlap of your services with the interests of a particular community of people. To get your message across most effectively you will have to talk on their terms in their language.

Some of the possible "publics" you might identify include existing clients, past and potential clients, the general public, your peers, your employees, vendors, the news media, students, civic groups, and related groups such as real estate developers, financiers, and contractors. Each of these groups will be interested in a slightly different aspect of your practice and you should plan varying approaches accordingly. You may need to emphasize some more than others simply for economic reasons or because some may be more closely tied to your firm and its activities.

The following are some of the public relations techniques you might consider in addition to brochures, newsletters, direct mail and advertising.

Press Releases

Press releases are one of the most economical ways to publicize your work, both in local newspapers and national trade magazines. Unfortunately, many releases never go to press because they are poorly written, incorrectly presented, or do not conform to the requirements of the publication. Here are some tips for writing an effective press release and getting it published.

1. It must be newsworthy. What constitutes news depends on the publication. Your release should be written with the proper slant. If you are announcing the receipt of a design commission for an office building, your release to local papers might emphasize the location, generally what it will look like, its effect on the community, local people involved, and so forth. The same announcement submitted to a national professional journal might emphasize the design, unique construction techniques, and other items of interest to the professional reader. Even among local newspapers, editors like to have a unique story, so rewrite the copy for each publication you submit it to.

2. Use the traditional "pyramid" newspaper style. Start out succinctly, giving the who, what, why, when, where, and how. After this, elaborate, giving the critical information first and least important data last. Editors have to fit the copy to the space available and it is usually the end of the story that is cut first.

3. Make it easy for the editor to do his or her job. Write each paragraph so it can stand alone when the editor cuts. Be concise and stick to the facts. A one-page press release is best; use a maximum of two if really necessary. If the story is so great that the editor wants more material, you will probably get a call for an interview.

4. If you are sending the release to two or more departments of the same paper, say so on the release or in a cover letter.

5. Start the piece with a concise, attention-getting heading. This should not be a headline—editors will write their own—but an easy way for those reviewing the press release to know immediately what it is about. Some public relations people advise against this, but I think it is helpful to let the editor quickly know what is in the body of the copy. You can put the first sentence in all caps if you like.

6. In the upper left-hand corner give your name, the firm's name, address and telephone number.

7. In the upper right-hand corner place the release date. This can be a specific day or "For Immediate Release" if you want the paper to publish as soon as they receive it.

8. Leave ample margins on all sides for the editor's notes. Double-space the copy and use only one side of an 8½″ by 11″ sheet of paper.

9. After the last line of the story place a *″—30—″* or *"*****"* to clearly indicate the end of the copy. If you use more than one sheet, place "more" at the bottom of the page and place a "slug line" with a "page 2" at the top of the next page. The slug is simply a two-or three-word title to identify that page with the rest of the story in case the two sheets get separated.

A few additional comments are worth noting. Keep in mind the schedules of those publications you are submitting your article to if timing is important. Monthly magazines have copy deadlines four to six weeks or longer before publication so you need to have your material to them well ahead of time. Try to coordinate your release with other parts of your marketing effort. When more than one communication about the same subject reaches your audience, its impact will be greater than a single item alone. Finally, target your press release to the appropriate media—those publications whose readers will be interested in your story.

Writing for Publication

There are many reasons for writing (ego gratification, peer approval, money, etc.). As a public relations tool, writing allows you to get your name and your firm's name in front of potential clients within a select marketing group, illustrates your expertise in a particular area, and provides you with a third-party endorsement (the publication in which your work appears) about your qualifications.

As a promotional tool, writing should be limited to the business press, those periodicals which are read by your potential clients, not your competitors. Save publication of your work in the architectural and design press for reprints and peer approval. If you are trying to market your skills and experience in school design, write for magazines that are read by school administrators, physical plant directors and others in the field.

When you decide to try writing, first consider content. Editors have their readers' interests in mind as a priority; if they do not, the magazine does not sell. What you may think is the most important article available may not interest the editor at all. To be a saleable commodity, your idea should appeal to your readers: it should help them do their jobs better, easier, faster, for less cost, keep them current with developments in their field, give them a step up on the competition, or in some way offer a tangible benefit. Your idea should also be timely and fit into the editorial plans of the publication. All magazines plan far ahead as to the general content of each issue. If what you submit does not fit into that plan or cannot be used as filler material, it will not be used. Don't be discouraged, however. Six months later your idea may be just what the editorial board is looking for.

The next step is to establish your list of possible markets. There are several sources you can use to do this.

The Design and Building Industry's Publicity Directory

Lord & Welanetz, Inc., eds.
Box 11316
Newington, CT 06111

> Co-published by MRH Associates, publisher of the *A/E Marketing Journal,* this directory lists more than 250 national publications read by purchasers of design services and others involved in the building industry. It gives the person to contact, address, readership, circulation, editorial direction, submission requirements, and editorial calendar for the upcoming year.

Business Publication Rates and Data

Standard Rate & Data Service, Inc.
5201 Old Orchard Road
Skokie, IL 60077

> This publication lists nearly every business journal produced in the United States. It is indexed by title and subject matter with detailed information about each journal.

Ayer Directory of Publications

Ayer Press
210 Washington Square
Philadelphia, PA 19106

> For broader coverage, this directory includes all the nation's daily and weekly newspapers and magazines including contacts, circulation, editorial content and deadlines.

Bacon's Publicity Checker: Magazines and Newspapers

Bacon's Publishing Company, Inc.
14 East Jackson Boulevard
Chicago, IL 60604

> Includes information on periodicals including such items as deadlines, editors' names and editorial scope.

Ulrich's International Periodicals Directory

R.R. Bowker Company
1180 Avenue of the Americas
New York, NY 10036

> Contains information and brief description on foreign and domestic periodicals.

After you have established a list of the most likely periodicals to approach, get a copy of them from the publisher or review some sample issues at your local library. Get a feeling for the magazine or newspaper. Determine what the articles are about, their length, how many are written by staffers as opposed to contributing writers, and what slant they have. Many magazines will also send you on request a guide sheet with submission requirements and style guidelines.

When you have convinced yourself that you have a marketable idea and some prospective publishers, set down your proposal in a query letter. Very few magazines want unsolicited manuscripts anymore—especially the professional and business journals. This is actually to your advantage since you do not have to waste your time researching and writing something that will not sell.

The query letter is simply a *brief* outline of your idea to see if an editor would be interested. When writing a letter of inquiry keep the following points in mind.

1. Include a statement of your idea, why it is relevant to the publication's readers, probable length, if you would provide any illustrations with it, and your qualifications for writing the piece.
2. Conclude with some kind of request for a response. "May I send you an outline and sample photographs?" is one possible way of ending the letter.
3. Keep it brief: one page, double-spaced, should be the maximum. Editors are busy people and they don't have time to read a lot of letters.
4. Be direct. Do not make assumptions about what the editor is thinking or what you think he or she should do. Offer your idea simply and succinctly and let the editor decide.
5. Make sure your idea has a definite slant toward the readers of the periodical. The basic information contained in the article may be the same for several possible submissions, but the emphasis should be placed to match the interests of the magazine's readers.
6. Submit an absolutely perfect letter in terms of spelling, grammar and style. If you cannot write a letter, why should the editor think you can write an entire article.

If your idea is sound, your query letter appealing, and you are accurate in your list of publications to which you submit, you will probably get an assignment. Expect a lot of rejection letters, but if you are persistent chances are you will see your name, and possibly your firm's name, in print.

Seminars and Workshops

Conducting seminars and workshops is an excellent way of offering the community a useful service while exposing the availability of your service to a potential market. Organizing and conducting a workshop is not an easy task, but allows you to talk to a number of *interested* people at one time. There are many ways of setting up a seminar or workshop. At a minimum, however, consider these guidelines:

- Offer the attendees some tangible benefit. You want them to go away with more knowledge than they came in with.
- Organize a group of people with different viewpoints and information to offer on the same topic. Not only does this take the burden off one person, but it makes the session more interesting, more useful, and makes it seem less self-serving.
- Provide handouts with usable information. These make note-taking easier, offer more for the money, and serve as a reminder of the seminar after it is over.
- Keep fees to a minimum, or free if possible. These kinds of seminars are usually not intended to be profit-making enterprises; they are a way of publicizing your firm. If you can make a profit, fine, but generally registrations should only cover the costs of producing the affair: meeting hall rental, meals, audio-visual rental, and so forth.
- Consider your audience when scheduling times and lengths of seminars. If you are offering one for busy executives, for example, a breakfast seminar or late afternoon or evening workshop may be the best time. If your market consists of large companies with a sizable number of employees who may be interested, you might consider taking the seminar to the business.
- Although seminars and workshops are useful marketing tools, do not use them as a soapbox for your sales lecture. If you present a good meeting, are knowledgeable in the subject matter, and generate interest in the audience you will probably get requests for more information or an interview for work.

Professional Committees

Offer your time to serve on committees either in your own profession or in allied professions. Not only will you provide much needed volunteer time for the organization, but the education you receive and the contacts you make will prove to be valuable.

Political Office

Either elective or appointed positions in local politics are ways to both serve your community and become known as a design professional. The contacts you make in these kinds of positions often are not available in any other way. Politics is not for everyone, of course. If you are not inclined to working within your local political system, stay out. You will not be useful and your experience will be frustrating at best.

Civic Activities

Donating your time and belonging to clubs are usually not as time-consuming as political office (or as volatile), but often produce similar results. Some professionals question the value of belonging to the country club, the chamber of commerce, athletic clubs, service organizations and the like. The simple fact, however, is that your clients and potential clients belong to these same groups. Meeting them on common ground directly, or through referrals, is still one of the best traditional ways of making a contact.

Open Houses

Another traditional method of public relations is the open house. Holding a Christmas party, showing off new offices, introducing people with recent promotions all offer some reason to invite people to your office who might not otherwise come. Most open houses, however, are downright dull and unmemorable. Show some creativity. Hold it at a building you designed that is under construction. Center the idea around a theme. Give away tote bags, note pads, or something your guests can use. The ideas don't have to be expensive; they should just show some thought and concern for offering an interesting party.

Design Awards

Design awards are one of the best ways to gain the acknowledgement of your peers. They are also useful as implied third-party endorsements and give added credibility to your marketing presentations. If you decide to enter design award programs with a marketing purpose be prepared, as with writing, for a lot of rejections. Be prepared, also, to spend some of your own money. There are often entry fees and always the cost of preparing a first-class entry with little tangible reward other than a plaque or certificate. To guide you in your search for award programs, get a copy of *The Design and Building Industry's Awards Directory,* companion to the *Publicity Directory,* published by Lord & Welanetz, Inc., and MRH Associates, Box 11316, Newington, CT 06111.

Speeches and Talk Shows

As a design professional you are an expert in your field and a credible source of information, knowledge, and opinion. Organizations, from neighborhood clubs to major conventions, are always looking for speakers. If you can give an informative, interesting talk in the language of your audience, you can use this public relations tool as a valuable addition to your marketing program. You can speak before live audiences and on radio or television talk shows.

If you decide to pursue this actively, concentrate on those situations that will give you the most exposure. Local broadcast shows can be found in almost every city, regardless of size. They are always in need of guests to fill air time as long as they have something that fits the station's format and is of interest to their listening audience. Possible topics might include informational discussions of the actions of the local urban renewal authority or planning commission and their effect on the community, announcement of an exhibition of a local architect's work, or a review of the activities of a volunteer group of which you are a member.

If you are a specialist in one area, are involved with some national program, have written a book or otherwise feel that you can expand your geographical range, consider that. A good source for reviewing the possible outlets for your appearances is the *Talk Show Directory for Radio and Television* published by the National Research Bureau, 310 South Michigan Avenue, Chicago, IL 60604. This directory lists both local and national shows, the name of the show, the station, address, phone number, air time, host's and producer's name, the format, criteria for guest appearances, and whom to contact for scheduling an appearance. The information is indexed by subject matter preferred, type of guests preferred, metro areas, drive time and AM/FM/VHF/UHF.

ADVERTISING

For practical purposes, advertising by architects and other design professionals is no longer a legal issue and has little substance as an ethical issue. The Department of Justice, state court decisions and the American Institute of Architects have all contributed toward making advertising by architects a fact of life. In the *Voluntary Statement of Ethical Principles* adopted by the AIA in 1981, Article VI states:

> "Members should be candid and truthful in their professional communications. The integrity of the profession depends upon truth and candor in all forms of communication. There is no justification for misleading discourse. This principle applies to advertising, promotional endeavors and presentation . . . "

It is no longer a question of whether you legally can or ethically should advertise, but whether you want to and how good of a marketing strategy it may be. Advertising is expensive. Before spending money on such an endeavor, you should carefully consider if you need it as part of your organized marketing plan, if you can afford it, and if it is the best way to reach a particular audience. Remember, one disadvantage is that it does not have third-party credibility. Find and consult with a competent advertising agency. They can advise you about whether to do it, and if so, how.

Keep the following ideas in mind when you begin to deal with an agency.

1. It is critical to first decide what the *purpose* of the ad is to be. What are your objectives? Is it to establish an image, change an image, get leads, announce a special service, or something else?

2. Based on your purpose, sell only one idea in each ad. Everything in the copy and illustration should be oriented to that one idea.

3. Generally, professionals can make the best use of advertising by emphasizing and selling their uniqueness. Tell what is special about your firm.

4. In broad terms, an advertisement must, a) get the attention of the reader, b) maintain his interest long enough to read the message, c) show benefits the reader will receive if he uses your service, and d) prompt some kind of action, whether that is a verbal or written response or a positive change in the reader's image.

5. The basic components of an advertisement in printed form are the headline, the copy, and the illustration. An advertising agency will be able to design these for the desired effect. Since most architects are not accustomed to thinking in these terms in their communications, be prepared to see years of experience of your firm and volumes of things you want to say reduced to a few, well-chosen words. Headlines must "grab" the reader and show benefits, indicate the purpose of the ad and prompt the reader to go on. The copy should be brief with the active voice and strong verbs, and be easily understood by the reader. Once again, no professional jargon, just simple, straight talk.

Select an advertising agency as you expect a client to select your firm for design services. Ask local and national firms to submit brochures, query your colleagues and other people you know who advertise, and be aware of ads you like in the printed media and on television and radio and find out who did them. From this investigation, develop a list of potential agencies for personal interviews. Check their experience, especially with service-oriented businesses as opposed to product-oriented companies. Talk prices, of course, and schedule. See if they have had any contact with the building industry or architects. Also, query them as to results of similar campaigns.

CASE IN POINT

The firm of Morris-Aubry Architects in Houston started a campaign in 1981 by buying space in such magazines as *Texas Monthly*, regional editions of *Newsweek*, *Time*, and New York editions of *Business Week*, *U.S. News and World Report* as well as others. They had decided that better recognition of their firm by major money lenders, especially in Chicago and New York, was needed. When many of their developer clients sought financing, the lenders wanted an architectural firm that was more well-known. The advertising program was designed to overcome this problem as *part of* an overall marketing strategy that included personal contacts by marketing staff. Janet Goodman of Morris-Aubry reports that response to the ads has been good. Lenders are beginning to recognize the name and capabilities of the firm, and developers use the advertisements to show the stature of "their" architectural firm when talking to financial sources. The Morris-Aubry promotion illustrates a first-class, professional approach to the issue of advertising by design professionals. They are straightforward, accurate, and address the concerns of their target audience.

MAKING WINNING PRESENTATIONS

The personal presentation of your firm's capabilities to a prospective client is the most important part of the entire marketing cycle. For most jobs, getting to this point means that you have been successful at making the initial contact, following the lead and showing that your firm can probably do jobs similar to the potential client's project as well as other firms on the "short list." The task now is to shift emphasis from general capabilities to how you can solve the *client's* problem within *their* budget and within *their* time frame, and offer something better than the competition. There are, of course, presentations that are designed to give a general introduction to a firm, just as a general brochure would do. My emphasis here, however, will be on presentations planned to get a specific job for a specific client.

Making the shift from presenting general capabilities to presenting specific project expertise is where many firms fail, especially small and medium-size offices. When a client invites a professional firm to present, they are mainly interested in knowing what the firm can do for them and how it will approach their problem. Like a written proposal, the presentation for a job needs to be precisely targeted to the client's situation. Since presentations are time-consuming (and therefore, money-consuming) the design professional needs to be able to quickly assess the client's needs and have a system of organizing the most effective presentation to address those needs.

Types of Presentations

There are, of course, many types of presentation techniques. When a firm or individual finds the one that seems to work the best for them they tend to stick with it regardless of the type of potential client they are talking to. This is understandable in the interest of saving time and doing something that you feel comfortable with, but can be a mistake. Like the content of the presentation, the type and structure of it should be targeted toward the audience. It is surprising how many architects use a similar format of a slide show, for example, whether they are talking to a board of directors or a developer. In deciding on the type of presentation to plan for a job interview consider these questions.

1. What are the expectations of the audience? Would they expect a multi-screen, sophisticated audio-visual presentation or would they want a more informal, one-to-one "conversation"?
2. What is the background of the audience? Are they lay people who would find it difficult to understand some types of architectural drawings? Are they engineers who would relate more to detailed process diagrams and other types of technical drawings? What is their knowledge level?
3. How many people are going to be in the audience? Consider the person who will be the farthest from the presentation medium.
4. How much time is available for the presentation itself?
5. How much time is available for preparation of the presentation? How much money is available?
6. What are the skills of the person presenting?
7. How can the problem-solving process for the proposed project best be communicated? A slide show may be best for one problem, a film for another and drawings mounted on boards for yet a third.
8. What kinds of information does the audience need to see in order to make a decision? Models, numbers, examples of similar jobs, your design and production process?
9. What types of presentation material will best communicate *your* thoughts about the project? Are there complicated three-dimensional ideas that need a model, for example? If time and movement are important, would a film be best?
10. What will the physical setting be? Will it be possible to darken the space for an audio-visual presentation? Does the presentation need to be portable for an out-of-town show?

There are many possible formats for marketing presentations. Many can be used in combination with others. No single technique is appropriate in all situations, and you should carefully evaluate what approach is the most likely to communicate your message to the potential client.

Before the Presentation

Proper preparation is vital to a successful showing of your work and approach to the client's problem. Consider the following when you prepare for any interview.

1. Define the objective. What do you hope to accomplish?
2. Know your client. Find out who will be in the audience and who the real decision makers are. Often the interview is set up by an intermediary who may give you an inaccurate impression of what the decision makers want to see. Find out as much as you can about the client's company.

This not only flatters them, but can help you decide what to talk about and show.

3. Visit the site and become familiar with the surrounding neighborhood, views, topography, unusual problems and anything else that might impinge on the design. As simple as this sounds, it is amazing how many architects don't do this simple task. Going into a presentation with this extra bit of knowledge gives you a step up on the competition. Of course, for out-of-town work it is imperative.

4. Try to find out who else is presenting. Knowing who your competition is may help you address special points that the other firms may bring up or omit.

5. Try to be the last in a series of interviews. The client may remember more about your firm if you are closer to the time of the decision.

6. Plan for some type of visual display. Studies show that over 80 percent of learning is through sight. Additionally, research indicates that 50 percent to 75 percent of presented material is retained if both visual and audio senses are stimulated while only about 20 percent is retained if the presentation is purely verbal. This doesn't mean, either, that you must plan for an elaborate multi-media extravaganza—just have something to reinforce what you are saying.

7. Arrange to have the presentation in your office if possible. It is easier to set up, easier to maintain control, it can be combined with an office tour, and most important, it gets the clients away from the distractions of their office.

8. Know what the lighting in the presentation room will be. Can it be darkened for audio-visual? Can material placed on the wall be properly illuminated?

9. Is there tack board available for pinups? Do you need to take your own easels?

10. How far away will the most distant person be? Plan your visuals for that person.

11. What other aspects of the presentation room will help or hinder your efforts? Consider such things as the color of the walls, furniture obstructions, seating position of the audience, glare from windows, comfort of the chairs, lack of proper ventilation and the like.

12. Prepare to show a little extra effort for the client—something they may not expect. Give them a checklist of things to consider in their planning, two or three concepts if they have asked for only one, or something that shows you have really thought about the project even though you do not have the job yet.

13. Dress according to the situation and your audience. Generally, dress should be neutral and consistent with what your listeners expect. You want attention paid to your words and visuals, not to some flashy outfit or incongruous attire.

14. Be prepared to talk time and cost even if it isn't requested. Have a good idea of how long it might take to complete the client's project and at least some rough cost ranges for the kind of project they are contemplating. Point out any unusual conditions that may affect cost and schedule that the client may not have considered.

15. Have a trial run in your office with other staff role-playing as "clients." Have them play devil's advocate to respond and ask questions as the toughest client might. Check technical items such as the length of your presentation, equipment setup problems, slide sequence and so forth.

During the Presentation

Regardless of what type of presentation you are making or what audio-visual hardware you have backing you up, the following suggestions may help you polish your communication efforts.

1. Play to your audience. Show concern for their business and their building problem and how you can help.

2. Emphasize your problem-solving approach. There is an important difference between showing your past work to illustrate how great you are and showing your previous jobs to illustrate how you have solved similar design problems.

3. Be aware of the interactive nature of presentations. Even in a monologue by you there is always feedback to temper your actions as the presentation proceeds. People's movement, attention or lack of it, body posture, whispering, note-taking or doodling, and other types of non-verbal communication should all be valuable clues to the exact structuring of the presentation. For example, if some audience action suggests special interest, it might be an indication that you should elaborate on that part. Conversely, if you sense attention wandering, do not be afraid to change your plan and speed on to the next item. Once attention is lost, it is difficult to get it back.

4. Present your ideas in a logical sequence that makes sense for your audience. One idea should relate to the next. Also, don't try to cover too much too fast.

5. Present your material in a progressive way to lead your audience through the sequence. You want to maintain control of what your listeners are concentrating on. This is one of the great advantages of a slide show or film. If you set up a complete set of boards, for example, attention quickly goes to the most interesting and understandable, (usually a rendering) while you are trying to explain a list of programming considerations.

6. Maintain eye contact. This is something that takes practice, but is vital to making that "contact" with your audience that is so important. Most

designers feel more comfortable with what they are showing and tend to look at that too much. But do not just scan the audience, never focusing on anyone. This is as annoying as not looking at the audience at all. Practice looking at one person long enough to verbalize an entire thought. Then shift your view to another person for another entire thought.

7. If you have audio-visual material, save it until you have made a personal introduction and established a rapport with the group. No matter how impressive your props are, people still want to see and get to know the professionals who might be working on their job.

8. If you have handouts, pass them out only when you want them to be viewed or at the end of the presentation. You want your audience's attention to be on you and your visual aids, not on a piece of paper.

9. If there is a preliminary budget or discussion of fees, save it until last—once dollars are mentioned, people start mentally calculating and don't listen as well. Show them what you would do, how well you can do it and then the figures will seem reasonable.

10. Don't be afraid of humor. This is a touchy area since it can often backfire, but a light comment at the appropriate time can help foster a more receptive audience.

11. Know when, and don't be afraid, to say "I don't know." Never try to fake an answer. The client will appreciate your candor. However, it is critical that you say you will check into the question and get the answer as soon as possible.

12. Regardless of what happens, do not become defensive. This sets up an adversary situation rather than a cooperative relationship. It takes practice to think quickly on your feet and effectively handle unfriendly questions, comments and the like. If you honestly do not agree with something the client says, say so politely and suggest that it is an important point that you and the client would have to work out as a *team.*

13. Don't be afraid to move around and gesture. Not only is standing in one place often boring, but occasionally moving into the audience and viewing your own displays implies a closer contact and team idea that you should be trying to establish from the very beginning. The same applies to facial expressions, body postures and gestures. Use these non-verbal forms of communication to reinforce your ideas, give "punch" to your presentation and add variety.

14. Try to involve the audience if possible and if appropriate. This also reinforces the team idea—that you are *both* involved in a common goal. It also helps your listeners retain what you are saying. Ask questions, pass something around, solicit comments, anything to have them participate in your actions.

15. Keep track of the time allotted so that you can cover everything you want. If it runs longer, let that be the decision of the client.
16. Have someone from your staff take notes. Again, it shows concern for what your potential client thinks and says during the presentation and can be useful if you do get the job.
17. Make sure everyone on your team has a role in the presentation. Potential clients want to see everyone "in action" even though the majority of the presentation is conducted by one person.
18. Avoid aesthetic comments. The audience will make those kinds of judgments as you go along. You want to tell how you can solve their problem.
19. Summarize at the end of the presentation. Expand on points that the client may have brought out during the interview and briefly emphasize the things you see as being important.
20. End with what you think the client's next step should be or problems that they might not have thought about. Offer some advice if you think they really need it.

These tips generally apply to any type of marketing presentation (and many to design presentations as well) whether you are simply talking to a potential client, using a video recorder, presentation boards, slide show or any of the various techniques available.

SLIDE PRESENTATIONS

Slide presentations are one of the most versatile forms of visual aids available to a professional design firm. Typically, however, the color transparency medium is underused or misused. Some common problems are dull uniformity of images, illegible lettering, slow pace, narration that does not match the visual display, inconsistent formats and incorrect exposures. With the proper planning, these kinds of problems can be avoided. Instead, your slide show can have a powerful impact and help sell your firm and your ideas.

The basic planning concepts for a one-projector show produced in-house are the same as for a computer-programmed, multi-screen extravaganza produced by a professional production company. Assembling an effective slide presentation does not depend on thousands of dollars worth of equipment for multi-projector shows, although these are effective and have their place. Your particular communication needs and budget will determine where in the range of possibilities you should be. For sophisticated shows, you need to hire outside help with the planning, production and equipment purchases. If you want to explore the fine points of this topic refer to the list of sources at the end of this chapter. For works you prepare in your office, the following guidelines will prove useful.

Planning and Presenting the Slide Show

1. Review your objectives. Is the show to illustrate general capabilities, convince someone you can do a building type you do not have experience with, explain your technical expertise, or emphasize a unique service? Most professionals try to show too much in one show. What will be the central theme of the whole display?

2. Block out the organization of what you want to say in diagrammatic form. This will help you divide a larger problem into more manageable pieces and give you an overview of sequence. For example, will you show work chronologically, by building type, by services you offer or some other way? How will the organization contribute to the overall effect?

3. With a general format established, begin to itemize specific points you want to make. The most efficient way to do this is with a story board. Use three-inch by five-inch or four-inch by six-inch cards with a single idea noted on one card. These can be tacked on a wall or slipped into a special board with sleeves to make rearranging easy. The cards should have a small rectangle in one corner proportionate to the slide format you plan to use. Ideas on what the slide for that card should show can be sketched in this area. The remainder of the card is for numbering and script. You can add, delete, change and rearrange these cards until you have a sequence that meets your objectives. At this point you may have some definite ideas about specific slides to be used or new slides that will have to be produced. Some cards, however, may remain just an idea at this point.

4. For those cards that are still part of a script or a rough notion, decide what kind of visual image will complement and reinforce it. Generally, you should try not to duplicate in the slide exactly what you will be saying, nor should you simply explain the slide with your words. Each should reinforce, expand, and supplement the other. With the technology available today, it is easy to develop a wide variety of slides in addition to the standard photograph or reproduction of flat art. Multiple images on one slide, computer-generated optical effects, an approximation of motion through rapid-dissolve control units and others are possible to help you communicate and hold your audience's attention. For more information on the possibilities get a copy of *Images, Images, Images* published by Kodak. Its emphasis is on multi-image production, but contains a wealth of ideas.

5. Refine the ideas you have on the story board cards into a script so you know precisely what you are going to say. You should *not* read the script, but writing it down the first time forces you to think in detail about what you should say. Most architects typically talk too long about the slide on the screen. Some audio-visual consultants advocate that each slide should be on the screen no longer than an average of seven seconds. This keeps the pace of the show moving and is consistent with the idea of each slide illustrating only one discrete concept. If more words are required, more than one slide should accompany the script. Plan for about 120

words-per-minute narration. Some people suggest that the script should be done first, but since most designers think visually more than verbally, the images and words should be organized concurrently.

6. In laying out the slides use a consistent format to avoid the annoying distraction of jumping from vertical to horizontal. Horizontal is best since this is what most people are used to seeing and is compatible with the viewing angle of the eye.

7. When explaining a number of separate but related ideas, or going through a list, expose one idea at a time on the screen. Don't show the entire list on one slide. The audience will read ahead of you and not listen to what you are saying. Instead, show a slide with the first point and talk about it. The next slide should show the first point *and* second point as you explain that. The third slide would show three, and so on. With a dual screen show you can list on one screen, show an example of it simultaneously and talk while both are reinforcing what you say.

8. Use a combination of slide types and viewing angles for variety and to maintain pace. Architects have a treasury of subject matter from which to draw. Some of the possibilities include actual buildings, charts, graphs, construction sequences, people, aerial views, abstracts, schematic drawings, models, renderings, multiple-images, office views, montages and title slides. Viewing angles can be varied, closeups used, and images overlaid. Your imagination is your only limitation as long as you remember that you are trying to communicate an idea and not just to produce a flashy series of gimmicks.

9. Always use blackout slides at the beginning and end of each slide show to avoid the blinding "white out" that occurs in a darkened room without them.

10. Consider the legibility of artwork slides in terms of color, contrast, and type size. As a general rule of thumb, the *body* of lower case letters should be a minimum of 1/25th of the height to be photographed. Another rule of thumb is that if you can read the lettering on a slide without projecting it, then it will probably be legible when viewed on a screen. Eastman Kodak Company makes a legibility calculator that is part of publication S-30, *Planning and Producing Slide Programs.* It is very useful for determining the required size of lettering on artwork based on the size of the planned projected image and the distance to the farthest viewer. Keep the number of words per slide to a minimum, use a sans serif type style and make sure you have plenty of space between lines.

11. Include key personnel in the presentation. Clients like to see who will be working on their job, and what their capabilities are. Have stock slides of your staff on hand in various formal and informal situations so these can be quickly incorporated into any presentation.

12. Emphasize what is unique about your firm. What makes you different from the competition? Be specific in stating this, too. You need to say more than just something like "we are a design-oriented firm."

13. When giving the presentation, talk to the audience, not the screen.

Pre-Slide Show Checklist

- How much can the presentation room be darkened? If it is too bright you may have to consider using a smaller image or a brighter projection bulb.
- Are there suspended light fixtures or other obstructions?
- Know where the circuit breakers are if a circuit becomes overloaded.
- What is the switching of the room? Can you have enough light for note taking and still have the room dark enough for good viewing?
- Do you need a speaker's light? Will it cast an annoying glare onto the screen?
- Do you need a podium? Is one available?
- Will you need to take your own projector stand? Use the type that can be raised above the heads of the audience to avoid interference and keystoning.
- Know in advance how to unjam your particular brand of projector.
- Do you have an extra projection bulb, extension cords, tape, and electrical adapter plugs?
- Will you need a pointer?
- Mark the slides in one corner for easy replacement if some fall out of the tray.
- What is the size of the room? For best viewing the minimum distance to the screen should be no less than two times the screen height. The maximum viewing distance is recommended to be no more than eight times the screen height. Try to keep the audience within a 30-degree area on either side of the centerline perpendicular to the screen.
- Have you run through the show to double-check for proper sequence and slide orientation?
- Do you have a choice of lenses of different focal lengths to allow for varying projection distances to get the image size you want?

These, of course, are just some of the highlights of producing an effective slide presentation. For more information on many of the details, refer to the information sources listed at the end of this chapter.

SOURCES FOR MORE INFORMATION

Books

Atkin, William Wilson. *Architectural Presentation Techniques*. New York: Van Nostrand Reinhold, 1976.

Braun, Irwin. *Building a Successful Professional Practice with Advertising*. New York: AMACOM, division of American Management Associations, 1981.

Burden, Ernest E. *Visual Presentation: A Practical Manual for Architects and Engineers.* New York: McGraw-Hill, 1977.

Jones, Gerre. *Effective Audiovisual Presentations.* Washington: Glyph Publishing, 1977.

Jones, Gerre. *How to Prepare Professional Design Brochures.* New York: McGraw-Hill, 1976.

Jones, Gerre. *How to Structure and Give Effective Formal Presentations.* Washington: Glyph Publishing, 1978.

Jones, Gerre. *Productive Proposal Preparation.* Washington: Glyph Publishing, 1981.

Jones, Gerre. *Professional Design Services Marketing, an Introduction.* Washington: Glyph Publishing, 1980.

Jones, Gerre. *Public Relations for the Design Professional.* New York: McGraw-Hill, 1980.

Kliment, Stephen A. *Creative Communications for a Successful Design Practice.* New York: Whitney Library of Design, 1977.

Laird, Dugan. *A User's Look at the Audio-Visual World.* National Audio-Visual Association, Inc., 3150 Spring Street, Fairfax, VA 22031.

Nagan, Peter S. *How to Put Out a Newsletter.* Newsletter Services, Inc., 1120 19th Street N.W., Washington, DC 20036.

Peake, Jacquelyn. *Public Relations in Business.* New York: Harper & Row Publishers, 1980.

Rose, Dr. Stuart, Barr, Vilma. *Promoting Professional Services.* Washington: Professional Development Resources, Inc., 1978.

Travers, David. *Preparing Design Office Brochures: A Handbook.* Santa Monica, CA: Management Books, 1978. 1936 La Mesa Drive, Santa Monica, CA 90402.

Walker, Morton. *Advertising and Promoting the Professional Practice.* New York: Hawthorn Books, 1979.

Newsletters and Associations

The Presentation Advisor, 20 Waterside Plaza, New York, NY 10160. Bimonthly newsletter on techniques and equipment for design professional presentations.

Better Communication, Information Plus, Inc., Box 602, Livingston, NJ 07039. Newsletter covering general aspects of communication.

Newsletter Association of America, Inc. National Press Building, Suite 1008, Washington, DC 20045. Publishes *Guidebook to Newsletter Publishing.*

Public Relations Society of America. 845 Third Avenue, New York, NY 10022.

Society for Marketing Professional Services. 1437 Powhatan Street, Alexandria, VA 22314.

Publications from Kodak Order from Eastman Kodak Company, 343 State Street, Rochester, NY 14650

The Communicator's Catalog from Kodak. Publication # S-4

Designing for Projection. Publication # V3-141

Images, Images, Images, The Book of Programmed Multi-Image Production. Publication # S-12

Kodak Projection Calculator and Seating Guide. Publication # S-16

Planning and Producing Slide Programs. Publication # S-30

Visual Marketing: A Program for the Design Profession. Publication # V1-36

Directories

Bacon's Newspaper Directory. Bacon's Publishing Company, Inc., 14 East Jackson Boulevard, Chicago, IL 60604. Listing of all daily, weekly and semiweekly newspapers in the U.S. Published annually.

National Directory of Weekly Newspapers. National Newspaper Association, 1627 K Street N.W., Suite 400, Washington, DC 20006. Information on about 8,000 weekly, semiweekly and triweekly newspapers in the U.S.

O'Dwyer's Directory of Public Relations Firms. O'Dwyer Company, Inc., 271 Madison Avenue, New York, NY 10016.

Professional Guide to Public Relations Services. Richard Weiner, Inc., 888 Seventh Avenue, New York, NY 10019, 1980. Lists about 650 different kinds of services such as clipping bureaus, newspaper feature release services, and directories.

U.S. Publicity Directory. Norback & Norback, 353 Nassau Street, Princeton, NJ 08540. Two-volume publication containing business and finance editors and radio and television program news directors.

NAVA Equipment Directory. National Audio-Visual Association, 3150 Spring Street, Fairfax, VA 22031. Over 500 pages of various kinds of A/V hardware including list prices and comparative specifications. Write to the Association for the latest edition or check your library.

Audiovisual Market Place. R.R. Bowker Company, 1180 Avenue of the Americas, New York, NY 10036. Directory of over 11,000 producers, distributors, manufacturers, dealers, labs and other areas of the audiovisual industry. Includes names, addresses, and key personnel. Published annually.

Other Sources

Conducting Winning Presentations
Professional Development Programs
The American Institute of Architects
1735 New York Avenue, N.W.
Washington, DC 20006

> A home-study course offered by the AIA. It includes review of skill development exercises by the MGI Management Institute and a course manual.

PSMJ TV Video Presentations

Professional Services Management Journal
126 Harvard Street
Brookline, MA 02146

> Video tape presentations on a variety of topics. Titles include "Successful Presentation Strategies," "How to Do Video Presentations," "Negotiating Higher Fees," and "Face to Face Sales Technique."

CHAPTER 4

Action Ideas for a
More Productive Office

Productivity is one of the key administrative goals for the eighties. Rising labor costs, unstable economic conditions, consumer demands, and the increasing expense of doing business all require top management to explore ways of increasing output to stay competitive. For professional service firms, measuring and improving productivity are more difficult than for product-oriented businesses. Standard measurements such as profit, percent billable time, fees generated per employee and similar ratios give only part of the picture. (More on these in Chapter 8) Architectural and design firms produce a "product" that has qualitative as well as quantitative aspects.

Design firm productivity follows from the imaginative effort of people. The creative process in any type of design business includes nearly all the work that goes on because it involves solving unique client and business problems in ways best suited to changing circumstances. Creativity is required as much for effective construction administration as it is for completing schematic studies, as much for streamlining paperwork as for successful marketing. A necessary part of the well-managed office, therefore, is what I call "managing creativity."

Managing creativity is not dictating design or enforcing a style; it involves fostering maximum output of people to reach stated goals. Each firm must set its own design goals—the qualitative aspect of productivity against which performance will be measured. These goals are just as important as financial goals, marketing goals and others. Together, they form the foundation of a complete management plan.

Increasing productivity of this part of a management plan requires organizing the creative process, the environment in which it takes place, and the time available to do it. This chapter will discuss some of the essential elements of these three concepts.

ORGANIZING THE CREATIVE PROCESS

Several elements are common to managing the creative process in almost any type of design office. Each must be considered and an action plan devised for their implementation. This includes leadership direction, design process, human resources, and client participation.

Leadership Direction

Leadership in business is guiding the motivations of individuals toward the goals of the organization. The leader does not try to subjugate individual needs for organizational needs, but inspires a balance so that the objectives of the firm are pursued enthusiastically. Management differs from leadership in that it focuses on guiding and directing actions to meet the needs of the organization, with or without the interests of the individual in mind. Leadership rallies the spirit of people toward a common effort regardless of how that effort is organized.

The often subtle differences between leadership and management are important for a design firm. Both can occur separately, but for maximum productivity they need to occur together. Two typical situations illustrate the extreme cases. In one instance, the principal of a firm may have all the charisma, dedication, and concern for personal needs of a true leader with the office staff marshaled behind to tackle any project with great zeal. Unfortunately, work assignments are poorly organized, project management techniques weak, and quality control lacking—all the elements of mismanagement. As a result, time and money are wasted. In the other scenario, everything is run according to strict procedure, roles are clearly defined, time scheduled to the last minute, and personal needs sacrificed for the good of the office. Management is at its zenith but morale is low, turnover high. There is a different set of ingredients with the same result: wasted time and money.

Finding the right balance between these two extremes is one of the most difficult tasks for anyone in a management or leadership position to do, whether he or she is a principal of a 500-person A/E firm or a job captain on a small project. The following ideas may help you take a more decisive role in managing that part of the creative process for which you are responsible.

1. Determine if you are a leader, manager or both. Be honest with yourself. Some people can manage better than they can lead and few can really do both well. If you cannot be both, find someone else to complement your efforts. Since the two are necessary for long-term, maximum productivity, this evaluation is critical.

2. Decide whether you want to establish an authoritarian or democratic leadership style. Authoritarian leadership creates a "top down" method of directing actions to accomplish a goal. The person leading makes a decision and directs others to follow-through according to that decision. Democratic leadership places the decision-making process with a group of people who are ultimately responsible

for carrying out those decisions and accepting responsibility for the consequences. The choice depends on your own abilities as well as a sensitive understanding of those you are trying to lead and the goals you are trying to accomplish.

3. Know the personal goals of your staff and develop a feel for their motivations. Building on these motivations whenever possible is more productive than ignoring them. If you are in a position to evaluate performance of office staff, a discussion of employee goals should be part of the review.

4. Consider having one or more people on staff who are not assigned to particular jobs, but who act as "in-house consultants" in certain areas, assisting project teams and offering advice and encouragement independent of the pressures of any one job. Time would be billable since productive work would be done. One such position could be a technical reviewer who would help select products to specify, organize and oversee construction document production, assist with detailing problems and advise on similar concerns. A like position could be created for design and managing. If you have enough good people, they can rotate in and out of this position in order to stay fresh.

5. Encourage unconventional ideas, new ways of looking at problems. A design organization trapped in the *status quo* cannot prosper.

6. Let risk-takers be in charge of design teams. They may guide the team toward innovative *and* profitable solutions.

Design Process

Neither designers nor firm owners should be wary of the notion of managing design. The purpose is not to stifle creativity but to facilitate the full utilization of the creative process in solving the client's problems without damaging the fiscal and business stability of the firm. It is not dictating design, but setting standards of excellence, workable ways of achieving them, and monitoring performance to ensure that those standards are met. A clearly stated policy and consistency in its application are vital in making it work. Specific suggestions for creative thinking techniques are discussed in Chapter 5. For design *management* four components are essential.

1. Based on your firm's goals and design philosophy, designate a format for how the design process should proceed. This will not be a rigid checklist that limits design, but guidelines setting forth the collective knowledge of what worked on past jobs and how to avoid common pitfalls in performing your office's services. As a record of past projects it should not be fixed. It should be updated as new information and experience are gained. While allowing for individual creativity it helps prevent the prima donna development and encourages a standard of design excellence for your firm.

2. Order a goal statement to be produced for every job. This should include

goals of the client as well as for the firm and the people working on the project. These goals can be reviewed periodically during the course of the project to evaluate progress.

3. Include the client in early planning sessions when problem statements are formulated and preliminary design concepts are proposed. This not only establishes the correct problem to be solved but also helps set the right direction for schematic design.

CASE IN POINT

CRS in Houston pioneered the well-known "squatters" technique that makes maximum use of this idea. A team from the architect's office works closely with the client and consultants on or near the site in an intense design session that may run from three to ten days depending on the complexity of the project. Time is saved and the quality of the design improved since everyone has a chance to contribute to the definition of important concepts.

4. Have designs reviewed periodically by other people in the office not working on the project. In these design critiques, emphasis should be placed on constructive criticism and checking to see if the design is meeting the original goals and objectives of both the client and the office. It helps to have a set time and format for these reviews so they don't get out of hand. A policy should also be established as to who has the last word on design issues.

Human Resources

The human resources that are the core of any architectural or design office must be allowed and encouraged to carry out what they do best. Establishing an environment where this can happen is one of the most difficult aspects of professional practice. It is usually easier to rely on traditional modes of working. The results, however, are often high turnover, dissatisfied workers, low morale—in general, all those things that work against productivity.

Some of the important considerations in employee relations are discussed in Chapter 7, but productivity depends on more than an adequate salary and other benefits. Productivity of truly creative persons in an architectural office stems as much from their desire to exercise their talents, participate in the development of a project, assume responsibility, and grow professionally as from a large paycheck. It is the *balance* of these factors that maximizes productivity.

Influenced by the kinds of people available or recruited, the goals of the firm, and the overall office management system, you can set up a creative human resource program. Some of the following ideas may help.

1. Consider shifting duties of people occasionally. Let a designer act as project manager on a small job or a job captain help with programming. People stuck in the same niche for too long become stale, no matter how much they like

what they are doing. In many small offices, having staff perform multiple functions is a necessity. For firms that specialize, however, changing roles helps everyone see problems from a different point of view. Don't be afraid to experiment. What may be a temporary inefficiency may turn out to have long-range benefits.

2. Hold regular office meetings to keep everyone up to date, provide a forum for airing grievances, making suggestions and discussing common project problems.

3. Schedule retreats where designated staff can get away from the daily demands of the office to discuss issues, review progress of the firm, study goals and brainstorm ways to improve methods of working.

4. Hold in-house seminars and programs to keep staff current with new products, methods, ideas, and professional services. Many firms use the lunch hour for these kinds of sessions so that they are both convenient and do not take away from billable time. Sources for speakers can include manufacturers' representatives (who are always happy to have a forum), other professionals, people in related fields (contractors, attorneys, construction managers, etc.), teachers from local design schools, and staff members who may be working on a special project or have some special interest to share.

5. Budget for and encourage attendance at seminars, design conferences, and professional development workshops. Not only are these considered "perks," but they are vital to the continuing education of your staff and the cross-fertilization of ideas in the profession.

6. Budget for and encourage memberships in professional associations. These should include memberships in groups related to your areas of service as well as the usual AIA, CSI and others. Belonging to these associations serves the dual purpose of helping see problems from other points of view and as a place for making marketing contacts.

7. Encourage travel. Seeing how other architects solved problems similar to the ones you deal with broadens the perspective of your staff. If a particular job warrants it, travel to other parts of the country to study completed works that may be counterparts to the assignment you have. Clients will sometimes pay for this if you can convince them of the benefits. If not, consider financing it yourself. It can pay dividends in the long run.

8. Evaluate flexible work scheduling. The creative process doesn't always coincide with an 8 to 5 timetable. Some studies have shown that giving employees the flexibility of scheduling at least part of their work time improves morale and increases productivity.

9. Do not limit yourself to hiring only architects or interior designers. People with different backgrounds and skills often can contribute productively to your office's output as well as generate extra enthusiasm in the office. More and more firms are taking this multi-disciplinary approach as a way of improving their marketing position as well as the quality of their service. Graphic designers, industrial designers, environmental psychologists, researchers and others who specialize in problem-solving can contribute.

10. Agree on measures of performance to be used in evaluating productivity. A person has to know what is expected before he or she can fulfill that expectation.

11. Develop a list of roles and responsibilities for various job positions. This should not pigeon-hole anyone but clarify what each person in the office can expect of other people. This list can be incorporated in a personnel manual or in an office management manual. In either case, it should be readily available to everyone at any time.

Client Participation

In a design office, creativity must exist as a constructive relationship between the client and the designer. Some offices give the client exactly what he asks for without exploring possible solutions the client might not have considered. Other offices try to extend the client's thinking, probe new territory, and experiment with sometimes untested problem solutions. Exactly where on the range of possibilities your office lies depends on your professional goals, but you must establish some guidelines for relating to your clients so that the partnership is supportive of your own productivity.

Find out as much about your client as possible. Formal, published sources such as those listed in Chapter 2 are useful for business information, but you need to go beyond that. Talk to business acquaintances of your client, entertain them, observe their actions in business situations—in short, try to understand what and how they think, what their biases are, priorities, everything you can. Architecture is a service and this type of personal relationship is important to a successful—and profitable—project.

Insist on working on a day-to-day basis with someone in the client's organization who is authorized to make decisions and provide you with the kind of information you need. Know who is really in charge. Much of the wasted effort, time and money in designing for the wrong decision-maker or without the proper information can be avoided by understanding this concept. If the organization is layered with several tiers of bureaucratic procedure, regular meetings and approvals with the right people are crucial.

Have the customer participate in the early formulation of the project schedule. This kind of involvement encourages a realistic understanding of the schedule; if it has to be compressed, the client is immediately aware of the consequences: additional money, fewer alternatives explored, and so forth. Draw up a detailed schedule and distribute it to everyone working on the job. Communication is vital. A continually updated plan aids the process.

Finally, hold periodic reviews with the client and have approval in writing before proceeding to the next phase. If they have to sign off on something, they are more inclined to take a hard look at the progress to date. This procedure can prevent time-consuming changes later, and if problems develop can give you a solid basis for requesting additional fees.

ORGANIZING THE ENVIRONMENT

Improving the environment can improve employee satisfaction and increase productivity. That is the message architects and interior designers are telling their clients in the eighties, and they are supported by recent studies that have investigated the relationship. It is paradoxical, then, that so many design offices are counterproductive in the way they are planned. You often find overcrowding, poor spatial relationships, inflexible work areas, and an absense of time-saving equipment to support the necessary work.

Evolving methods of office organization, new management techniques and technological advances will all change the way the architect's office must be designed for maximum output. Some changes are simple and can be made at low cost and with little disruption to existing work patterns. Others take organizational planning and a commitment to productive change. Take an objective look at your office environment. Why was it really designed the way it was? How has it evolved (mutated)? Is it facilitating the work of your employees or making it more difficult? Are you lacking equipment to provide your services most efficiently? Use the following list of ideas as a source for discussion in your office. Then take some positive steps to improve your own workspace for increased productivity.

1. Analyze the work flow of a project as it moves through your office, just as you would for a client in planning their space. Does the overall layout correspond to the flow? Are you wasting time and motion moving people, drawings, paper and samples from one point to another? Even for medium-size firms, improvement in this area can make it easier for people to do their jobs.

2. Review your need for open or closed work spaces. The traditional open plan of almost every architectural office is supposed to make efficient use of space, provide for and encourage communication, and allow for flexibility in changing work teams and staff relocation. Often, the results are negative. In the quest for efficiency overcrowding often results. Designers sometimes pack more people into less space than they would ever dream of suggesting to their clients. The behavioral and productivity implications of overcrowding have been studied and the results are not encouraging.

The communication the open plan allows sometimes becomes excessive. Noise, chatter, and other distractions negate any advantages gained. Smoking is also difficult to control. With more medical evidence concerning the damaging effects of smoke on non-smokers and the increased militancy (supported by legislative and judicial rulings) of non-smokers, office management must decide how to solve the problem in the office. If it is addressed with physical solutions rather than administrative solutions (no smoking areas, etc.) then closed versus open plan becomes a consideration.

Subdividing the office into smaller group areas is one solution; using movable partitions is another. Some offices maintain private rooms for the use of anyone who needs an area for concentrated work.

3. Maintain one or more areas for the exclusive use of creative team efforts. Design sessions, for example, with several staff members, consultants, and clients require a space different from a collection of individual workstations. A conference room is usually not appropriate since it has to be available and "clean" for a variety of uses throughout the day. The creative work area should have all the support facilities necessary: adjustable lighting, drawing surfaces, work surfaces for spreading out drawings and models, projection screens, tack space, seating and supplies. The space should be able to remain messy for any length of time required by the project and should be isolated from the rest of the office to keep distractions to a minimum.

4. Decide if your workstations are appropriate for the kind of work that really goes on. Most workstations are relics from the past when the predominant tool was the T-square. While the drafting function is still important, the way projects are done and the tools used are rapidly changing. Does a project manager, for example, need the same kind of space as a designer? Should the specification writer's major tool be a CRT screen and keyboard? Do production staff have what they now need? New techniques in overlay drafting, paste-up, and other reprographic methods require a space much different from the traditional drafting station.

5. If yours is a small firm, consider a shared office arrangement. Dividing the expense and effort of maintaining a library, receptionist, word processing, presentation room, copy facilities, and other investments would allow you to concentrate your resources on more important areas of your practice. With tightening economic conditions, shared facilities will be making more sense for even larger firms.

6. Formulate a plan for the transition to computer use if you have not already done so. Since it is not a matter of whether you will be using computers but when, planning now is imperative. For maximum benefit, you need to consider all the factors office planners take into account for their clients: workstation height and layout, lighting, ventilation, power supply, location of peripheral attachments, and other ergonomic requirements.

7. Review the applicability of such time-and money-saving devices as "electronic mail," and teleconferencing. With teleconferencing, for example, it is possible to use teleprinters and "electronic blackboards" to transmit drawings and sketches while you are meeting. If you cannot afford the investment for some of these technologies, there are companies that maintain the equipment and facilities. You simply rent the space on an "as needed" basis. More of these services are likely to spring up in the future, too. You can save time and money in long-distance travel while still being effective in much of your long-distance communications.

ORGANIZING USE OF TIME

Time is an essential element of productivity in the business world. In the design professions productivity means a certain task must be accomplished within a given amount of time. Fees are set and a job must be done for those fees or the office loses money. Anything can happen within the time defined by the fees. If a large percentage of it is consumed by interruptions, socializing, unnecessary paper work and the like, there is less time to perform the task itself.

One difference between productivity and other measures is worth noting. The ratio of billable time to total time is not necessarily productivity. That is a score kept for the accountant and financial manager. Billable time can be productive or non-productive. People can be profitable in the design profession without being productive if the fees are high enough to allow for wasted activities. The goal of time management is to help you get as much done as possible within what is usually a limited amount of time, realizing that there is little margin for waste.

Most architects let circumstances control their time instead of controlling circumstances for maximum productivity. The following pages discuss ways to eliminate or minimize some of the major time-wasters in the design professions.

Planning

Even though architects and designers are in the business of planning it is surprising how little they do with their most valuable commodity—their time. The idea that things in the profession happen too fast and unexpectedly on a day-to-day basis to plan ahead much is nonsense. This is simply "management by crisis"—letting the circumstances get the best of you. Planning is the first step in organizing time for greater productivity. Consider the following points and see how your habits measure up. Even if you are trying some of these techniques now, analyze the results and try to identify areas for improvement.

1. Keep a daily journal of your activities and time spent on each for a week or two. The results may surprise you. Where do you spend most of your time? Are these the most productive and profitable activities for you? Are you doing things other people should be doing? This analysis can work for managers, principals, production personnel, specification writers or anyone in the office. Information from such a journal can help you decide where to spend more or less time.

2. Set objectives for your time. Just as goals are a necessary first step in a business plan or marketing plan so are they in a "productivity plan." If you are a specification writer, for example, one of your goals may be to have a certain number of hours per week for materials research not related to a specific job.

3. Begin planning for the long term. For recurring tasks set aside times every week or month when these need to happen. Knowing when you will give them your consideration lets you schedule your other time accordingly and prepare for them. Use a calendar or scheduling board in your workspace to see at a glance where you are, what you have to do and when you have to do it.

4. For short-term planning, use a daily "to-do" list. Itemize those things that you feel you want to accomplish on a given day. Often, the best time to do this is just before you leave the office so that you are ready for the next day. Don't stop with just listing, however. Assign priorities. Identify those things you must do,

those you should do, and those you would like to do but are not critical. Concentrate on important, high-profit tasks, even though they may not be the easiest or the most enjoyable. One of the biggest mistakes most architects make is spending time on activities that bring the least return. Start with the must-do items first and complete them before going on to the next set. If you date the list and bind it in a notebook, it can also serve as a personal journal for completing your time sheet and as a backup log for job progress—a time saver in itself.

5. Set deadlines for yourself. These are often set for you, of course, by other people or project requirements. For those that are not, it gives you something to target your efforts toward. Breaking up a large task with a single deadline into smaller, multiple deadline tasks helps you keep control of your work by charting progress with more manageable units.

6. Combine similar tasks. Efficiency usually increases when all phone calls can be made at once, trips outside the office grouped, or meetings placed back to back. Doing this is one of the supreme tests for a design professional. It is organizing your activities rather than having events disorganize you.

7. Discipline yourself to stick with one task until it is done no matter how unpleasant. Nothing can be accomplished by jumping from one thing to another. Only on rare occasions should the urgency of the situation pull you away from your planned activities.

8. Allow for the unexpected. This assumes that in the design business there are emergencies periodically or times when you want to deviate from your plan. Trying to schedule every minute can be as counter-productive as not planning at all. If you have your to-do list and long-term schedule, you always have plenty to do if the unexpected does not happen or a scheduled meeting is canceled.

Meetings

Meetings are one of the greatest time-wasters in the architectural profession. Their purpose is for exchange of information, coordination, problem-solving, and presentation of ideas to others. All of these are necessary, of course, but meetings tend to get out of hand and usually take about twice as much time as necessary. Next time you are in a slow-moving meeting list the people involved and their billing rate. Calculate how much money is being expended per hour by the meeting. Divide by sixty to calculate the cost per minute. You may be astonished. This does not even take into account the cost of preparing for the meeting, travel time, or wasted time before and after. Compare this with the progress (or lack of it) being made toward some goal.

Here are some techniques that are useful in making a meeting more efficient. Incorporating them into your standard procedures can eliminate wasted time and free you for more creative endeavors.

1. Make sure the meeting is necessary. Could the same thing be accomplished quicker with a memo, posted notice, or telephone conference call, for example? Also determine if regularly scheduled meetings are occurring at the right frequency. Weekly management meetings in architectural offices seem to be typical occurrences. Could management be as effectively served with biweekly meetings, thereby cutting the cost in half?

2. Develop an agenda and stick to it. This can be as brief as a list of three points you want the participants to consider or a detailed, multi-page outline of topics, alternatives to discuss, and background information. Whatever form it takes, the agenda helps people keep on track, provides the broad organizational structure required for efficiency, and lets everyone know when the meeting should be over. The agenda can also do double duty as an outline for the minutes of the meeting. With extra space below each topic or to one side, notes can be added as to people's comments, decisions reached, and follow-up required.

3. Start on time. Having several people waiting for a few latecomers is simply a waste of money besides being unfair and discourteous to those on time.

4. Set time limits for the length of the meeting. With a deadline, people tend to work toward completing their business in the allotted span. Without an end point, meetings tend to go on and on.

5. Try to keep the number of attendees to a minimum. Not only does it cost more to have more people attend, but greater numbers make coordination and interaction more difficult. Research has suggested that the maximum size for effective communication is seven or eight people seated at a round table. If you are afraid of offending some people, solicit their ideas, questions, and opinions in writing before the meeting and have the written comments presented during the conference. Conclusions reached or meeting minutes can also be distributed or posted for those who did not attend. If all or a majority of the office staff should be present, hold the meeting immediately after working hours, on the lunch break or in a social situation.

6. Every meeting should have a definite leader, whether self-appointed or not. Someone must develop the agenda, keep everyone on the subject, watch the time, and see that useful conclusions result from the gathering. Several people just "getting together to talk" may be enjoyable and pass the time but will hardly accomplish anything. Save that kind of "meeting" for informal sessions over a beer after work.

7. As a general rule, don't make the meeting environment too comfortable. This only encourages people to linger. Some architects hold stand-up meetings when the number of items to be discussed is few. It is a clear indication that a limited meeting is expected. There are, of course, exceptions such as a presentation to a client or a day-long charette.

8. Time your meeting for a period just before the end of the day or before

lunch. This is another trick to encourage short gatherings. Scheduling several meetings back-to-back accomplishes the same thing with the added advantage of making all of them more productive since you are in the same frame of mind and can do all your meeting preparation at once.

9. Do not let a meeting end without reaching a conclusion, making a decision, assigning tasks for completion or otherwise producing a tangible result.

Interruptions

Interruptions happen dozens of times every day, usually just when you are being the most productive. They destroy productivity, yet too many architects and designers continue to allow them to control their time. Some, of course, are unavoidable. The majority, however, can be managed. It simply takes determination and cooperation from everyone in the office. Consider the following checklist of ideas to minimize wasted time from interruptions.

TELEPHONE

The telephone can be either the worst time-waster in the world or the best time-saver—the choice is yours. The telephone is so pervasive in our lives that we let it dominate us. It allows us instant communication with anyone in the world, but also provides instant interruption. The best way to use it productively is only when you want to, not when it demands you stop what you are doing to answer it. Having a secretary or receptionist screen calls is the traditional way to keep some control over the phone. Some professionals go so far as never to answer the phone. They collect the messages from their secretary and return calls in a group when it is convenient for them. Others let it be known that they take calls only during a certain time, say 1:00 to 4:00 in the afternoon. One of the greatest advantages of electronic mail and other computer-based message services will be the ability for one person to send a message while it is fresh in mind without worrying if the receiver is there or not. Messages will be collected and dealt with at the receiver's convenience, thus eliminating the sometimes ludicrous and costly situation of two people trying for days to return each other's calls for what may amount to a two-minute conversation.

SALESPEOPLE

Never let a salesman or manufacturer's representative drop in unannounced. Require that they make an appointment with the receptionist. Even a specification writer who needs to keep up-to-date with the latest products should set aside a time to see reps, with meetings grouped at his convenience. Some offices direct the rep to the librarian or junior staff person in charge of the sample room where the sales person can update catalogues, replace samples or make a quick presentation. The librarian then assumes the responsibility to disseminate the information to the right people in the office.

VISITORS

Visitors come in many forms, but like the telephone, when they make their presence known they demand some kind of response. The best strategy is to avoid unexpected visitors completely—stay in control of when and where. If you must see an unexpected visitor, do it in the reception area standing up. The caller will quickly get the message that he or she cannot take up much of your time. Some people have prearranged agreements with their secretaries for them to break in after a certain period to remind them of "another appointment."

PRIVACY

Have one or more separate rooms available for office staff to use when a secluded, concentrated effort is required. These should not be conference rooms since those are built-in interruptions. If your office is mostly open, this gives people a chance to get away from noise, movement, the telephone and other distractions.

QUIET HOUR

Consider establishing a "quiet hour" in the office when no telephone calls are received, visitors are not allowed, no meetings scheduled or any socializing permitted. It gives everyone a chance to concentrate on some task without outside interference. Making such a time takes some effort initially, but once staff and outside people know when this period is the increase in productivity is worth it.

SHORT WORK

Use interruptions creatively. Identify those tasks that you must do every day that are of short duration and do not take a great deal of concentration. Schedule their completion for those times when you are most likely to be interrupted. If you receive several intermittent phone calls while you are going through your mail, for example, the disruptions are not as great as if you were trying to write a programming report. Similar interruptible jobs can be scheduled to make use of brief blocks of time such as on airplanes, waiting or while commuting. Always have on hand a stack of such work for those moments when you really can't be doing anything else. You will be surprised how much of it you can complete so that other time can be freed for more important matters.

Paper Work

We have become a nation of paper shufflers. With the majority of workers engaged in the processing of information in one form or another the handling of paper becomes one of the worker's most time-consuming activities. Even with the increased use of computers we will still have a lot of paper to deal with, probably more. In the architectural office, paper is necessary to record ideas, develop design solutions, communicate, and to record information for legal purposes. Unfortunately, paper work often controls too much of the architect's time. Here are some tips to help you cut through the stacks of paper on your desk and prevent generating unnecessary paper.

1. Develop the habit of handling a piece of paper only once. If you do not have an "in-box" now, get one. For many architects this may seem to be the height of bureaucratic slavery, but it works. When you take something out of the box, either throw it away, act on it, or save it for consideration at a later time if you need more information. For example, something may go into your stack of light reading for the evening. Or you may need more information before you can respond to a letter. For that kind of item, set up a chronological file with a place for each day. Place the item in the slot for the day when you intend to act on it.

2. Classify paper work according to its urgency. The tendency for most people is to deal with the easiest things first and procrastinate with the others. Instead, identify which pieces of paper are urgent, which must be dealt with soon, but not immediately, and those that can wait. Act on the urgent first. Many times the remainder turn out to be not so important and don't need responses at all.

3. Make generous use of your wastebasket. Most of the paper that crosses your desk is not as important as it may seem. If you are among that group that believes that they will need something the day after they throw it away, set up a "mellowing" stack. Keep things stored that you are not sure of. After a few weeks if you have not needed anything, chances are you never will. Throw it out. After a period of time you will convince yourself what a time-saver the wastebasket is.

4. Have your receptionist or whoever handles mail in your office do initial screening. Make sure it goes to the right person the first time.

5. Avoid memos. Too often, people get into the habit of playing games with memos. They are used to cover themselves, show other people how "busy" they are, or any number of other reasons other than their primary one of communicating something in writing. Most of the time spent thinking about writing, typing, transmitting, reading and filing memos is wasted in the architectural office. Unless you absolutely need a written record, communicate your memo thought on the telephone or by a quick personal visit.

6. Analyze your method of dealing with correspondence. Many incoming letters do not need to be answered at all; others can be handled simply by writing a reply on the face of the letter you receive. A copy can be quickly made for your

files and the original sent back to the sender. With the cost involved in writing one letter it makes sense to sacrifice the polished appearance of an original reply for a savings in your time and money. For longer, detailed letters that may be revised several times before sending, a word processor is a must. Any architect that does not yet have one is a century behind.

7. Use a pocket dictating machine. The small, portable kind are great time-savers for dictating letters, making punch lists, field reports, and recording ideas.

8. Make forms work *for* you. Like the in-box, many forms symbolize a bureaucracy and not a professional design firm. The simple fact is, however, that most of the activities of an architectural project need to be recorded for legal purposes as well as to improve communication. They are also repetitious. Efficiently designed forms can streamline much of the recording and transfer of information. Refer to Chapter 10 for more guidelines on form design.

9. Keep your workspace organized. A cluttered desk is not proof you are busy or productive. Keep projects you are not working on at the moment in a drawer at your desk or in the office files. With all the filing systems and support equipment available today, there is no excuse for wasting time rearranging papers on your desk or trying to find a buried letter.

Work Habits

Sloppy work habits account for much of the professional's wasted time. In addition to the techniques mentioned above consider reviewing your business routine with the following suggestions.

1. Beware of the excess perfection syndrome. This is a common problem among architects and designers. There is a tendency to want to work and rework a problem or design until it is perfect. There is a point, however, at which greatly increased effort results in very little improvement. Working beyond this point just wastes time and money for little or no benefit. Further explanation of this can be found in Chapter 9.

2. Learn to delegate. One of the greatest time-wasters is doing tasks that other people should be doing for you. For someone who has come up through the ranks and is used to "doing" rather than "managing" this is sometimes difficult. It is critical, however, to work at the level where you can make the best, most effective use of your experience and knowledge.

3. Related to delegating is *not* doing the work of others. This involves letting the other people on the building team do their own work. Architects often try to do too much: coordinating tasks that the contractor should really be handling, tracking down samples and information that a sales rep could—and should—do for you and similar jobs. It is nice to help people, but do it judiciously.

4. Do not let procrastination make your decisions for you. The longer you

wait to do something, the fewer choices you have. If you wait long enough, you may have only one remaining choice, and that may be an undesirable one. Quality then suffers. We all fall prey to the danger of putting things off to avoid an unpleasant or difficult task. All the excuses, delay tactics, worrying and avoidance behavior do nothing but waste time and take energies away from what could be productive endeavors. Attack the problem by focusing on one thing and working on it until it is done, no matter how unpleasant. This is especially important if what you are doing is on your first-priority list. If the problem seems too big, break it up into smaller units that may not be so difficult to face.

5. Be realistic with your time commitments. A person trying to do too many things at once does none of them well and runs the risk of making unnecessary mistakes.

6. Avoid impulse reading. If the latest issue of *Progressive Architecture* lands on your desk it is tempting to stop what you are doing and leaf through it. Don't. Schedule a time for that kind of reading—commuting, evenings, lunch breaks or whenever is convenient for you. If your reading list gets too long, you might consider having your secretary or assistant in the office list the contents of every magazine and other material your office receives. When the list is distributed, check the articles you think might be of interest and have them photocopied for your review.

7. Develop the ability to decide what *not* to read. There is enough information you must keep up with without compounding the problem by unnecessary reading. In many cases it is simply enough to have a system of knowing what is available and where it is so it can be read when needed. Published indexes such as the *Architectural Index* are useful for this purpose. You may want to consider developing your own in-house system for the information you receive.

8. Be prompt and expect others to be. Tardiness is nothing but a bad habit and the result of poor planning. We all hate to wait and know what a non-productive use of time it is. You cannot expect others to be on time, however, if you are not. If your schedule is tightly planned, announce at the beginning of a meeting, for example, when you have to leave. This sets the ground rules and avoids the appearance of leaving in the middle of the meeting. Be realistic in your scheduling, too. If you are not sure how long a session may take, plan for a non-critical activity after it. If time is available you can proceed; if not, you can put off the non-critical activity until later.

All of these suggestions may not work for all people, but trying some of them may help you replace non-productive time with *billable* time. Not only will this increase your profit, but also free you for more of the things you want to do in your professional career.

SOURCES FOR MORE INFORMATION

Lakein, Alan. *How to Get Control of Your Time and Your Life.* Bergenfield, NJ: The New American Library, 1973.

MacKenzie, R. Alec. *New Time Management Methods.* Dartnell, 4660 Ravenswood Avenue, Chicago, IL 60640.

MacKenzie, R. Alec. *The Time Trap.* New York: McGraw-Hill Book Company, 1972.

Uris, Auren. *The Executive Deskbook.* New York: Van Nostrand Reinhold.

Chronolog. Newsletter devoted to time management. Available from Guidelines, Box 456, Orinda, CA 94563.

CHAPTER 5
Streamline the Design and Production Process

Since design and construction documents usually re-
QUIRE the greatest amount of time of all phases of a project, improving methods
of production can increase the overall productivity of the office while advancing
the quality of service. With marginal fees, short time schedules, and demanding
clients, architects and interior designers must improve these aspects of practice if
they are to remain competitive. This chapter will briefly outline some of the approaches you might consider to increase the efficiency of your office in these areas.

TARGETING DESIGN EFFORTS

One of the greatest challenges for design professionals is that such a wide
range of creative and problem-solving approaches must be used during the course
of a project. Thinking must extend from the sometimes wildly outrageous to the
most analytical reasoning. At one time solutions must be sought by branching out
and at another by filtering down. The design process is one of continually shifting
from one level to another. Many times a designer gets locked in at one level and
attempts to solve all aspects of a problem with only one approach.

In order to produce good design *and* be profitable you have to get to the
heart of the problem *quickly,* analyze it, generate alternative solution concepts, select
one for development, and refine it to satisfy the criteria. Professional design firms
do not have the luxury of making too many false starts or letting designers work
at a leisurely pace until the perfect solution is worked out. The best offices are
those that have developed systems in which design is not *compromised* by the desire
to get a job in and out factory-fashion, but *enhanced* by a process that allows the
right kind of effort without wasted motions.

Pitfalls in the Design Process

Certain problems in the design process seem to recur frequently. Check your office's operation against the following list of pitfalls to see where improvements could be made.

1. Starting with a stylistic bias and molding the problem to fit the designer's goals rather than letting the problem focus the direction of the solution.
2. Selectively (and sometimes unconsciously) considering only that information that the designer or other team members want which supports *their* image of the design; not rigorously recording *all* the goals, objectives, program information, and ideas of members of the team and setting them in order of priority.
3. Solving problems in physical terms before solving them in performance terms; designing with labels rather than attributes. This amounts to deciding exactly how a problem is to be solved before deciding what criteria are to be met by *any* kind of solution. For example, specifying a "window" rather than first specifying what kind of wall penetration is needed—view, light, contact with the outside, status of the room occupant, etc. The word "window" immediately forms images in your mind and may discourage other approaches to solving the problem.
4. Not thinking conceptually during the beginning phases of design; losing track of broad issues, problems and general approaches to their solution.
5. Becoming to specific too soon; not "seeing the forest for the trees." Details have a way of capturing our attention and steering it away from what it is those details are supposed to be doing for us.
6. Stopping at the first adequate solution. This usually happens when too much time has been spent developing one preliminary idea before many concepts have been reviewed. Time then runs out and you must go with what you have.
7. Putting off decisions. Commitments are sometimes difficult to make for a designer, but the longer you wait to make a decision, the fewer alternatives you have available to you. If you wait long enough, only one possible course of action will be available. Waiting until more information is available or to gain more time to think about the problem often lessens the quality of the decision. One of the skills of a good designer is knowing when to make a decision after a period of data gathering and study.
8. Losing sight of original intentions, goals, and objectives. A lot can happen between the time of the first meeting with a client and later stages of the design process. Problems are modified, people on the team come and go, and solutions take on a life of their own. Without

the right discipline, the solution becomes more important than the original problem.

9. Succumbing to the "project perfection syndrome." This is discussed in more detail in Chapter 9, but it is particularly troublesome in the design process. The problem is worked and reworked repeatedly to refine it to an idealized state of perfection. In many offices the designer is still trying to change the design during construction! Any office that allows this is courting disaster.

10. Not coordinating or managing the efforts of the team; letting the designer and other members of the team work in a vacuum without interaction between them and without direction from a project manager.

11. Not resolving conflicts among team members when they first occur and letting them grow to the point where they are a detriment to the project.

12. Not breaking large problems into smaller, manageable units. If this happens, the tendency is to simplify the large problem so it can be solved.

13. Not getting approvals on time and in writing. This almost always leads to misdirected and wasted effort trying to design to the wrong criteria.

14. Designing outside the bounds of the budget. When the cost constraints are especially tight this can easily happen, but ignoring them and trying to cut back later only results in a severely compromised design.

DIRECTING EFFICIENT DESIGN PROCESSES

There has been a great deal of research done on creative thinking—how it operates, what personality traits are found in creative people, and how creativity can be encouraged. Two of the frequently held myths have been dispelled: that creativity is something people are born with, either you have "talent" or you don't, and great ideas always occur in an instant of "creative insight." What is generally agreed on now is that creativity requires training and practice and can be learned like any other skill. One of the reasons it seems so elusive for many people is that our child-rearing methods, educational system, and economic/social/political environment all contribute to retard the creative potential. Instead, conformity and the quick, cookbook solution to problems are encouraged. While a *portion* of the second myth is true—the coalescence of a creative idea may happen unexpectedly in a flash—generally speaking, creative thinking is often a slow process during which any number of processes or methods of thought may be used to reach an objective.

Creative thinking is, of course, vital to the environmental design process, but one of the biggest problems is that the time and money pressures of business encourage the quick, final solution approach rather than the exploration and development of several solutions in a search for the most appropriate one. People then rely on past methods of problem-solving (and sometimes past solutions!) because these are the quickest ways to arrive at a resolution of both the design *and* business problem. Design professionals caught in this trap must either have more time, and therefore more fees, to explore problems sufficiently or must improve their current methods of problem-solving.

There are hundreds of design techniques an architect can use during the course of a project. These range from methods of lateral thinking for generating ideas to statistical analysis of completed work. The possibilities are vast, yet too many designers limit themselves to just a few, usually the simulation techniques of sketching on paper or building models. The following group of ideas lists only a *few* of the techniques you may find useful to loosen up your thinking and improve the quality of your design. Use them as a starting point to develop your own in-house procedures. You should explore the subject further with the references given at the end of the chapter.

Question Assumptions

In any design problem there are two basic kinds of assumptions: those that are actual constraints that are more or less fixed and those that are of the designer's own creation. Assumptions are necessary to limit any problem enough so that alternatives for its solution can be found, but the danger is getting locked into them. Looking back occasionally to verify if original assumptions are correct is a useful technique. Even if an assumption is "fixed," viewing a problem as though it were not helps stimulate new thinking. For example, how would a building be designed if the site were three times its actual size? If it were three times smaller?

Think in Five Senses

Environmental design affects all the senses of a person experiencing it, yet designers have a tendency to think only in visual terms. Consider each sense separately. What would your design be like for a blind person? What kinds of surfaces do people like to touch? How can you manipulate the sonic environment? Use the wealth of resources at your disposal to help solve the design problem.

Use Brainstorming

Brainstorming is a common, but underused, method of generating ideas. In the design office it is useful for encouraging free thinking among several people with different points of view and for producing many concepts for exploration. It prevents a single interpretation of a problem or its possible solution. In order to make brainstorming work you should state the problem in one sentence. Make it specific enough so you can concentrate on one area but broad enough so you don't limit solutions to one type. Six to fifteen people should participate for about twenty to thirty minutes. Have someone record the ideas while they are happening. There should also be a group leader to keep everyone on track and to keep things moving.

Remember that all judgments should be suspended while the session is taking place. Any idea, whether crazy or commonplace, should be recorded. It may serve as a springboard to another, more practical, notion. This should be encouraged. Most of the best solutions are developed by modifying or improving on other people's thoughts. After the session, evaluate all the ideas to sort out those that need more exploration, those that are outlandish but have some germ of a valid concept, those that are directly useful, and those that can be discarded. If used properly, brainstorming can generate a wealth of valid ideas and concepts in a very short time.

Restructure Patterns

Man is a pattern-seeking creature. Perception depends on the ability of the mind and sensory organs to structure stimuli into meaningful patterns. They occur not only in how things are actually laid out in the world, but also in how every person sees those things. The Rorschach inkblot test is a well-known example of this. In architecture and interior design the pattern concept comes into play in three areas. The first is how the elements of design are actually laid out: bricks set up to form a wall, classrooms arranged in a school, or furniture set in a waiting room. The second is the expectation a user of architecture has about how the environment should be arranged: a corridor should lead somewhere or a window at eye level should have a view. The third is the mental process a designer uses to solve a problem. It is in this area that patterns can either be useful or a hindrance since once a pattern is impressed on our memory our minds tend to block out other patterns. One aspect of creativity in the design process involves exploring many different patterns, not just fixing on the first one that comes to mind.

Figure 5-1 illustrates this with simple graphic shapes. The four hemicycles shown in (A) form one pattern. The most likely regrouping is into two circles (B) since this is a shape common to everyone and very prevalent in the world of experience. Others are possible, however. The ones shown illustrate the gestalt ideas of figure-ground, closure, grouping and projection. Projection is the assignment of meaning to a pattern apart from its denotative meaning. For example, to an interior designer, the grouping in (C) could be seen as four chairs in plan around a non-existent table. Viewing the patterns of problems in various ways will often free you from the trap of single-minded thinking.

Think Performance Criteria

A designed object, building, or space is the result of deciding *how* something should be done. Preceding the "how" should be the question of "what" needs to be done. Train yourself to think of the object or space you are designing in terms of how it has to perform rather than jumping directly to specifying something familiar that has worked in other circumstances. Listing all the attributes of the object or space is often a good way to start. For instance, the usual response to

**Figure 5-1
Patterns**

designing someone's office workspace is to call for a "desk" rather than a work surface with certain necessary attributes and support features. The physical response to the performance criteria may or may not be a "desk." Under the pressures of time and fee availability there is a natural tendency to fall back on previous successful responses to problems, but you should resist it when more comprehensive solutions are being sought.

Change Frame of Reference

There are times when one or more members of the design team will get stuck. Attempts at solutions become fruitless and time is wasted in trying to continue on one line of thinking. When these mental blocks occur it is sometimes useful to change how you view the problem, the solutions you have generated so far, or the relationships between the various parts of the problem or solution. Some of the ways to change your frame of reference include changing scale, reversing, turning images upside down, distorting, combining unlikely parts, changing uses, changing viewing position, and rearranging. While these may seem like "tricks" they are useful when other approaches produce few results. They may not lead directly to a solution by themselves, but may suggest more productive directions for your thinking.

Play Roles

Another way to change your frame of reference is by role-playing. Each member of the team assumes the role of someone else, designer, client, consultant, building inspector, project manager, and so forth and looks at the project from those points of view. Like brainstorming, this is another under-utilized technique of design firms. It is especially useful for critiques, design reviews, and as a dry run for formal presentations.

Record Goal Changes

Goals often change, are modified, or abandoned as a project progresses. Priorities shift. The client's organization changes, people come and go, attitudes and wants change, the economy turns, technology advances, or any number of forces cause amended project objectives to alter design parameters. These changes in goals are sometimes subtle and easily overlooked. Design proceeds as though nothing has happened until the end of the project when the client asks why all of his needs have not been met. This is especially likely to happen on projects of long duration. Keep track of goals and objectives throughout the project. At each project milestone, re-evaluate where you are and review this with the client. Keep a written record of these reviews with a copy sent to your client. It is useful to keep your office's design work on the right track and can be helpful later if disputes arise.

Balance Wants vs. Needs and Resources vs. Constraints

All environmental design problems have conflicts between wants and needs and between resources and constraints. An effective design results only when these are brought into an acceptable balance (Figure 5-2). They continually change during the course of a project, too. Needs may really be "wants," constraints may be turned into resources, or resources may be depleted and become a constraint. Each member of the team will have a differing view of this balance, as well. It is the job of the designer (or project manager) to identify the conflicts and bring them into proper balance.

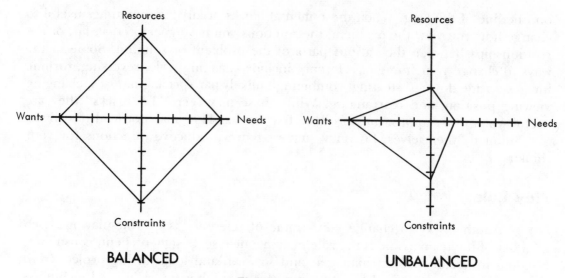

Figure 5-2
Wants/Needs—Resources/Constraints

Use a Story Board

This is one of the simplest, yet most effective tool in the design office. A story board is simply a large board or tack surface on which can be attached individual cards. A five-inch by seven-inch size is convenient although you can use other sizes. The story board is utilized for developing ideas, organizing information or planning work. For the design process each card may contain one idea, either graphic or verbal. They can be displayed, grouped, rearranged, discarded, added to, changed, and written on. In one glance you can see the status and progress of a design. The flexible nature of the board makes developing design concepts easy. It is also invaluable as a communication aid for the project and the office.

Assemble Standard Information

A great deal of design time can be saved by building your own library or reference notebook of standard data your office uses repeatedly. It becomes your own version of *Architectural Graphic Standards* and can contain such things as space standards, equipment information, typical adjacency diagrams, source contacts, building code information, and standard details. The time spent assembling it can pay dividends later on by eliminating repetitive research work.

Maintain a Project Board

This can be a board located near the team's workstations or a separate room if the job is large enough to warrant it. It can be used in conjunction with the story board and should include such things as the project schedule, fee or man-hour allocations, project goals, design concepts, ideas, messages, reminders, and anything else that would help project communication. It keeps everyone informed and encourages others in the office to lend ideas and suggestions.

Evaluate Alternatives

Every office should have a formal method of evaluating alternatives and recording this evaluation. It should be used during all stages of the design and design development process and be an automatic part of the project management sequence. Figure 5-3 shows one possible format where the criteria for the design under review are listed and a rating scale for each laid out. The alternatives are plotted based on how well they meet the particular criteria. This shows at a glance how the alternatives compare. Requiring documented evaluation encourages everyone on the design team to look carefully at each component of the solution and helps prevent adoption of one alternative based on personal bias.

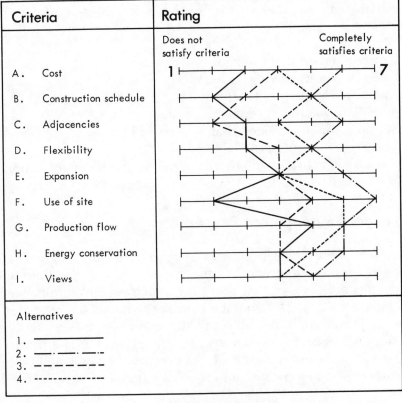

Figure 5-3
Alternatives Rating Chart

DIRECTING EFFICIENT PRODUCTION PROCESSES

Design office production techniques are in an evolutionary process if not a revolutionary one. Methods such as registration drafting, photo drafting, and computer-aided design and drafting are causing fundamental changes in the way architects and interior designers provide services. However, the revolution is not a uniform one. While some firms use state-of-the-art computer graphics others still struggle with draftsmen drawing and redrawing every job from scratch. Regardless of where your office stands within this wide range, there are steps you can take to improve this time-consuming and mistake-prone aspect of professional practice. Even if you are using computer-aided drafting there are still small jobs or special tasks that must be completed by hand. The work of doing these kinds of jobs can be streamlined to further increase your productivity.

There are five basic stages in improving production processes. I have listed them generally in order of simplest to most complex, least expensive to most expensive, and those that are easiest to implement to those that require more time and effort to implement. There is no fixed order for their completion and more than one may need to be put into effect at the same time. This will depend on the particular needs of your office and whether you have already established procedures in some areas. The five stages are:

1. Improve design development procedures
2. Develop better drafting techniques
3. Establish master specifications
4. Organize a master coordination system
5. Set up a computer-aided drafting capability

Steps to take are briefly discussed below. For more information on any phase, refer to the sources listed at the end of this chapter.

Improve Design Development Procedures

More efficient document production begins with the design development phase. All design decisions and many of the major detailing questions should be resolved during this phase so working drawings are almost an "automatic" process. Many offices have a tendency to continue to make design changes while the documents are being produced, or put off resolving detailing questions until this time. The results are usually wasteful: design changes cause downtime for the production people (and lead to mistakes) or the detail that everyone thought could be "worked out later" proves to be impossible and requires a major change in the building construction.

A better approach is to spend more time on the design development phase finalizing all aspects of the design and getting the client's final approval based on this. By using registration drafting techniques you can even complete many of the base sheets during this phase for reuse on the working drawings. At the end of design development the major portions of the site plan should be finalized, the structural grid set, most wall locations determined, elevations resolved, major mechanical components marked out, and details affecting major appearance points verified.

The following items should be determined at the end of the design development phase if you want to improve your document production process. All drawings, of course, should be at the same scale as the working drawings will be.

1. Building location and major site features, including grading, with all major dimensions worked out.
2. Utility connection points (with utility company approval).
3. Landscaping plan.
4. Structural grid with final overall dimensions and major framing components.
5. Floor plans with final wall locations, doors, millwork and fixed equipment. Dimensions of critical components controlling other dimensions should be worked out.
6. Detailed floor plans of critical areas or repetitive units (like hotel rooms) determined with dimensions shown.
7. Reflected ceiling plans with light layouts and changes of ceiling plane. Sections of special ceiling configurations drawn at a large scale showing coordination of structural, mechanical, electrical and architectural elements.
8. Interior elevations of special areas with details and dimensions determined.
9. Exterior elevations with floor elevations fixed, windows and other openings determined.
10. Wall sections of typical walls that affect overall design of both interior and exterior treatment.
11. Furniture layout.
12. Mechanical plans showing duct sizes and other items that will affect other trades.
13. Plumbing plans with stack locations, drain pitches, and space requirements worked out. These should be coordinated with other trades.
14. Telephone service requirements.
15. Electrical and signal distribution plans showing method of supplying power to all areas. Especially critical in open plan offices or buildings subject to change.
16. Special details or features that will affect dimensioning or other building layout. These features may be such things as monumental stairs, atriums, fixed subsurface or site conditions, and the like.

17. Building code requirements double-checked and approved.
18. List of all specification sections that will be required with accompanying outline specifications.
19. Samples of all major building components as a double check of client approval, compatability with other materials, appearance, dimensioning, and so forth.
20. A statement of probable construction cost that accurately reflects the detail outlined above. If the cost exceeds the client's budget, it is much easier and less expensive for the designer to know at this point so that changes can be made before more fee is spent on document production. This is an additional advantage to more specific design development drawings. If a cost overrun is found at bidding time and exceeds what may be considered reasonable (about 10 percent to 15 percent, often less!) the designer may have to redesign at no increase in fee.

Develop Better Drafting Techniques

With very little investment in money or learning time any office can improve its productivity in producing working drawings. Even firms that are already using some of the time-saving techniques like registration drafting can probably make further advances by carefully evaluating their present methods. The following suggestions briefly outline some of the ways to streamline working drawing production.

The first method, which many offices have adopted, is registration drafting. A different sheet of polyester drafting film is used for each component of a drawing and later reassembled photographically to create the final reproducible for printing. For example, one sheet may contain the title block and border, another the structural grid, another the wall layouts, another may have the room names and numbers on it and yet another would contain the dimensions and notation. All of these would be combined to form the architectural floor plan. Only the title block, wall layouts and room name sheets would be assembled to provide a base sheet for the mechanical engineer. See Figure 5-4. Repeat drafting is eliminated and changes made much more easily and quickly. Properly planned, this process can even begin in the design development phase as mentioned above. One firm reported completing as much as 20 percent of the working drawings during design development simply by using this technique.

Another labor-saving technique is to use composite drafting. This is sometimes refered to as cut-and-paste drafting. Various individual elements such as repeated units (hotel rooms, offices, etc.), catalogue cuts, previously drawn details, standard notes and the like are taped on to a full-size carrier sheet which is photographically reproduced to give a base sheet transparency that can be revised and completed to make up a new original. Tracing, redrafting, and generally "reinventing the wheel" is done away with, letting the reproduction shop do the work for you.

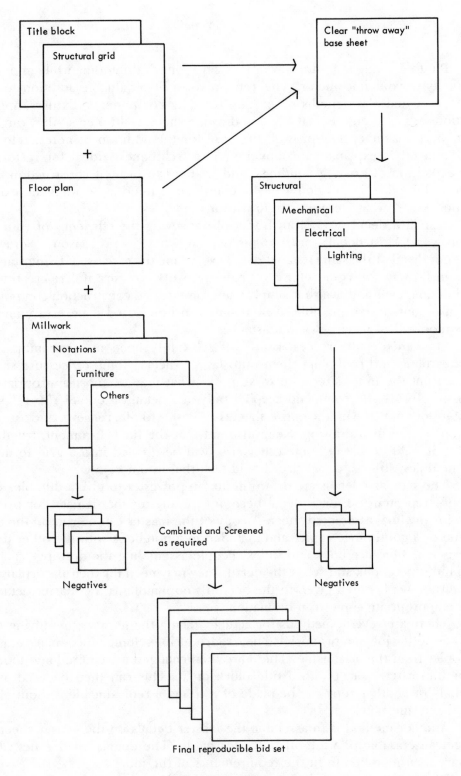

Title block

Structural grid

+

Floor plan

+

Millwork

Notations

Furniture

Others

Clear "throw away" base sheet

Structural

Mechanical

Electrical

Lighting

Negatives

Combined and Screened as required

Negatives

Final reproducible bid set

**Figure 5-4
Registration Drafting Process**

Photo-drafting is a third way of reducing your drafting time while improving the quality of your documents. This can prove to be a valuable addition to your repertory. Actual photographs of existing building components, fixtures, and site conditions are used on the final working drawing sheet. Halftoned so they can print in any diazo machine, they provide the base for the addition of notes, reference details and other explanatory comments. The technique is ideal for restoration work, expansion of existing buildings, and changes to present construction. With a picture, there can be no doubt in the contractor's mind as to what the existing condition is and what you want to do with it.

Standard details are a fourth way of improving the efficiency of your production work. Most detail work is repetitive and there is no reason to draw the same door detail or the same parapet detail every time they are used. Using standard details in no way will compromise your design work; you are not re-creating the same building over and over but simply using time-tested construction components that make your design possible. New details can be created if necessary and old details modified to meet new circumstances.

Standard details are best kept on 8½″ x 11″ sheets at a maximum. This facilitates filing and compiling them onto larger sheets. Some offices use smaller modules, but the exact size is up to you and what may be most appropriate for your kind of work. I recommend keeping only one detail on one 8½″ x 11″ sheet even if it does not take up the entire sheet. It is easier to file, retrieve, and assemble mock-ups of the final drawing. Keep in mind that the final document, whether it is 24″ x 36″, 30″ x 42″ or some other size, will be divided into a grid format of equal modules, so each detail size should take that into account.

The standard details are drawn in ink on polyester to give a durable, sharp image for repeated use. Each detail becomes the master that is used for printing copies for the final assembled sheet. A copy of the master can be run on the diazo machine or a good office copier and included in a notebook with the other details to serve as a reference book and index. People assembling the drawings can look through this notebook and select the details they may need for their particular jobs. A list of numbers is then given to the person who maintains the master details so that the appropriate copies can be made.

There are several methods for actually taking the masters, modifying them to fit the specific job and producing a new reproducible. Some offices make erasable film copies from the master file. These are then changed as required and taped to a clear film carrier sheet with a title block on it. This can then be used as the "original" or another copy can be made of it to get a reproducible without all the loose sheets and tape.

Another method is to assemble the master details on the carrier sheet and then get an erasable or wash-off polyester made. The details on this new, large sheet are then modified to fit the requirements of the job.

Whatever method you choose, it must be thought out before proceeding. You will be using the system for a long time and it will be difficult, and costly, to change later. The best way to get started is to review drawings for past jobs. Study the details and determine which types are used repeatedly. These are probably the ones to standardize first. You must also develop your own graphic standards. The details will be drawn over a long period of time by many different people and there should be consistency from detail to detail since they will always be compiled in different ways. Lettering height, line thicknesses, orientation of inside and outside surfaces, dimension lines, and the like all should be specified.

Someone should also be designated to oversee the maintenance, production, filing, and use of the standard detail system. This is the only way to maintain consistency, see that the system is utilized to its fullest potential, and keep it organized. New details must be checked for accuracy, old ones updated as technology changes and new staff members educated in the use of the system. Management commitment to the system is absolutely essential.

The use of a standard detail system *can* save time, increase production and improve the quality of the final drawing set.

CASE IN POINT

The firm of Gresham, Smith and Partners in Nashville, Tennessee has been using a standard detail system for several years now and reports a time savings of 25 percent on some of their work.

Other firms cite examples of forty-hour jobs being reduced to four-hour jobs. An added benefit of using standard details is that it prepares your staff for computerized drafting. The concept of reusability is the same, it is just that the computer does the assembling of the various components and lets you change them as necessary very quickly.

If you need some help starting a standard detail library, *Guidelines* offers a master detail system for hundreds of the most commonly used details. They are base details which a subscribing office completes to fit its own unique needs and drafting style. For more information, write to Guidelines, Box 456, Orinda, CA 94563.

There are a lot of fine points in using a standard detail system, registration drafting and the other techniques mentioned above that are beyond the scope of this book. The best reference on these is in *Systems Drafting* by Fred. A. Stitt (McGraw-Hill, Inc., 1980). Another handbook you might find useful is *Unigrafs* by Edgar Powers, Jr. (Gresham, Smith and Partners, Nashville, 1981). Both of these provide detailed, step-by-step procedures and tips for vastly improving drawing production.

As you are organizing and setting up better systems for drawing production (it takes time to do it right) consider the following checklist of steps you can take almost immediately to improve drafting room production.

1. Provide the proper environment for work. This includes correct task and ambient lighting for the various production tasks, colors, exterior views, rest areas and all the other considerations you would apply to designing an office for one of your clients.

2. Plan the workroom so that all reference aids, tools, and other support facilities are close at hand. The time taken to walk across the office to use a light table or find a handbook adds up. There is the added time-waster of socializing when someone walks past a number of other workstations.

3. Take a close look at the efficiency and ergonomic correctness of each person's workstation. Are the chairs correct? Is the drafting table adjustable? Are reference tables in the best location? Is there enough storage in the right place? Eliminate all the factors that may place an unnecessary strain on the draftsperson.

4. Get the right tools for everyone. For a nominal investment you can reap larger benefits. Consider buying tools that are often supplied by the employee. This encourages the use of methods that work best for *your* office and is an added benefit to the employee. Electric erasers, technical pens, pencils, and the like should all be selected and provided with an eye toward supporting your production methods.

5. Consider substituting drafting machines for the standard parallel rules. With one tool you can eliminate the fumbling required with multiple triangles and straightedges and at the same time keep the drawing medium cleaner. It takes some getting used to for people that have worked for years with parallel rules but the benefits may be worth the effort.

6. Use lettering machines for titles. They are not only faster than hand lettering of large print or stenciling but look better and highlight the title in a way that hand lettering seldom can. Used with the right reproduction techniques, the type can also be used for presentation drawings instead of dry transfer lettering.

7. Invest in an in-house vacuum frame or flatbed printer. It gives more accurate reproductions when making check prints as you combine base sheets with multiple overlays using a registration drafting system. Running a few sheets together through the standard diazo print machine is possible, but the registration will be slightly off due to the curvature of the exposure drum. There are several other jobs the vacuum frame can do for you as well. Making wash-off intermediates of paste-up sheets, simulating screened prints, and providing base sheets for consultants are all possible. Being able to do these in-house often saves time and allows you to do work at night or on weekends when the repro shop is not open.

8. Use fine point leads. The most popular is the .5mm size. These can be used without the need for continually sharpening them as is the case with the larger diameter leads. Many people claim that ink drafting on polyester can actually be faster than any kind of pencil drawing with the added advantage of yielding much better line quality for reproduction and half-size reduction.

9. Use polyester film. This is almost standard today in the design office, but there still are a few firms that use paper for small jobs. Polyester should be used for *all* working drawing production. It can take repeated erasures and stand up to general abuse that all drawings receive. It is also dimensionally stable, being little affected by humidity and handling.

10. Think reusability from the start. In any drafting work you should consider how the same effort can be put to more than one use. If you are developing a detail consider it a "standard" detail that can be modified on a future job. If you are starting an interior elevation for a design development presentation plan on using it for the working drawing set as well. In the same way, base sheets of floor plans can be used for design presentations as well as working drawings. Work smarter, not harder.

11. Consider freehand detailing. With a little practice it can be faster than the old two-step process of someone's freehanding a detail and then giving it to someone else to hardline. Combine the two operations into one. Done on tracing media with non-print grids at a large scale and then reduced, it produces a perfectly good drawing.

12. Keep track of drafting time on each sheet. Preprinted title block sheets can have a small matrix or chart in the non-print areas for every draftsperson to mark how much time was expended on the drawing. This not only makes everyone more aware of the time spent on a drawing but provides office management with invaluable information for future job cost budgeting.

13. Use typewritten notation on sticky-back film. For standard notes or lengthy wording, this is much faster than hand lettering. For repetitive work, a secretary can type up multiple copies and have them ready for instant use or, if it is the right brand, the office copier can be used to make multiple transparent copies off an opaque original.

14. Use graphic arts tape and shading films. These products are much faster than hand work for indicating wall types, areas not in the contract, boundary lines, match lines, material indications and a host of other features on drawings. Just remember to put them on the back side of the original so they will be protected when run through the print machine.

15. Use preprinted title block sheets, schedule forms, north arrows and any other item repeated from job to job. Again, this is standard in almost every office now, but some people are still drawing unnecessary lines on every job.

16. Number sheets in groups rather than consecutively. This makes it easy to slip in an additional sheet if required without disrupting the entire numbering sequence. For instance, you may have a site development group, an exterior enclosure group and an interior finishes group, each with a unique prefix number. The individual sheets within each group

are then separated from the prefix number (or letter) with a period and numbered sequentially from that point. Planning, cross-referencing and making changes are done much faster.

17. Have enough storage files for drawings. Shuffling through drawers overloaded with prints and original drawings is both frustrating and time-consuming. It also has a tendency to damage drawings. Vertical files are more efficient in use of space and are generally easier to use.

18. Do not overdraw. If adding detail, shading, or extra notes does not help explain or describe the subject being drawn, don't waste your time. Keep in mind, also, the entire process of production and the various roles played by others. For example, if you know you are going to get detailed shop drawings on millwork, do not waste time drawing every connection detail, piece of hardware or item of blocking unless it is unique to your design. The mill shop will do this for you and you always have the opportunity to check what they draw when you review the shop drawings.

19. Reuse old drawings. Even if you have not yet set up a formal standard detail library and system you can still use details from previous jobs if they are appropriate to your current project. Instead of redrawing or tracing it send it to the reproduction shop for an erasable film copy. Make modifications as necessary and paste it up on your new original.

20. In your staffing, consider hiring graduates from technical drafting schools rather than recent architectural graduates whose interest may not be in production work. If you can find a school in your area that teaches architectural drafting, it may be able to supply you with good candidates for in-house training according to your methods and standards.

21. Establish a drafting standards manual. There is no need to reinvent the wheel when it comes to reference marks, material indications, dimensioning methods, and similar conventions. Such a manual also saves time in training new staff.

22. Use drafting services. They can be useful in helping with rush work or drafting overload without forcing you to temporarily staff up with all the attendant overhead costs that entails. Some offices even use drafting services exclusively for all their production work. The service is under contract to produce a given amount of work for a fixed fee and this kind of cost budgeting can be valuable for firm management. Total personnel numbers are also reduced, thus saving overhead costs and the problems that come with managing a large office staff. The critical variables, of course, are getting a service that does quality work and organizing *your* management processes to make it possible. This includes having all decisions made at the end of design development and having the drawing set planned out in great detail before giving it to the service. Done properly, these procedures should overcome the most common objection of "losing control" if work is sent out for production.

Establish Master Specifications

Every office should have a master specification. This does not necessarily mean purchasing one of the standard specifications available, but having a complete, accurate, comprehensive base document from which to build specifications for individual jobs. No office should attempt the old "cut-and-paste" method any more. The chances for mistakes and potential liability problems are simply too great to make this a standard business practice. Additionally, assembling new specs from old ones is a wasteful use of the limited time you have to complete a job.

Master specifications do not necessarily mean automated specifications although this should be the ultimate goal because of the time-saving potential of word processing equipment now available. The first step for an office that has no master specification should be development of those sections that are used on most every job. General Requirements, Insulation, Gypsum Wallboard, and Painting are examples of these kinds of sections. Additional sections should be targeted to the particular kind of work your office does or the kinds of materials you typically use. If, for example, you do a lot of schools, sections on Chalkboards and Tackboards, and Lockers will be helpful.

Unless you have a lot of time and money to spare, these sections will probably need to be written over a period of time until you have assembled all of the typical sections you need in sufficient detail to allow for deductive editing; that is, editing of the master by deleting those items you do *not* need. For the small or medium-size office the commercially available specifications may be a good place to start if you do not have the resources to write your own from scratch, but even these need to be modified to fit your particular needs. It is impossible to write one specification to fit every office and every circumstance.

There are several master specifications available. The most popular are the following:

MASTERSPEC 2
>Production Systems for Architects & Engineers, Inc. (PSAE)
>1735 New York Avenue, N.W.
>Washington, DC 20006

SPECTEXT
>The Construction Specifications Institute
>601 Madison Street
>Alexandria, VA 22314

Spectext is a copyrighted document of the Construction Sciences Research Foundation. Bowne Information Systems, 435 Hudson Street, New York, NY 10014, has the exclusive license to maintain *Spectext* on computer. CSI is licensed by CSRF to sell *Spectext* in hard copy form. Contact Bowne Information Systems for information on computerized versions of *Spectext.*

STANDARDSPEC
Construction Specifications Service
530 North McClurg Ct.
Chicago, IL 60611

One significant advantage to these products is the updating service available—a job your office may not have time to do. All of these are available in printed versions and SPECTEXT and MASTERSPEC 2 are available for use in some brands of word processors and microcomputers. In addition, MASTERSPEC 2 is licensed by PSAE to many automation services around the country. A current list of these services is available by writing to PSAE. For more information about any of these services write to them directly for the most up-to-date information.

There are also independent specifications consultants who can assist you in developing your own in-house master specifications or you can hire them on an as-needed basis for each project. For a list of these consultants write to:

Specification Consultants in Independent Practice
5000 First Avenue South
Minneapolis, MN 55419

If you choose to develop your own in-house master specification and then decide to put it on a microcomputer or word processor first make sure the software will support a few of the editing needs unique to specifications. Just about every program will do the standard functions of deleting words, lines, and paragraphs, search and replace one word for another and the like. Additional criteria for specifications software should include disappearing notes (guidelines that print on the master specification for the editor but that do not print on the final), choice of selecting one block of text from among several, and automatic paragraph renumbering. Many word processing programs do not include some or all of these features.

Organize a Master Coordination System

Construction document production should not exist as an isolated phase of service. Since it is the summation of hundreds or thousands of decisions made from the beginning of the project there must be some way of coordinating those decisions with what is actually shown on the drawings and specifications. This is where many of the typical errors and ommissions occur—some piece of information generated two months previous gets lost or a client's comment at a meeting is forgotten and does not reveal itself until move-in.

Developing a coordination system is difficult because there is such a variety of components to organize: drawings, specifications, meeting notes, programming information, consultant data, building department requirements, design development decisions, and the like. One aspect of the design may also change many times during the course of the project. For example, the finishes of a building lobby may start as a preference of the building owner, change as the designer develops schematics, be modified due to fire code requirements, downgraded during design development because of cost, have some details revised during working drawings, respecified slightly when the specifier finds the particular finish is no longer manufactured, and finally revised again when the contractor submits an acceptable alternate. Tracking all of these modifications and the changes they imply is difficult, but imperative if problems are to be avoided. Knowing who made what decision when and *why* is critical, too, if disputes arise.

One commercially available system to help in this kind of coordination is *The Guidelines Systems Management Manual Series,* published by Guidelines, P. O. Box 456, Orinda, CA 94563. It includes a five-volume set of checklists, worksheets, notation and keynoting manuals, and other information useful for the project manager during the entire development of the job. Write to them for more information.

Set Up a Computer-Aided Drafting Capability

The final stage in improving your production processes is to implement computer-aided design and drafting. As costs come down and the technology is refined for architectural and interiors work such a system makes more sense for more firms of all sizes. Not only can productivity be increased, but firms with this capability will be able to take on work they could not have even considered before. Getting started with computer-aided drafting will be discussed in more detail in Chapter 12.

SOURCES FOR MORE INFORMATION

Books

Bloomberg, Morton. *Creativity; Theory and Research.* New Haven, CT: College and University Press, 1973.

de Bono, Edward. *Lateral Thinking, Creativity Step by Step.* New York: Harper & Row, Publishers, 1970.

Gordon, William J. J. *Synectics: The Development of Creative Capacity.* New York: Harper & Row, Publishers, 1961.

Halprin, Lawrence. *Taking Part: A Workshop Approach to Collective Creativity.* Cambridge: MIT Press, 1974.

Issac, Arg. *Approach to Architectural Design.* Toronto: University of Toronto Press, 1971.

Jones, J. Christopher. *Design Methods.* New York: John Wiley & Sons, 1981.

Moore, Gary, ed. *Emerging Methods in Environment Design and Planning.* Cambridge: MIT Press, 1970.

Powers, Edgar Jr. *Unigrafs.* Nashville: Gresham, Smith and Partners, 1981.

Raudsepp, Eugene. *How to Create New Ideas for Corporate Profit and Personal Success.* Englewood Cliffs, NJ: Prentice-Hall, Inc., 1982.

Rosen, Harold J. *Construction Specifications Writing.* New York: John Wiley & Sons, 1981.

Stitt, Fred A. *Systems Drafting, Creative Reprographics for Architects and Engineers.* New York: McGraw-Hill Book Company, 1980.

Seminars and Workshops Contact each for current schedule and topics

SYSTEMS '84. International Conference on Production & Management in A/E Firms. Annual conference and trade show on production and design office automation., P.O. Box 11316, Newington, CT 06111.

Guidelines Systems Drafting Workshops, Guidelines, P.O. Box 456, Orinda, CA 94563.

University of Wisconsin Extension, Department of Engineering and Applied Science, 432 N. Lake Street, Madison, WI 53706.

Newsletters

A/E Systems Report, MRH Associates, Inc., P. O. Box 11316, Newington, CT 06111.

The Guidelines Letter, Box 456, Orinda, CA 94563.

Plan and Print, International Reprographic Association, 10116 Franklin Avenue, Franklin Park, IL 60131.

Others

American Institute of Architects, Practice Management Office, 1735 New York Avenue N.W., Washington, DC 20006. The Professional Development office offers a home study course in "How to Reduce Production Costs with Systems Drafting."

Construction Specifications Institute, 601 Madison Street, Alexandria, VA 22314.

CHAPTER 6

Avoiding Legal Problems Through Quality Control

LEGAL ISSUES CONSTITUTE ONE OF THE MOST PERPLEXING AREAS of architectural practice. Despite the precise nature of the law and the vast collection of written statutes, there are often no fixed answers to guide the design professional in exactly the right direction. Laws vary among jurisdictions, change constantly, are applied to unique situations, and are interpreted by people who must make judgments in applying the written word to human conditions.

Legal issues are also very complicated. Basic precepts appear simple and straightforward, but their variations, exceptions, relationships, applications, and nuances require a specialist to understand. Architects and designers are typically given little or no exposure to the law in school and very little in actual practice. The professional's first experience with the law usually comes when it is too late—when a dispute has arisen.

The extent of legal issues in practice is great. Not only are there the contractual agreements between the architect and owner, and the owner and contractor, but also issues in such areas as office organizational structure, employee relations, consultant agreements, copyright, arbitration, expert witness involvement, extended services, professional conduct, and obligations to the public. The sources of the law are varied. Law is established through legislation by the states, federal and state constitutions, by administrative regulations such as zoning ordinances and licensing boards, and through court decisions where a vast body of precedent rulings are set. These rulings may or may not be followed depending on the specific facts of a case.

It would be impossible in the space of one short chapter to address the many legal problems design professionals can, and will, encounter in their practice. Instead, my approach will be to highlight some of the ways to avoid legal problems in the first place in the area where most difficulties occur—in the delivery of professional services under the traditional architect/client relationship. Discussion of specific cases, either in summary or detail, has been avoided as the many texts on construction law are more appropriately oriented to this function. Instead, my purpose in this chapter is to emphasize concepts and the idea of risk management— maintaining control on the inevitable risk position that every design professional is in when in business. However, I have included references at the end of the chapter for those readers who want to explore some of these issues in more detail.

One word of caution. Because the nature of the law as it applies to design professionals is both complex and unique to each situation, you should seek professional legal advice whenever necessary. When you do, find an attorney who is familiar with the unique problems of design professionals. Ideas suggested here are intended to help you establish a conscientious, rigorous program to minimize the possibility of encountering legal problems.

AVOIDING PROBLEMS DURING PREDESIGN

Initial Client Contact

A job started wrong seldom gets any better. The first critical step for an architect or designer in avoiding legal problems is to know his or her potential client. Too often the professional jumps at any job offered, especially during slack periods, without sufficient regard for the viability of either the client or the project. One important concern, of course, is the client's ability to pay the professional fee. Past clients will have established a record of payment habits that usually remain consistent. However, if some time has passed since your last contract with a client, check for any change in his financial status, increase in size of the proposed project, and financial success of past projects.

You should also note unreasonable expectations or demands in your first meetings with a potential client. With a client requesting professional services for the first time, some of this can be attributed to lack of knowledge of the design and building process and what services architects offer. Patient clarification of some of the fundamentals should clear up most confusion. If, however, the client persists in unrealistic ideas about budget, time, a set design idea, or otherwise has an impossible program it should be a clear signal not to enter into a contract. Expecting that you will be able to "educate" the client as the project progresses and work out the problems may be unrealistic thinking on *your* part.

For new and unfamiliar clients, a credit check is well worth the cost. Dun & Bradstreet is one commercial firm that offers such checks. Contact your local office for information and rates. Also check with business associates and past clients of your potential client. What were they like to work with? Did they pay promptly?

Do not be afraid to require an advance payment on fees up front. If the amount is reasonable and the client's organization does not have any specific restrictions against advances, reluctance to pay a retainer is usually a clue to later problems. Every project needs some up-front money and there is no reason for the architect to be ignored.

One possible way to minimize your risk is business credit insurance. The insurance company verifies the potential client's credit for you and insures payment of the account for a fee. Check with your insurance agent for this kind of coverage. The small premium is well worth the cost if it helps you avoid non-payment of just one client or assists in collection of late payments.

During the negotiation phase, understand the implications of the legal structure of the entity you are dealing with. The person or persons with authority are generally clearly defined in a sole proprietorship or partnership. With large corporations, however, be sure you are dealing with someone who has authority to make representations during negotiation. As a precaution, keep these points in mind:

1. Make sure all items which have been negotiated are incorporated into the final contract. Representations made by someone without authority to make them and which are not included in the contract may become the subject of a dispute.

2. Make sure the contract is signed by an officer of the corporation. If you have any doubts, you can ask to see the articles of incorporation to verify who does have authority to contract.

3. If the contract is submitted by the corporation to you, don't be afraid to insist on changes if you and your attorney feel they are needed.

4. For unincorporated associations, such as labor unions, social clubs and churches, verify that the persons you contract with have authority to request commencement of professional services. If you are in doubt, ask to see some evidence of their authority and insist that a resolution by the governing board be passed authorizing the contract.

Architect/Client Contracts

Many of the legal problems that originate with architect/client contracts can be avoided by understanding some of the fundamental concepts of such contracts: those that define the expectations, duties, responsibilities, and conduct of the architect or designer. An awareness of these concepts can help guide your actions correctly regardless of the specific form of agreement or phase of service you are in. Detailed discussions of the various agreements between parties (those published by the AIA, for example) have been examined in detail in other sources. For an item-by-item review, refer to the sources listed at the end of this chapter. The following discussion outlines some of the basic concepts to remember.

Contracts

A contract is basically a bargain between two or more parties who agree to exchange something each desires to obtain. For example, the client desires to have the architect design a building and the architect desires to be paid for his or her time. An analysis of this meeting of the minds suggests there are two parts to this process: an offer by one party and an acceptance by the other. In general, every contract, whether written or oral, should have both to be valid. If one person offers to do something and does it without acceptance and an agreement to do something in return, a contract may not exist. Relief in the form of damages may not be possible.

Generally, contracts in writing tend to minimize misunderstandings in this area since signatures and the language of the document will set forth the terms of the offer and acceptance. Proposals, it should be noted, are not contracts if the person to whom the proposal is made is not authorized to "accept" the proposal or does not promise to do something in return for the person who made the proposal.

Contracts can be either express or implied. Express contracts may be either oral or written. Implied contracts are those which are suggested by the actions of the parties. Architects often overlook or are not aware of their implied contractual duties or those of the contractor. Some of these are enumerated in the next section and the section on Avoiding Problems During Construction.

In settling disputes, the courts will generally scrutinize more carefully the party who drew the contract *if* both parties negotiated the terms of the contract from roughly equal bargaining positions. For example, if two people both negotiate terms knowledgeably and by mutual give and take, then both will be treated similarly. However, if one party has dictated the terms of the contract, he or she will be presumed to possess a superior knowledge of its terms. This situation may occur when employing the standard AIA contract forms. Additional problems with using standard contract forms are that they are not specific to any particular architect's mode of operation and may include responsibilities not anticipated by either party.

Consider having your attorney draw up a contract drafted specifically for *your* practice. Make it a balanced one. The client has rights and expectations just as you do. Have it tailored to fit the precise needs of your method of operating and the kinds of work you do. Consider, also, having the contract clearly worded in plain English. Highlight those portions that you and your attorney feel should be emphasized. The extra time and money involved will more than pay for themselves in reduced misunderstandings and possible litigation.

Agency

The architect or designer typically acts as the agent of the client. The legal concept of agency involves three parts: the "principal," the "agent," and the "third party." In the typical situation, the principal is the client and the third party is the contractor. Generally, the law holds that when the agent consents to act on behalf of and represent the interests of the principal the agent is empowered to create legal relationships between the principal and third parties. In the course of his conveying information to the contractor, it is easy for the contractor to assume that the professional speaks with authority for the client (which, in fact, he may). In such situations the law may hold the contractor (third party) *may assume* the architect (agent) has all types of authority to bind the client (principal). This is especially true if the contractor can show several specific instances when the architect did act with authority for the client.

The problem usually arises when the contractor does not perform as intended by the client who, in turn, goes to the architect and demands correction of the problem saying that is why he retained the design professional in the first place. The contractor says he just did his work as directed and blames the architect. In the middle is the architect—the focus of bad feelings as well as exposure to legal liability if the contractor is successful in shifting the blame.

Disputes can also arise when the architect or designer exceeds authority. If the client is unwillingly bound to the contractor by some decision or act of the architect, the client usually will seek relief by claiming the architect is liable.

There are four ways that the legal system can view the source of authority for the architect or designer as agent, a few of which most architects are unaware. The first is express authority. This is written or verbal direction given by the client (principal). Typical examples of this are the listing of responsibilities given in Article 2 of the AIA General Conditions of the Contract for Construction or services to be performed as enumerated in an Owner-Architect agreement.

The second is implied authority. This stems from those actions that are incidental or reasonably necessary to the performance of the job for which the architect has express authority.

The third source is apparent authority which results from the representations of the principal (the client) to the third party (the contractor). In other words, what the client may say or do in dealings with the contractor may lead the contractor to believe that the architect does have the authority to authorize or perform certain actions. In this case, the client may be liable to the contractor as a result of the actions of the architect, *but* the architect may in turn be liable to the client.

The last kind of authority is inherent. This principle exists mainly for the protection of the third party when the agent may exceed his or her authority without the third party's knowledge such authority has been exceeded. If the architect does go beyond authorized limits and binds the client and contractor into an agreement, the architect may once again be liable to the client for damages caused by such an agreement.

These sources of authority in the agency relationship should serve as a guide for written correspondence, words, and actions of the design professional during all phases of the project, especially the construction administration portion. Just because something is or is not written down does not necessarily mean it will be applied by the third-party judge or arbitrator if disputes come up. The lesser-known concepts of implied, apparent and inherent authority can create problems for the architect not aware of their implications.

Of course, all the intricacies and related legal issues surrounding agency cannot be elaborated here. What has been intended in this section is to illustrate that an agency relationship can develop in a number of different ways not always intended. However, if you are aware of the circumstances by which the relationship can be established it is possible to at least document the extent of any liability.

The following guidelines may help you avoid some of the common problems that seem to plague the profession. Disputes usually arise with agency concepts when the client questions if he or she is responsible to the contractor for the acts of the architect. If it appears from the client's perspective that he or she is so bound, the client may then seek reimbursement for losses from the design professional.

1. Remember that the architect or designer as agent usually does not have the authority to change the contractual rights of the parties to the contract. He or she normally is only authorized to do what is reasonable to accomplish what the client wants done as reflected in the design, plans or specifications. Change orders, for example, altering the contract in any significant fashion, especially in terms of time or money should be signed by the client and contractor. Other express authorities should be listed in the agreement, such as in Article 2 of AIA document A 201. This document does give the architect express authority to make minor changes not involving time or cost.

2. Communicate often and extensively with your client. Too many design professionals think part of their service should be to "take care of things" so that their client does not have to worry about the details. Avoid getting yourself in this position—it can only lead to problems. Generally, this type of client will seek to get you to make decisions and then hold you responsible when they are not to his or her liking.

If the client is constantly aware of the architect's (agent's) actions and does nothing to countermand them, applying the doctrine of ratification may offer a limited defense for the architect if questions of authority come up. The doctrine generally holds that the client is deemed to have ratified the agent's actions by not acting to the contrary when and if he or she was fully aware of the activities taking place. The client *may* then be bound by the architect's acts even if the authority may have been exceeded. Notify your client of even minor changes before they are made or at least as soon as possible after they are made.

3. If your client does want to assume less involvement than is normal and give you more authority, consult with your attorney before reaching such an agreement and have the exact limits of this grant of authority outlined in writing *before* the project begins. However, this practice is risky at best. You should carefully weigh the advantages against the risk.

4. Request written authorization from your client on actions you may feel need to be taken if they are not specifically and clearly spelled out in your contract.

5. Request written authorization *not* to do something if inaction would put you in a possible position of ratifying something the contractor may say or do.

6. If your agency position should be terminated by your client, notify other people who may still assume you have apparent authority.

Duties

The law recognizes that the professional undertakes certain responsibilities when he or she contracts to perform services on behalf of the client. The law attempts to define and set limits on what one person "owes" another in a given relationship.

The concept of duty developed in this context, and is critical in the construction process because there are usually multiple relationships, all with varying degrees of liability involved in getting a job done, some contractual and many not. There are basically three ways the duties of an architect may be defined.

The first is by the terms of an express contract, whether oral or written. For example, Article 1 of the AIA Form of Agreement between Owner and Architect attempts to outline the services and responsibilities of the architect, states that these duties may not be modified or extended without written consent of the owner, and provides for defining additional services (read duty) if agreed by both parties.

The second way is by the architect's conduct. The courts often look to implied duties based on the conduct of the parties and what can reasonably be expected of each in the course of performing their respective responsibilities. Many situations which arise during a project are *not* addressed by the contract or the General Conditions of the Contract. Just because this is true doesn't mean you are free to act unilaterally without discussing matters with your client or are immune from the reasonable consequences of either your actions or inaction.

The classic example of this involves the responsibility of the architect to stop the work if there is an unsafe working condition during construction. Although most contracts place the responsibility of maintaining a safe job site and supervising the methods of construction on the contractor, you as the professional on the job may have exposure to liability. The general rule of thumb applied by the courts is the more apparent or flagrant the unsafe condition or violation, the greater the degree of exposure. Rulings on this particular point vary, but this example does serve to illustrate the possible extent of the architect's responsibility. Additional duties which may be implied are listed later in this chapter in the discussion on Construction Administration.

The last way duties are usually defined is by legislative enactment. Architectural licensing laws and building codes are examples of this.

In order to avoid some of the common pitfalls in this area, the first step should be to require everyone working on a project to read the Owner/Architect contract to know what their express duties are. As fundamental as this seems, once the Owner/Architect agreement is signed, it is usually filed away, never to be seen again until a dispute arises. It is tedious reading, but essential to the entire project team. Your office may want to spend some time developing a "contract highlights" checklist for the people on the team that briefly spells out the pertinent points of the contract you use. Holding a meeting at the beginning of each job for the appropriate team members to discuss the office's legal responsibilities on that job is another way of emphasizing the critical points. From time to time it is good preventive medicine to have an attorney hold a seminar for the office on current legal thinking in the area of construction law. Paying for a few hours of legal advice could reap vast dividends if it helps avoid a protracted legal dispute.

Liability

Liability is one of the foremost topics on the architect's mind today. With the increasing instances of lawsuits against professionals in general and the subsequent increase in professional liability insurance, everyone wants to know how to avoid or at least minimize the problem. You should start from the perspective that you *cannot avoid liability,* but you *can limit your exposure* by careful planning and implementation of your own standards of professional conduct. The courts have held an architect is one who holds himself or herself out to have special knowledge or skill.

The prevailing legal concept at the moment is that the professional is not expected to be perfect; he or she is expected to exercise the degree of skill, knowledge and judgment normally possessed by other professionals in similar circumstances in similar communities. The standard to which an architect or designer is to perform is that of the professional community and the generally accepted knowledge, practice, and procedures of that community. If the design professional is found to be negligent in performing to those standards, he or she can, and probably will, be held liable for the damages caused.

Liability laws vary from state so you should check with your attorney to suggest the ground rules under which you may have to operate. Generally, to show liability the claimant must establish a duty and demonstrate that the duty was breached by the professional. This is why understanding the concept of duty previously discussed and the various sources of it are so important. Additionally, and of equal importance, is to understand that liability is not limited to some gross breach of the written contract. It can, and will, arise from the sum total of the contract documents, the conduct of all parties, conversations, observations, and financial considerations.

Most liability claims are a result not of intended negligence, but rather the failure of the architect or designer to do something to fulfill a duty that is expected of a reasonably prudent professional. The unfortunate part of this is that in many cases the failure to act could be readily avoided and usually involves a relatively simple task, such as a letter that should have been written, a careful review of a drawing, notification of noncompliance or noting a problem, time made in a busy schedule for coordination, or something that is usually planned for in the execution of a project anyway.

One of the most effective ways to minimize your exposure to liability claims (and greatly improve the level of office efficiency) is to start and maintain an active quality control program—a checklist of standard minimal procedures used on all jobs. The fundamental components must include:

1. Commitment by top management to the program
2. In-house standards and procedures
3. Designation of one person, preferably a principal of the firm, to co-ordinate and administer the program
4. Enforcement of the program on a continuing basis
5. Feedback from use of the program to continually improve it

More and more architectural firms are developing quality control programs and most of the major insurance companies encourage and support such efforts. Establishing quality assurance not only helps to lessen potential liability exposure, but also gives you an added component to add to your marketing program.

CASE IN POINT

The firm of Gresham, Smith and Partners in Nashville, Tennessee has an extensive quality assurance program. Two key elements of their efforts include an extensive systems drafting process and complete checking procedures.

All of the components of systems drafting are used: overlay drafting, cut and paste, standardized details, photodrafting, and half-size, color offset working drawings. Master specifications are used as well. With this system errors are greatly reduced, there is better project pricing since the documents are easily interpreted, and overall the level of quality control is high. As an added bonus, the completed set of color offset, half-size drawings gives them a valuable marketing tool that impresses potential clients.

For checking, only the most qualified people are used and a set of drawings may go through six different people before being issued. First, the set is reviewed by the project architect. Next is a technical check to review the details and other construction components. Then they are checked for coordination with the specifications. A spot-check of dimensions is followed by an examination of the drawings from a contractor's standpoint. In special areas, such as medical work, another specialist may be involved, too.

The bottom line to these elaborate procedures is that to date, Gresham, Smith and Partners has not had any legal problems due to errors in construction documents and has received other benefits as well.

In summary, keep the following additional points in mind to help avoid legal problems during the predesign phase.

1. Establish and maintain client awareness. In the predesign phase this involves explaining the inexact nature of construction, pointing out that no project is perfect, that problems will most certainly develop, that changes will be requested and made, that cost will almost certainly increase, that the schedule will probably be too short, and that the client will have to be closely involved for the duration

of the job. Most seasoned clients who have been through a building program know this, but it is always prudent to repeat it. Clients who enter into an agreement with an architect or designer with these expectations are less likely to look for guilty parties when the inevitable problems arise.

2. Do not create expectations that cannot be met. Most design professionals are so eager to please their clients at the start of a job they often give the impression they will deliver more than they should or can. A client will respect you more for being forthright about the project and realistic in what he can expect than for making too many unrealistic promises. Unfulfilled expectations will cause nothing but bad feelings and set the stage for other problems including non-payment of your fee.

3. To avoid false expectations, spell out in detail what services you intend to perform as part of your contract. A dollar amount should be assigned to each phase of service rather than a lump sum total so it is easier to determine what money is owed if a dispute comes up in the middle of a project and only partial payment is made. This scope of services is also useful in establishing your basic compensation and claims for additional fees if extra work is requested. You may even want to be more explicit in your contract for services than what is included in the standard AIA Owner/Architect Agreement.

4. Don't be afraid to enumerate the responsibilities of the client in your contract. The client must be actively involved and these contract provisions establish the extent of his involvement. Although Article 2 of the AIA Owner/Architect Agreement lists the owner's responsibilities, most of these are in the area of what the owner will furnish, such as soil tests, surveys, budgets, and the like. Be sure he understands the extent of these responsibilities. There should be additional requirements for the day-to-day participation of the owner, including times of review of progress, written approval required at each phase, inclusion in project meetings and similar involvement. You should have the client initial drawings, diagrams, sketches and other documents as they are approved at various stages of the design. This is especially applicable to requested changes in design.

5. Have your attorney review any proposed contract which contains items that are unique or with which you have not had prior experience. Do not rely on standard forms, even the AIA agreement, without studying how they apply to your project. Each job and client is a little different. Consider having your attorney draft your own office's "standard contract" to customize it for your needs.

6. Do not proceed with a project until you have an explicit program. Inadvertently solving the wrong problem or not satisfying all the client's requirements seems an unlikely mistake to make but it happens. Develop a checklist of wants and needs with your client. If the client gives you a completed program, do not take it at face value. Question what it says to make absolutely certain it is what you should be designing for. When you have completed the problem definition phase have the client sign off on it. If you have approval in writing, the program can serve as the basis for negotiating later changes and justified increases in your fee.

7. Document all your actions. This applies to all phases of the design and construction process. Architects are notoriously bad record keepers. Trying to reconstruct a series of events or prove a point when disputes arise is difficult or impossible if it is not in writing. No one can argue that careful documentation is tedious, unenjoyable and time-consuming, but no other single administrative task you can do is more important. Keep a daily journal of each job, noting what was done or what decisions were made, by whom, why, and any follow-up actions. This should supplement the usual documentation of meetings, telephone calls, transmittals, notifications required by contract, and other standard forms such as change orders and field reports.

8. Know what your responsibilities are, both express and implied. The predesign phase is the best time to clarify these with all members of the team working on the project. During this phase as well as for the duration of the job, do exactly what you are required to do—no more and no less.

9. Consider carefully the inclusion of an arbitration clause in your contract. Discuss this with your attorney. Experience in some areas of the country indicates the arbitration process can be substantially more cumbersome, expensive and fraught with delay than the available legal counterpart.

AVOIDING PROBLEMS DURING THE DESIGN PHASE

When an architect begins the design phase of a project he or she represents that certain obligations will be carried out. Foremost among these are that the design will result in a structure that meets the requirements of the client, is suitable for its intended use, conforms to applicable codes and regulations, and is buildable within the cost constraints of the client. There are others, of course, but these four requirements are usually where most disputes arise between owner and designer. Being suitable for intended use includes a wide range of design aspects from general conformance to a program to applicability of details to function properly.

One aspect of cost is worth highlighting. The standard form of agreement between owner and architect published by the AIA, as well as other typical contracts, contains a disclaimer about the architect's not warranting that project bids will not vary from the architect's statement of probable construction cost. While this puts the owner on notice concerning the proper place of the designer's budget and affords some protection if the bid price does exceed the budgeted cost it does not make the professional completely immune. You should be aware that the courts strongly dislike such attempts to limit liability and will attempt to discount these efforts whenever possible.

The courts have held that when the designer's estimate is significantly below what the lowest bidder's price is and not due to changes requested by the client or other circumstances out of the designer's control, the designer may be liable for negligence. He or she may in turn be assessed for any damages the client might have suffered as the result of the underestimation as well as having to forfeit design fees claimed due.

What is meant by "significant difference" will be determined by the third party adjudicating the dispute; each case is unique. Remember, the third party is probably not going to be an architect who understands the problems of architecture. Instead, he or she will apply the facts as related by witnesses on both sides to the applicable principles of law. Often, points you may take for granted are not brought out and therefore will not be considered by the court. Take care in checking your work and the work of others. It is far simpler to spend a few minutes reviewing your work than days or weeks educating a judge or jury in the entire evolution of the project.

Differences of 50 percent or higher would usually be considered grossly in variance, for example, but on public projects where a strict limit is set, any discrepancy may create a substantial problem. With the disclaimer in a contract concerning the architect's statement of probable or estimated construction costs, an overrun of 5 to 15 percent *may* be reasonable and expected (although not liked!). Anything over this amount will probably create problems and possible litigation.

To help you avoid falling into common traps during the design and design development phase of a typical project, review this list of suggestions.

1. As in other project phases, each person on the architect's design team should have read the agreement or at least a summary checklist prepared by the project manager.

2. During the design phase maintain active communication with the client. This starts with scheduling review and approval points up front, before design begins. Give the client a copy of the overall schedule and stick to it. Document these review meetings with complete notes and send a copy to the client for verification.

3. Hold periodic in-house design reviews. Check your progress against the contract requirements, the program developed for the project, office goals and the client's budget. No one should be allowed to hide away and one day emerge with the "design." Problems are more easily spotted by a team with different objective viewpoints than by one prima donna.

4. Provide design alternatives for the client. Architectural design is a process of exploring alternatives and no matter how much the client (or you) may like the first try (and often the only try) they always have the nagging feeling later that maybe something else should have been looked at. This usually happens late in the design development phase when much time and effort have been expended to finalize that first "great" design concept. Most clients cannot respond well until they see something on paper, a model, or some firm representation of an idea. Do this early when it costs less and is easier to change. A client involved in this way is less likely to demand costly redesign later and say that the architect did not adequately discharge his design duties.

5. Often, questions of choice between similar alternatives come up. This can occur with design concepts, product selection, or building systems. When this happens, explore, research, and present the pros and cons of each alternative. You may make your best professional recommendation supported by careful reasoning. Once the presentation is complete ask the client for his decision. Later, if problems develop, the client is unlikely to question a decision in which he took part or made. Should the decision later be the subject of litigation the logical best defense is that you not only acted with reasonable skill and knowledge typical of others in your profession but also with the participation and approval of your client—a difficult defense to overcome.

6. Develop a method of feedback from past jobs. Learn from your mistakes and successes. Most designers do not do this since there is seldom any money set aside for this. It is critical, however, and part of the job fee should be devoted to it. Knowledge gained should be formally documented and available to all office personnel, not just filed in someone's memory.

7. Stay current with products and technologies. This is one of the implied duties of an architect if he or she expects to practice with the same degree of skill as other similarly placed professionals. Having used an out-of-date roofing system when more reliable methods were available would put you in a vulnerable position if you were involved in litigation for designing a roof that leaked.

8. Know industry standards and trade customs. They can play a significant part in court proceedings as one of the measures by which your design may be judged. If you design below or above typical standards or require performance deviating from normal trade customs, you should document the reasoning as to why you took a specific action or deviated from the standard, including how you endeavored to ensure that you acted with reasonable skill and care. Have copies of current standards in your office and know when and how they apply to your project. Be knowledgeable in the skills and abilities of the workmen in your area of practice. Consider having contractors hold seminars for your office on design and construction from the contractor's point of view.

9. If you have any doubt as to the adequacy of your design, do not hesitate to build models, make full-size mock-ups or perform other testing of the product, system, or design configuration you plan to use. This will often point out problems before they happen.

10. With unfamiliar products and systems, always check several sources for information. Do not depend just on manufacturers' literature—they are trying to market the product. See where they have been used before, under what conditions, and how they have performed. Write to the manufacturers of the products or systems stating how you intend to utilize them and obtain specific recommendations on use or implementation. Review independent sources such as testing laboratories and trade associations. Then present the information to your client. Explain that the products or materials are new or untried. Provide him with a summary of the data you have synthesized and seek his opinion, or better yet, his participation in the

decision-making process. With this kind of in-depth research you have not only minimized your exposure to the claim by performing with reasonable skill and care, but also greatly lessened the chances of problems developing. If something goes wrong later, you have once again laid the groundwork for a strong defense.

11. An architect or designer has the duty to see that a building or interior is designed according to code regardless of checking and approval by the building department. Perform building code and zoning ordinance research before beginning design. This should include the usual review of the applicable code in your area as well as special regulations pertaining to the project type under design such as health care facilities, housing and the like. Develop a checklist for your areas of practice and require its use on all projects. There will be questions and even doubts about the interpretation of provisions of the code. Don't hesitate to talk to the appropriate person at the building department about the problem. Document the meeting with notes and if the building official will not sign off on a set of drawings (as they usually will not) at least send a copy of the notes to the department and to your client. If requirements are changed later, you have proof of why you proceeded as you did.

12. Never include a fixed limit of construction cost as a condition of agreement with your client. Stick with the standard AIA language or similar contract provisions regarding statements of probable or projected construction costs. If the client insists on having a guaranteed cost, suggest that he negotiate with a contractor or construction management firm and find another architect.

13. If you do not feel confident in providing a statement of probable construction cost, get help. There are independent cost estimators that provide this kind of service and who are usually accurate. Remember, courts have held that if the building cost does not reasonably approach the designer's budget (excluding change orders and other unusual conditions) the designer may stand liable at law for a malpractice claim. This can result in a loss of fees, and/or the requirement that the architect redesign the project at no additional cost to meet the budget.

14. In your early discussions with the client, explain how cost budgeting is done and carefully enumerate the factors beyond your control that affect construction cost. Emphasize the importance of having some contingency funds available for unforeseen changes and problems.

15. Think cost alternatives from the start. One of the axioms of design is that there is never enough money to do what you, or the client, wants to do. Trying to cut the cost after the bids are in by picking at the design seldom works and is highly risky from a liability standpoint. Either the costs are not reduced enough or the design concept is severely compromised. Work with your client early in the design phase to determine priorities and establish what is absolutely necessary for the successful solution to the design problem.

16. Always refer to your work with estimating cost as a "budget." Avoid the terms "estimate," "price," "cost" or other words that might imply a fixed amount.

I even prefer not to use the AIA's phrase of "probable construction cost." Unfortunately for the architect, clients tend to only see and hear "construction cost," not the all-important word "probable."

17. Communicate with the client, in writing, what the cost effect will be of each change that the client makes during the design and design development phases. Clients do not always understand the full implication of what may seem like a minor change. An early and prompt addressing of each additional cost will not only discourage frequent requests for modifications but also make the client aware that each change costs money. Notification should, of course, explain possible increases in your fee as well as adjustments in the construction schedule.

18. Document all decisions made during the design phase. This includes meetings as well as day-to-day decisions that seem minor at the time but can blossom into full-scale disputes when everyone is relying on memory. Keep a daily journal and note the who, what, why, and how of the situation as well as follow-up required.

19. Have the client sign off on design drawings as work proceeds. Sit with the client and take him or her through every part, every room, every elevation, so you are sure he has studied what you are doing.

AVOIDING PROBLEMS DURING CONSTRUCTION DOCUMENT PRODUCTION

Defective plans and specifications account for the majority of claims against architects and designers. The professional has the duty to both the owner and the contractor to produce an adequate set of documents. Since the design contract is between client and architect or designer, the architect impliedly warrants that satisfactory results can be obtained if the contract documents are followed.

Of course, no set of documents is perfect and none ever will be. Deciding whether the liability rests with the contractor or the design professional is often up to a third party adjudicating the dispute. This third party generally has limited knowledge in both construction and design. Obviously, each case must rest on the facts peculiar to the situation, but as a general rule the design professional is liable for extra cost or time extension due to errors in the construction documents. The architect clearly is liable if there are substantial errors contrary to the normal standards of practice or if the architect did not act with reasonable skill and diligence in preparing them. The best insurance is to avoid the problems in the first place with a good quality control program.

Compare your existing methods of producing construction documents with the following checklist. The items listed represent some of the areas that commonly precipitate legal disputes. Included are ideas for maintaining better control over document production.

1. *Control.* One person should be responsible for overall planning, coordination, and implementation of the office's quality assurance program. This person should set up in-house procedures and standards, verify them against prevailing professional standards, monitor work for conformance to standards, and make sure that information gained from past jobs is incorporated into the system.

2. *Coordination between plans and specifications.* These two parts of the contract document set are often produced at different times by different people and when changes are made they are frequently made on the drawings only. If there are two or more reasonable interpretations possible from a complete set of documents, the law usually gives more weight to that interpretation which is most favorable to the party who did not draft the documents. Having one person, either the project architect or project manager, responsible for overseeing both is one way to minimize this problem. Another way is to use one of the master specification systems avilable such as *Masterspec* published by Production Systems for Architects & Engineers, Inc., which includes a drawing coordination sheet with each specification section, highlighting what aspects need to be included in the drawings. Another company has developed a standard detail management and indexing manual to help coordinate drawings, specifications, filing, feedback system and quality control. This is in conjunction with their published sets of standard details. For more information contact Guidelines, P.O. Box 456, Orinda, CA 94563.

3. *Industry standards.* Standards developed and accepted in the construction industry and normal trade customs are given a great deal of consideration when legal disputes develop. Whether they are published or simply a matter of normal practice, the design professional should make it a point to remain current and knowledgeable on the industry standards of quality and workmanship. If standards higher than the normal are desired, they must be spelled out exactly in the drawings and specifications.

4. *Work procedures.* Utilize a working drawing checklist to minimize the possibility of omissions. Tailor it to the kind of work your office does. Add to it as you learn from past successes and mistakes. More and more offices are turning to the use of standard details, too. They build a file of construction configurations that are accepted in the industry and that work and use them as the basis for modification as needed for particular jobs. Not only does this reduce the time and cost of producing a set of working drawings, but it helps prevent mistakes that are made when every draftsperson re-invents the wheel.

5. *Professional standards.* With the legal emphasis being placed on performing with the same standard of care as other similarly placed professionals, there is a trend to use standard master specifications such as *Masterspec* previously mentioned or *Spectext* by the Construction Sciences Research Foundation. The use of these industry-accepted specifications is increasingly being recognized as one way to reduce the design professional's exposure to liability. Additionally, courts give more consideration to the credibility and professionalism of an architect who has utilized

these kinds of specifications than one who has cut and pasted his or her own. For the small and medium-size offices who may not have the time and resources to develop their own well-researched master specifications, these products are a cost-effective way to improve the quality of their office's specifications and minimize problems. With the advent of low-cost microcomputers and word processors there is no reason to use the typical, and dangerous, cut-and-paste method of assembling new specs from old.

One word of caution, however, on the use of word processing for specifications. The word processor can become an extremely dangerous tool. Instead of assisting the design professional it can lead to an area of liability that he never envisioned. The problem arises when the architect or designer becomes lazy or attempts to cut corners by not carefully reviewing the generated document. He or she may have had several successful specifications run and begins to rely on the machine to produce an error-free document without scrutinizing each line. If a mistake or omission is critical, you will receive little sympathy from the client, judge or the jury when you attempt to explain it was the machine's fault.

6. *Conflicts.* Check and recheck for conflicts and confusing instructions. When the construction document set is complete, it should be reviewed by a qualified person who has not worked on the job. Time for this check should be budgeted into the schedule, a day or two for small jobs, up to a week or more for large, complex projects. A great many errors, conflicts, and confusing items can be caught with this simple, but often underused, technique.

7. *Consultants.* Require that your consultants perform the same kind of checking you do. During drawing and specification production, exchange progress prints weekly. That way each part of the team is aware of the current status of the other disciplines even if someone forgets to phone or write to the other with new information.

8. *Owner-supplied specifications.* Be wary of owner-supplied specifications or requests to use a particular product. You may become liable for damages caused by specifications or requirements which are not your own if they are included in the project. If you cannot dissuade the client from his insistence that you employ the request or specification, ask him to sign a letter acknowledging you have advised against the request. In the letter set forth your reasons and have it clearly stated that the client is directing you to proceed contrary to your advice.

9. *Project schedule.* A great many construction disputes center around time: too short a construction period, delays, inaccurate schedules, and the like. Although most of the causes of these problems are beyond the control of the architect or designer some of them can be averted by requiring, in the specifications, that the contractor provide a critical path method schedule rather than the familiar bar chart. Most competent contractors do this anyway on large jobs, but perhaps its use should be expanded to smaller projects. It forces the contractor to think through the schedule more closely and gives the architect and owner a firm basis by which to

judge progress. Additionally, in your contract with the client, you may require a provision that the time parameters be clearly spelled out including date of construction commencement, due dates for various phases and any deadlines you as the architect or designer are required to meet.

10. *Ambiguity.* One of the weakest positions to be in as a designer is to see something being built not according to your intent, but as the result of unclear drawings or specifications which allow the interpretation employed by the contractor and for which you may bear ultimate liability. There are many ways contract documents can be ambiguous:

    a. The same item drawn or described two or more different ways.
    b. Details drawn at a scale too small to be clearly understood.
    c. Items omitted in the drawings or specifications permitting the contractor to assume an industry standard or make his own interpretation of what you intended.
    d. Unclear words used with vague or multiple definitions.
    e. Confusing, wordy or incorrect specification syntax.
    f. References made to out-of-date industry or association standards.

11. *Impossibility.* Showing something on the drawings or specification that may turn out to be "impossible" to accomplish may relieve the contractor from his obligation to do it, especially if the contractor attempts to accomplish the design. Although the concept of "impossibility" is primarily a legal one to be interpreted by the courts, it is generally demonstrated if something is physically impossible, extremely difficult to accomplish, or if there are expenses associated with accomplishment of the design substantially in excess of those originally contemplated.

12. *Product failure.* There is an increasing number of instances in which designers are being held liable for the inclusion of manufactured products or design concepts that subsequently fail. Design professionals have not yet been subject to concepts of strict liability, that is, liability without the need to prove negligence. However, this concept is being applied to an increasingly larger number of product designers. It may be only a matter of time before we see the legal doctrine applied to the design professional. Although, to date, its broadest application has been to product suppliers and not suppliers of services it is not difficult to see the possible application to structures.

If it can be shown that the architect selected and specified a product that was not appropriate for its intended use, did not investigate it thoroughly or in some other way did not act with the same standard of care as other professionals would have in the same situation, negligence most likely will be shown and the professional held accountable for damages in the failure of the structure. However, a substantial portion of this exposure can be minimized simply by following the guidelines given in the previous section concerning product and system selection.

13. *Evaluation.* Perform a walk-through of your projects immediately after occupancy and about six months later. Note problems, complaints or criticisms and how they could have been prevented. Incorporate this information into your detail

system, specifications, and production manuals so that the same mistakes are not made again. Also keep track of information on contractors, subcontractors, material suppliers, manufacturers' representatives, and consultants. Note their strong and weak points so that others in the office will know about their qualifications for future jobs.

AVOIDING PROBLEMS DURING CONSTRUCTION ADMINISTRATION

The AIA Owner-Architect agreement and the General Conditions of the Contract spell out in some detail the responsibilities and duties of the architect. Other forms of contracts usually list them as well. However, many implied duties also exist that have developed through years of court rulings in literally hundreds of cases. These are often overlooked by architects and designers, and apply to both the design professional and the contractor.

During construction, under a typical owner-contractor agreement, the architect's main function is to represent the owner's interests, see to it that the construction proceeds according to the contract documents, and to administer various approvals. From these seemingly basic responsibilities spring a myriad of potential legal pitfalls for the unwary or naive design professional. The most common categories include:

- Exceeding scope of authority
- Failure to keep the owner informed
- Failure to perform expressed and implied duties
- Exposure to third party claims
- Waiver and acceptance of defects

By becoming entangled in any one of these pitfalls, the architect or designer runs the risk of being liable for construction cost overruns, forfeiting fees, or being sued for breach of contract, all of which may lead to substantial legal fees and costs, even if the professional prevails.

Exceeding Scope of Authority

Because of the agency relationship, actions taken by the design professional may legally bind the client even though the actions may have exceeded the express and implied authority of the professional. For example, the contractor may be led to believe, in the course of a project, that the architect has the apparent authority to make changes during construction in the specified work without the approval of the client. Unfortunately, as the result of the pressure to resolve field problems and keep the job moving, modifications, changes, and directions are given by the architect to the contractor without confirmation by written change orders. Even though many of the changes may be incidental to the normal duties of the architect, many are not. Although the owner will be held accountable to the contractor for the cost of these changes, the architect may find himself or herself in the uncomfortable position of forfeiting fees or the cost of the results of the exceeded authority should the owner decide to press the matter seeking reimbursement from the design professional.

Failure to Keep the Owner Informed

During construction, the architect is specifically charged with the responsibility of keeping the client informed of the progress of the work. All clients are different: some want to be constantly in touch with the project while others would like the architect to "take care of things" and call them when the job is finished. It is the latter category of client that poses the greatest problem and danger. Avoid this delegation at all costs. Even with such apparent authority to "take care of things," when problems develop (and they always do) the client will first look to the architect as the guilty party. For your own protection do not let the client divorce himself from the job. You will almost invariably be the loser. To help avoid these problems try the following techniques:

1. Remember that the design professional cannot make any changes in the contract, which includes, of course, the drawings and specifications, without the express approval of the client.
2. Insist on formal change order procedures even if the client approves changes verbally.
3. Complete written field reports at least once a week with copies to the client and contractor.
4. Keep a daily log of the job progress, noting what was decided, why, and who was involved.
5. Emphasize changes and problems that you feel are especially critical by addressing those concerns in a letter to the client. If the client does not respond, you will have at least performed your duty by placing him or her on notice. It is then possible, at a later date, to assert that the client's failure to act or authorize you to address your concern precluded you from taking further action on the matter. This will afford you a limited degree of protection if problems develop. Remember, however, that if the problem is one of substance, especially involving matters of health or safety, you may not be able to avoid responsibility by pointing to your client's silence.
6. Insist that the client attend regular project meetings during construction to hear directly from the contractor and others about the progress of the job and the decisions being made.

7. Notify the client, in writing, if you observe the contractor is not complying with the plans and specifications.

Failure to Perform Express and Implied Duties

Not fulfilling the stated duties in the owner-architect agreement and the owner-contractor agreement can set the design professional up for legal action by either the client or the contractor. This is why it is imperative that all members of the architect's team read the contracts to know the extent of their expressed duties. A strong project management system can also help maintain compliance with contract requirements in a timely manner.

Implied duties present additional pitfalls. Although such duties are not stated in most contracts, courts may apply these principles to both contractors and architects alike. The following are some of the more important ones to keep in mind.

1. The architect has the duty not to interfere with the contractor's work. This includes actions which might cause delay, additional costs, or cause the contractor to modify standard methods and procedures of construction. The architect may become liable for the results of such interference.
2. The architect has the duty to cooperate with the contractor. This includes timely response to questions, approvals and other problems as they arise.
3. The architect has the duty to inform the contractor of relevant information that may affect the progress of the job, including errors observed.
4. The architect has the duty to assist the owner in coordination with the schedules and requirements of other contractors and vendors not under the control of the general contractor. This might include furniture dealers, drapery suppliers, landscape contractors, and the like.

Exposure to Third-Party Claims

Traditionally, through the concept of privity, the design professional was protected from claims by parties with whom he had no direct contractual relationship. However, this is no longer true and the professional may find himself the subject of claims by one or more of the participants in a construction project.

The response to this problem by the design profession has been an attempt to include unequivocal indemnification clauses in the contract documents. These clauses are an attempt to limit liability. They purport to hold harmless both the owner and architect for any damages, claims and losses resulting from the performance of any work on the project whether by the contractor, or others. Paragraph 4.18 in the AIA General Conditions of the Contract is one example of this kind of clause. Although this sort of escape provision may appear to be highly beneficial for the architect, an increasing number of courts are extremely reluctant to support its enforcement, often finding technical reasons to avoid its effect. The results may lead to a greater exposure than had the indemnification clause been eliminated in the first place. An additional complication, from the architect's point of view, is that many states, by law, prohibit the use of such indemnification clauses in construction contracts.

Generally, design professionals will not be indemnified (even with an unequivocal contract clause) or be allowed to limit their liability if the problem stems from their preparation of drawings, specifications, approvals and the like or if the giving of or failure to give directions or instruction is the primary cause of the damage. Because of these and similar provisions, there is no absolute way to avoid third-party claims, whether justified or not. At a minimum, however, you may wish to consider the following:

1. If permitted by the laws of your state, you may want to consider including an indemnification clause in your contract. Consult with an attorney who is knowledgeable in the construction contract field concerning its inclusion and to determine the exact wording in order to protect yourself to the fullest extent possible.

2. Be careful not to include any language in your contract with the owner or in the owner-contractor agreement that would expressly state or even imply responsibility on your part to provide management, supervision, coordination, or planning of the construction unless you are, in fact, providing construction management services. In the latter case, an entirely different set of risks and insurance requirements prevails. The recommended procedure is to include a provision in your standard design contract specifically excluding such services unless a second agreement for construction management services is executed by the client. This clearly avoids any confusion on what is expected of the design professional.

3. Be aware that by your actions or directions during construction you may inadvertently imply your responsibility extends to portions of the work beyond what your contract requires or what might reasonably be required of you by application of the standards of your profession. Such actions may make you a target of liability claims. Do not give directions concerning methods or techniques of construction.

4. Point out obvious construction safety problems to the contractor. Put your notification in writing and send a copy to the owner as well. If the contractor does not correct the situation, notify the owner and recommend that the owner stop construction until the problem is corrected.

Waiver and Acceptance of Defects

Most well-written construction contracts, including the AIA General Conditions of the Contract for Construction, A201, provide for conditions under which one party waives certain rights or conditions either expressly or by actions. Final payment by the owner constituting waiver of all claims (with exceptions) is one example of this. Where the owner and architect may be particularly vulnerable is failing to speak out or notify the contractor of unsatisfactory performance. AIA document A201 specifically tries to eliminate the possibility of this kind of waiver in paragraph 7.6.2 stating that any action or failure to act does not constitute acceptance or approval of non-complying work nor does it constitute a waiver of other rights under the contract.

Clauses of this type offer some protection, but are not waiver-proof. Courts may hold that failure to point out obvious defects in the contractor's work during the course of regular visits to the job site may constitute acceptance of the work. This type of action, especially if it is consistent and forms a pattern, may also apply to procedural matters as well, such as giving verbal orders without writing a formal change order. The contract requirement that all changes be directed by a written change order may be construed by a third party to have been modified by the conduct of the people involved in the normal course of completing the project.

Avoid these problems by careful observation of the progress of the job and written notification of problems to the contractor with a copy to your client. Make sure that the contract does include a clause precluding waiver of rights due to any action or inaction on the part of the design professional or owner. Finally, follow the requirements of the contract to the letter. Deviation from it by either the owner, contractor, or architect is usually where misunderstandings occur and legal problems begin.

One final caution: the material contained in this chapter is intended only to highlight, in basic terms, some of the legal problems design professionals may encounter and ideas on how to avoid them. Obviously, much has been omitted. Legal issues are complex and vary among states, counties, and municipalities. You should discuss the topics addressed here with legal counsel in terms of your particular practice, clientele, and applicable laws of the state and local jurisdiction in which you practice.

SOURCES FOR MORE INFORMATION

Books

Cushman, Robert F., ed. *Avoiding or Limiting Liability in Architectural Design and Construction*. New York: John Wiley & Sons, Inc., 1982.

Hauf, Harold D. *Building Contracts for Design and Construction,* 2nd ed. New York: John Wiley & Sons, Inc., 1976.

Hohns, H. Murray. *Deskbook of Construction Contract Law—With Forms.* Englewood Cliffs, NJ: Prentice-Hall, Inc., 1981.

Hohns, H. Murray. *Preventing and Solving Construction Contract Disputes.* New York: Van Nostrand Reinhold Company, 1979.

Jellinger, Thomas C. *Construction Contract Documents and Specifications.* Reading, MA: Addison-Wesley Publishing Co., 1981.

Lambert, Jeremiah D., White, Lawrence. *Handbook of Modern Construction Law.* Englewood Cliffs, NJ: Prentice-Hall, Inc., 1982.

Sweet, Justin. *Legal Aspects of Architecture, Engineering, and the Construction Process.* St. Paul: West Publishing Co., 1977.

Walker, Nathan, Walker, Edward N., Rohdenburg, Theodor K. *Legal Pitfalls in Architecture, Engineering and Building Construction,* 2nd ed. New York: McGraw-Hill Book Co., 1979.

Reports

Design Professional Liability Insurance: A Survey. AIA Architects Liability Committee. Washington: American Institute of Architects, 1980.

Lien Laws for Design Professionals: A Survey and Analysis. Washington: American Institute of Architects, 1980.

Loss Prevention and Control for Design Professionals. Professional Design Insurance Management Corporation, 222 N. New Jersey, Suite 200, Indianapolis, IN 46204.

Professional Liability Insurance. Survey of California Architectural Firms' Insurance Coverage and Analysis of Major Insurance Carriers. San Francisco: California Council, AIA, 1979.

Untangling the Web of Professional Liability. San Francisco: Design Professional Insurance Co., 1976.

Newsletters

Building Failures Forum. P. O. Box 848, Ithaca, NY 14850.

Guidelines for Improving Practice and *A/E Legal Newsletter.* Victor O. Schinnerer & Co., 5028 Wisconsin Avenue, N.W., Washington, DC 20016.

Legal Briefs for Architects, Engineers and Contractors. McGraw-Hill Book Company, Inc., 1221 Avenue of the Americas, New York, NY 10020.

Seminars and Workshops Contact each for current schedule and topics.

American Institute of Architects, Continuing Education Programs, 1735 New York Avenue, N.W., Washington, DC 20006. The Professional Development Program also offers a home study course in "Reducing Professional Liability in Your Architectural Practice."

Battelle Memorial Institute, Seminars and Studies Program, 4000 N.E. 41st Street, P.O. Box C-5395, Seattle, WA 98105.

Office of Professional Liability Research, Victor O. Schinnerer and Co., Inc., 5028 Wisconsin Avenue, N.W., Washington, DC 20016.

University of San Francisco School of Law, Seminar Division Office, 1120 20th Street N.W., Washington, DC 20036.

Others

American Society for Quality Control, Inc., 230 West Wells Street, Milwaukee, WI 53203. Publishes *Quality Progress* magazine.

Professional Liability Insurance Companies

Continental Casualty Co.
Victor O. Schinnerer & Co., Inc.
5028 Wisconsin Avenue, N.W.
Washington, DC 20016

Design Professional Insurance
Corporation
Union Bank Building, Suite 545
50 California Street
San Francisco, CA 94111

Imperial Casualty & Indemnity Company
Thomas F. Sheehan Inc.
460 South Northwest Highway
Park Ridge, IL 60068

Insurance Company of North America
INAX
10 South Riverside Plaza
Chicago, IL 60606

International Insurance Company
International Surplus Lines
Insurance Company
PCM Intermediaries Ltd.
90 William Street
New York, NY 10038

Lloyd's of London
Illinois R. B. Jones
175 West Jackson Boulevard
Chicago, IL 60604

Northbrook Insurance Company
Shand-Morahan & Company
1 American Plaza
Evanston, IL 60201

CHAPTER 7
The Architect's Most Valuable Asset

THE SUCCESS OF ANY PROFESSIONAL DESIGN OFFICE depends, in large part, on the quality and cooperative effort of its people. Design professionals have historically recognized this fundamental concept as less of a management priority than many other service organizations. The relatively low pay of architectural and design employees compared with other professions, high turnover, and other problems are well-known to every architect who has "come up through the ranks."

People problems only reduce efficiency and eat into profits, yet many firms continue to operate with employee management practices that discourage full utilization of human resources. Some of the most significant gains in profit and productivity can be made by improving the administration of the design professional's most valuable asset: the people who provide the service that is sold. However, this is one of the most difficult areas of practice because employer/employee relations do not exist as an isolated entity. They are part of a whole system of an individual's professional development as well as a firm's effort in providing design services. In order to understand where and how improvements can be made in the management of human resources it may be helpful to view the situation from this perspective; that is, employer/employee relations within the larger context.

A vicious cycle has developed preventing many firms from achieving their maximum potential. Figure 7-1 illustrates some of the major components of this simplified model.

Within the inner circle you may start anywhere. With antitrust rulings preventing standardized fee quotes, architects are free to bid competitively in the marketplace, quoting fees high or low, but often on the low end. As a result this limits the amount of money they can offer employees in salary and benefits. According to the 1981 Firm Survey conducted by the AIA, the average base compensation (not including bonuses, etc.) for *principals* of AIA firms was about $35,000 per year; for supervisory staff, including project managers and project architects, the average was about $24,000. These figures are substantially less than for other professionals with similar education, experience, and responsibilities.

135

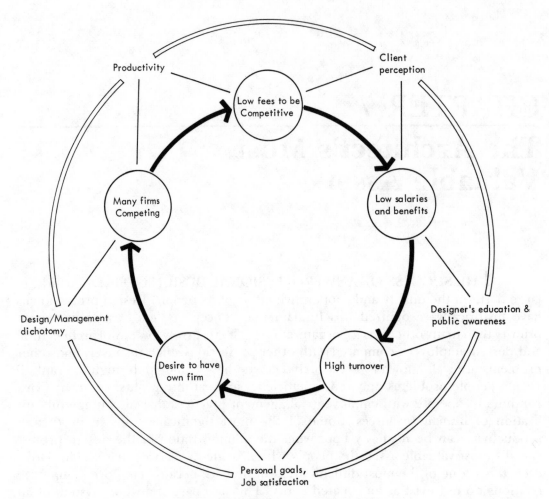

Figure 7-1
Employee/Employer Milieu

Low salaries and benefits are one of the primary reasons (although not the only ones) why employees typically seek to improve their situation and income by moving on. Frequent personnel changes create inefficiencies all employers know too well. The progression of turnover over time often develops to a point where the up-and-coming architect wants to have his or her own firm for economic reasons as well as others. A survey by *Architectural Record* of 1981 graduates, for example, found that nearly 90 percent wanted to someday own their own firm. (*Architectural Record*, January, 1981, pages 84–89).

This leads to many firms competing for the same work. The same 1981 AIA survey also found that about 82 percent of the AIA firms employ ten or fewer people. This is interesting in light of the *Architectural Record* finding that about 86 percent of the 1981 graduates would prefer to work in a small or medium-size office.

With increased competition owners must keep their fees as low as possible to keep the doors open, and we are back full circle. Fresh graduates become discontented employees who become employers who have the same problems their employers had before them.

The outer circle in Figure 7-1 indicates some of the additional factors impinging on the salary-turnover-competition cycle. The perception of the architect's worth by the buyer of the design services tends to keep fees and salaries low. Clients often are not willing to spend the same kind of money for professional design services as they are, for example, for legal services. This perception, I think, goes hand-in-hand with the educational system. There is lack of public education as to what the design professional has to offer and the public still tends to perceive the architect as "designer" rather than problem-solver and businessman.

The educational system turns out graduates who many firms feel are not capable of jumping right in and assuming much responsibility without further on-the-job training. This becomes the well-known justification to pay low starting salaries compared with other businesses and industries for new graduates. Unfortunately, salaries usually stay low even with more experience. The educational system is also limited in what it can offer in a five, six or seven-year education. The knowledge required to be a competent architect or interior designer is vast. Much of it can only be gained through practical experience. This, in turn, encourages high turnover, as young graduates move around to gain the kind of practice experience they need and to fulfill the image the educational system often fosters: that of "master builder" and designer rather than only one member of a larger building team.

Personal goals that architectural and design employees have then become additional reasons for high turnover and the desire to have their own firms as they seek to develop job satisfaction, design control, and firm ownership in addition to economic rewards.

Once in an ownership or high management position, the traditional design/management dichotomy becomes evident. The young graduate trained with design as the primary focus is usually more interested in design than in management and wants to oversee the creative efforts of the firm. There is little knowledge of, or experience with, architecture as a tough, profit-making business. Without a good business sense the employee-turned-employer finds it difficult to generate business and be competitive no matter how low the fees are.

Lack of management knowledge then affects productivity and development of human resources. With inefficiencies in office practice, fees alone are left to be lowered to meet the bottom line in order to stay competitive. This kind of business practice, compared to the other commercial organizations the client is used to dealing with, then contributes to the client's (and public's) poor image of the architect. We are again back to our starting point with vicious circle feeding on vicious circle. The net result is that many firms do not survive or barely survive from year to year, victims of the vagaries of the economy and the people who buy services.

This cycle *can* be broken or at least slowed with improved management of human resources in three areas. Productivity of the professional team can be boosted, better use can be made of existing salary and benefit budgets, and job satisfaction can be enriched for the benefit of both employer and employee. This chapter will discuss ideas for improvement in these areas for increased profit and career satisfaction.

INCREASED PRODUCTIVITY OF THE PROFESSIONAL TEAM

There has been a great deal of attention recently concerning the decline in productivity in the United States. While most people tend to imagine less output from the assembly line, the decline is actually in the white-collar sector and that includes professional service organizations. Architectural offices can be made more productive without any sacrifice in design quality. The key is to first make the best use of the available talent you have. Principals, for example, should be managing and directing, not troubleshooting daily problems. Experienced architects should be designing and directing production efforts, not drafting or running prints. A goal is to have everyone performing the kinds of tasks they are best suited for and that their billing rate reflects.

The combined talent of the professional team should then be backed up by clear management guidelines and communication, rigorous project management procedures, appropriate tools and equipment, and the use of the latest production techniques.

Assessing Your Current Situation

Since offices vary in their structure, size, philosophy, and services, the first step in improving the management of human resources is to evaluate your office. Problem areas can be pinpointed and an action plan will begin to emerge from this assessment. Have staff rate the office separate from management, then compare. Figure 7-2 lists some of the items that can be evaluated. You may want to use them as points of discussion or actually assign a scale to each and have everyone rank where they think the office is.

Management and Communication

The basis for a productive professional team is sound management and a continuous exchange of ideas. Review the following suggestions to see if any improvements could be made in your office.

- Office goals clearly stated and communicated to staff

- Definate sense of long-term direction at all levels

- Clear task definition on a daily and weekly basis

- Salary and benefits comparable with other offices

- Opinions and ideas of staff actively sought

- Motivation from recognition, growth, advancement, etc.

- Two-way communication (bottom up as well as top down)

- Evaluations of staff and office held regularly

- Ample opportunity for advancement

- Staff challenged with projects and responsibilities

- Office up-to-date with production tools and techniques

- In-house training provided for new staff members

- Continuing education encouraged

- Low absenteeism

- Minimum turnover

- Employee policies fair and clearly stated

- Attitude of office generally good

- Top quality employees aggressively recruited

Figure 7-2
Office Assessment Rating

1. Insist on good management throughout the office. This starts with a sound and workable business plan that includes direction for all phases of office operation as well as policy statements concerning personnel. It continues with a stable financial plan and rigorous project management procedures. All members of the team need clear direction, from understanding how a particular job is helping the firm to how the most productive use can be made of a morning's work. Good planning makes this possible. Morale is kept high and less time wasted.

2. Keep up-to-date with new techniques of design and production. Give your staff the kind of physical support it needs to do the job at peak efficiency. For example, are you still using the cut-and-paste method of producing specifications?

With the availability and low cost of microcomputers today, this procedure should be as antiquated as the T-square, yet many small and medium-size offices continue this kind of wasteful practice. Architectural firms traditionally have lagged behind other businesses in their adoption of labor-saving procedures and equipment. It makes sense only if you look at the short term. Long-term consequences of this kind of thinking can be disastrous.

3. Share the goals and objectives of the organization. Employees need to see the big picture if they are to understand how their efforts are contributing. Let them know the prospects for work for both the short and long term. Outline marketing strategies and how staff may help achieve them. Review the general business plan so everyone knows where the firm is heading.

4. Listen to employees' complaints and suggestions. Opening up the lines of communication is one of the best ways to get everyone working as a professional team rather than struggling with a "we" (employees) and "they" (management) situation.

5. Continue your own education in the area of personnel management. Virtually all architects and designers never receive this kind of training in design schools. Several universities and trade groups offer seminars in this area of practice. Some are more theoretical than others so select the kind that will be the most helpful to you.

6. Call in a personnel management consultant if you continue to have problems. They can advise you on everything from dealing with marginal employees to constructing compensation packages. A useful listing of management, employee relations, and other types of consultants is available from *Professional Services Management Journal*, MRH Associates, Inc., P.O. Box 11316, Newington, CT 06111.

Involvement by Employees

Nearly all professional service firms can benefit from increased participation by staff in both the short and long-range governing of the office. Most employees want to do more than receive orders from "management," carry them out, and go home. They want to be actively involved in all aspects of producing a job and know that they are making an important contribution to the overall effort of the office. This kind of involvement is crucial to the spirit of the firm and ultimately its productivity. Architectural and design firms that support and encourage it will be a step ahead in their management of human resources.

The functional organization of the office and the desires of the owners will, of course, help determine exactly how employee participation can be the most useful for both the employee and the employer. It may range from the simplest "gripe session" to actual financial ownership. The following are a few ideas you might consider.

Establish "quality control circles." This concept is becoming more common in other industries and has the potential for improving design businesses as well.

These QC circles are small groups of employees who meet regularly among themselves and with management representatives to identify and resolve issues that affect their area of work. The philosophy is that employees know better than management what their immediate problems are and how to solve them. Quality control circles are not set up in response to an immediate situation, but are on-going groups that attempt to improve the quality of work output. More than being just a suggestion group, the employees organize the full range of the process from identification of the topic to its implementation.

When specific problems do not exist, the group can take on special research activities in areas that may improve productivity. A group of administrative staff, for example, could explore ways to speed clerical activities or how automation could improve their work flow. Project managers could study methods for streamlining job administration.

Quality control group meetings may take an hour or two per week of company time, but the benefit to cost ratio is usually high. The overall results can be great because employee-generated actions produce more enthusiasm for their implementation and pull company goals and personal goals closer together.

In order to make quality control circles work there are a few important variables that must exist:

1. The idea must be supported all the way by the principals of the firm. It cannot be a token gesture.
2. If the organization is large, any middle management that exists must also support the idea and participate in the implementation.
3. Hearing complaints is a part of the process but not the only part. Definite actions must result.
4. The activity of the quality control circle must be on-going. It should not be allowed to die for intermediate periods of time.
5. Quality control circles are voluntary.
6. The groups should not be overloaded with people. In small offices the circle may represent a high percentage of the total number of employees while in medium or large-size firms they should be representative of a larger group of staff. It is better to have several small groups working in different areas than a large one trying to do more than it can handle. Three to six people would be about right for a design office.

There are other ways to keep employees involved with the functioning of the firm. Instead of continuing quality control circles you can set up special study groups to work on specific projects. Ideas are generated, evaluated, and submitted to the firm principals for study and implementation. Some firms have committees made up of the heads of each department that meet regularly to coordinate actions and do long-range planning.

Another possibility is to give employees partial ownership in the firm. One of the ways to do this is with an Employee Stock Ownership Plan (ESOP). A company sets up a trust to which it gives stock or cash to buy stock. The contributed stock is then allocated to each employee based on one of several allowable formulas. Over a period of time, usually from ten to fifteen years, the employee becomes fully vested. Usual vesting is 10 percent per year. Voting rights may or may not be given depending on how the plan is set up and the amount of stock the trust holds for the employees may range from 1 percent to 100 percent.

In addition to the benefits of ownership and significant participation in the firm, ESOP's also offer tax advantages and financing opportunities for the business. There are also several disadvantages that must be considered when contemplating an ESOP. It is definitely only for the architectural office that is on a stable financial and management footing to begin with.

Employee Stock Ownership Plans are complicated and often expensive to set up, requiring legal advice and careful planning. They are only for the firm that is truly interested in the value of the employees and the mutual benefit of everyone involved. If properly established, however, evidence indicates that ESOP's can result in greater job satisfaction and increased profit and productivity.

For more information on ESOP's contact the National Center for Employee Ownership, 4836 South 28th Street, Arlington, VA 22206 or the Employee Stock Ownership Plan Association of America, 1725 DeSales Street N.W., Washington, DC 20036.

Project Staffing Alternatives

One of the most difficult aspects of human resource management in professional design firms is maintaining a reasonably constant number of staff. Alternately hiring and laying off people to match the workload demand is both inefficient and demoralizing. As an alternative to the traditional method of having most of the required expertise on the payroll consider trying some of the following ideas. You may be able to minimize the number of employees you need so you can concentrate on creating a productive workplace for those you do have.

Make use of independent consultants. These are not just the usual engineering kind of consultants, but people who contract to do work like drafting, design, specifications, energy conservation and dozens of other services. Both the design firm and the consultant benefit from this arrangement. You only contract to get a specific amount of work done and do not end up paying expensive personnel overhead costs or for all the nonproductive time typically encountered in an office.

The usual objection most firm owners have is that working with consultants is more time-consuming and lessens the control and immediate contact management likes to have with the team. With proper working procedures and clearly defined agreements, however, these objections can be easily overcome. Keep the following points in mind.

1. Develop a list of reliable people in your area that you can call on when the need arises. Have several contacts for each type of work so if one is too busy you have an alternative.

2. Check references before hiring a consultant. Only a small percentage of the total number available will be just right for you. You should know which ones before you have them start working.

3. Plan and outline the work required before giving it to the consultant. This may seem like extra work for you at first, but should actually improve the final result. This planning forces you to study the job in more detail than you would normally. The result is better coordination and reduced risk of omissions.

4. Establish a lump-sum contract price for the work to be farmed out. This is usually possible with tasks like working drawings, specifications and the like. This allows you to budget accurately for the job. If the consultant runs over that is their problem; if they complete the job in less time and do it well they have made extra money. However, be explicit in your written agreement as to the extent of the work to be done and its quality. Again, checking references and past work is a must.

5. Set up a strict schedule of progress meetings and reviews. This is the only way to catch problems before they develop into major catastrophes.

6. Do not assume that all work is being done for you. You still must have overall coordination control and spend the time to review all the work the consultant does. Since someone in the office would be doing this anyway you are not losing any ground. Remember that you are still legally and financially liable for the work of these consultants just as you are for the work of structural and electrical engineers.

Investigate joining or setting up a network. This is a group of firms who pool their talents and resources for particular jobs. Each one remains a separate entity, but joins with others when extra personnel or expertise is needed. It allows smaller firms to compete with larger offices on specific jobs without the impossible expense of maintaining a large staff of specialists. It is an effective way to expand the kinds and scope of services you offer while allowing you to make the best use of your available employees.

CASE IN POINT

Design Network, Inc. in Denver, Colorado operates a diverse practice, providing services from graphics to development consulting. Within a basic corporate structure and with a very small office, Design Network, Inc. works with a network of affiliates who provide construction documentation, space planning and interior design, graphic design, landscape architecture, and other support services. The various affiliates are listed in the company brochure and included in proposals on an as-needed basis. While fee budgeting is done jointly with the affiliated offices, legal liability and insurance coverage is carried under the Design Network company. Full-time employees are kept to an absolute minimum while allowing involvement with a diverse range of projects. The key to the operation is good organization and management of the various members of the team.

Re-evaluate the *kinds* of employees you now have. If you are uncomfortable going outside the firm for assistance with usual production tasks, make sure you have the right person for each job. One of the most common problems design firms have is the constant search for good production people. Fresh out of school they usually start on drafting and minor design tasks. Although this is an excellent way to expand their knowledge they want to move up and are not satisfied for long with the pay of a starting production staff member. Just when they become proficient they are lost to a new entry-level person.

Consider, instead, hiring an architectural technician. This is a person who may come out of a two-year technical college rather than a professional school. The legal profession has made effective use of this idea for years with "para-legals" assisting much higher paid attorneys. Advancement and salary increases can be made within their task group, but there is less likelihood of their moving on as fast as a young architect eager for his or her own office.

GETTING THE MOST FROM SALARY AND BENEFITS

Regardless of your firm's size or profitability a significant portion of your budget is devoted to compensating your employees for their efforts. Your particular financial plan may allocate more or less to this line item than other firms, but you still have a fixed expense to deal with (not including profits, of course). *How* you make the best use of this budget amount is the critical point.

You need to tailor the use of salaries and benefits to fit both the firm's goals and organizational structure as well as the goals of the employees. This is especially important if you expect to attract and keep the best people. To be competitive in this area, architectural and design firms are going to have to be more creative in their monetary rewards than in the past.

Salary and benefits alone, of course, are not always the primary motivators in a professional service firm, but without a competitive remuneration level all of the other parts of a human resources program are of little consequence. Some of these will be discussed in the next section.

Salary and benefit provisions required by labor laws and other statutory mandates have been covered in other sources (such as in the *Personnel Practices Handbook* published by the American Institute of Architects, Catalog number 2M138) so they will not be repeated here. In addition to statutory requirements consider implementing some of the following ideas if they are consistent with your office's goals. Some require a moderate investment while others can be set up with little extra cost. Remember that no matter what you spend it is an investment in the most important commodity you have to sell to your clients—the skill and talent of people.

Salary and Benefit Ideas

1. Offer flextime. This allows employees to set their own hours within certain limits and is a big plus for many workers. Since most offices have to be "covered" during the standard five-day week, half or full days off are usually alternated among staff. The simplest option is to allow variable starting and quitting times in a standard eight-hour day with a core time when everyone should be there, say from 9:00 to 4:00. The other variation is to work nine- or ten-hour days to allow for a half or full day off every week or every other week.

2. Establish a flexible benefit package plan. Under this system, required statutory benefits are provided and then the employee can assemble the benefits that make the most sense to him from a lump-sum allowance. For example, extra paid time off for an unmarried person may be more important than a larger contribution to a medical insurance plan for an employee with a large family. Check with an employee compensation consultant for more details.

3. Sponsor social events for your office. These may include parties, weekly wine tastings, skiing trips, educational programs, seminars and similar amenities.

4. Institute two or three days per year as "floating holidays." It is then up to the discretion of the employee to use them as desired. This allows someone to take off the Friday after Thanksgiving or extend the Christmas break without cutting into regular vacation time. A variation of this is providing a certain number of days of "personal leave" for emergencies or "mental health" days. These kinds of options are vital for morale and can help alleviate the use of sick days for the same thing.

5. Provide a sabbatical every three to five years to allow a refresher break. This gives an added incentive for someone to stay with the company and furnishes time for travel, special study or simply a break from the demands of the design profession.

6. Establish a set number of days that employees can use in any way they want: for sick days, vacation, or unused for cash.

7. As an added perk for larger firms, buy and maintain a vacation retreat. It can be used by clients as well as employees and may offer tax benefits for the office as well.

8. Investigate giving compensation to employees in ways other than salary. A straight raise or bonus is taxable income for the employee and offers no deduction for the employer. Consider instead such things as offering educational reimbursements, paying for travel to conventions and seminars after which the employee takes extra time for a vacation, merit awards, day care services if they are offered

to all employees, or group term life insurance. Check with your accountant or an employee compensation consultant for details.

9. Maintain a yearly performance bonus system. Of course, money is not the only thing that motivates, but recognizing outstanding performance, average work, or less than adequate labors *is* one way of encouraging a good job.

10. Base profit sharing on individual project performance. If the team produces the job on schedule and is profitable, then each member receives a percentage of that profit in addition to a base salary.

CASE IN POINT

Ebert, Hannum & Volz in San Francisco uses an incentive plan based on individual, fixed-fee jobs. At the start of a project a portion of the total fee is allocated to profit and everyone on the team knows what this goal is. If the team manages and produces the job well, meeting the targeted financial goal, a percentage of the profit is allocated to each person based on his or her role on the project. This extra compensation can amount to one-month's pay or more in the best situations. Although this kind of program can have its problems, the firm reports that this method of immediate financial reward helps provide added incentive to produce each job in the best way possible. Additionally, it supports the strong studio approach to design the office maintains.

11. Offer "wellness" programs in addition to the traditional medical insurance. Many see this as a way to reduce the rising costs of health care by preventing problems before they occur. Having employees who are following a good health care program pays dividends on the job in fewer sick days, more energy and a better attitude.

12. Arrange for financial counseling for employees as an option. This helps them make the best use of the monetary compensation they receive and is something most people do not spend money on themselves.

13. Evaluate the economics of providing one or more company cars. If extensive traveling is required of some of your employees, they appreciate saving wear and tear on their personal automobiles. An added benefit for employees in large urban areas is that they do not have to bother with driving and parking problems just to bring a car to work.

14. Give time off for professional and civic activities. Besides improving the employees' development your firm gets added exposure among peers and potential clients.

15. Encourage membership in professional organizations by offering to pay dues.

16. Promote licensing of staff by paying exam fees and registration fees. You might also consider paying NCARB dues.

17. Give time off for conventions, seminars and other educational programs. The people you depend on need to keep up with the latest developments in their field.

18. Contribute to continuing education programs. Pay all or part of an employee's tuition if the program improves his or her value to the firm.

19. Consider reinstatement of benefits for former staff. Good employees whom you wanted to keep but who left for one reason or another will continue to be valuable if you can get them back. Giving them seniority, vacation time earned, vesting in profit-sharing plans and the like as though they had not left the firm will let all your employees know you place high priority on people.

CASE IN POINT

HDR in Omaha, Nebraska has found that reinstating benefits to former employees who left voluntarily and then came back to work saves in recruiting and training costs and lets all of their employees know the value the firm places on human resources. Exactly what benefits are reinstated depends on how long the employees have worked for the firm and how long they have been gone. For example, if someone has been gone longer than he has worked, he does not receive credit for the pension plan, but does maintain vacation time. The bottom line benefits greatly outweigh the additional costs to the firm: money is saved in the long run, employee morale is boosted and the benefit is unique among A/E firms.

JOB SATISFACTION

Satisfaction and motivation of the office staff is the third area in which human resource management can be improved. Volumes of research have been published on this topic; I will only touch on some of the highlights here and suggest ways to improve job satisfaction in the professional design office. In architectural firms money is usually not the primary motivator. Practically any architect or designer will readily agree with this assertion. This is consistent with one of the classic research studies done in this area by Frederick Herzberg in 1961 for Texas Instruments.

In studying both white-collar as well as blue-collar workers Herzberg found that job satisfaction and motivation (and productivity) were related to two sets of factors. There were "dissatisfiers" and "motivators." The dissatisfiers included such things as salary, benefits, personnel policy, and working conditions. The motivators included such items as recognition, growth, advancement, participation, and other factors related to the self-actualization of the individual.

Improving the dissatisfiers did not increase motivation or productivity, but failure to maintain a reasonable level did increase dissatisfaction. In other words, having a good salary and favorable working conditions are necessary prerequisites to job satisfaction but these kinds of factors cannot stand alone. The second part of the equation, the "motivators" must also be present. Simply adding more money and benefits will not improve the situation. The following topics discuss some ideas on how to improve motivation and job satisfaction.

Matching Firm Goals with the Employee's Goals

We all have different reasons for being in the design profession and we all have different goals for our professional careers. Too frequently firm owners or those doing the hiring think only in terms of what the employee can do for them. The employee comes with certain expectations and hopes of fulfilling his or her goals, too. If they are not met, he leaves, to the detriment of both the employer and employee.

Recognizing this, trying to establish a plan whereby both the firm's and employee's goals are met generally results in a more productive staff and lower turnover which, in turn, can result in less time and cost involved with training new people. Some of the important components of a "career development" plan include the following:

1. Extensive interviewing of likely job applicants to determine their goals, plans, needs, and whether these are consistent with those of the office. No one should be hired on the basis of just a resume and one interview. Initial impressions should be verified with a second and possibly third discussion. Potential personality conflicts are also likely to be discovered at this time as well.
2. Sensitivity to individual differences and the particular "motivator" in each employee. Some people are motivated by achievement, better jobs, more responsibility and the like. Some are motivated by power and other by affiliation with peer groups. These should be identified and incorporated into the career plan of each person on staff.
3. Establishment of a plan in consultation with the employee that outlines how you are both going to meet your objectives.
4. Promotion within the firm whenever possible to provide the advancement potential of those capable and desiring of it.
5. Provisions for continuing education to provide the necessary skill levels.
6. Recognition that no one stays forever. This management mind set is important to plan for the most effective use of the time that an employee is with the firm.

Communication

The importance of clear communication lines within the office was mentioned in the beginning of this chapter. It is as important for maintaining job satisfaction as it is for productivity of the professional team. Many firms still keep long-range plans, job progress information, even equipment purchases a "secret" from the staff until the final moment of unveiling. To alleviate some of the communication problems, check your office's performance against the following list.

1. Do you inform the staff of the overall goals and objectives of the firm and how you plan to meet them?
2. Do you hold regular staff meetings to exchange information, ideas, gripes, and suggestions in a two-way interchange?
3. Do you solicit participation in solving problems or implementing new procedures in the office?
4. Do you keep a project status board somewhere in the office so everyone knows how each job is progressing and what jobs are coming up?
5. Do you have a clearly stated and consistent policy concerning evaluation, promotions and raises?
6. Do you use the term "key employees" to suggest that some of your people are *not* important?
7. Do you tell the bad news as well as the good news such as impending layoffs, financial problems, work slowdown and the like?
8. Do you hold regular performance reviews and evaluations to see if both you and your employees are on the career development path you should have planned?
9. Do you encourage informal gatherings such as parties and other social events to provide a forum for casual interchange of ideas?
10. Do you actively help new employees become familiar with the office by assigning a senior staff member to that person to assist with general orientation, questions and the like?
11. Do you provide recognition for outstanding performance by featuring such employees in the company newsletter, bulletin board, or simply with a pat on the back?
12. Do you provide vital job information such as contract requirements, job budget, and schedules to all members of the design and production team?

Personnel Policy Manual

A personnel policy manual should be a positive statement of the firm's commitment to its people. It should be viewed as a tool to aid in maintaining clear communications in the firm rather than a rule book threatening disciplinary action if the rules are violated. The occasional disruptive employee is best dealt with on a personal, one-to-one basis. All of the concepts discussed in this chapter that you would choose to implement, as well as others, are spelled out formally in the manual.

Everyone then knows the ground rules and is treated equitably which is in itself an important part of any human resources plan.

Every personnel manual will be a little different because of the office's philosophy and method of operating. A general outline of possible topics for such a manual is illustrated in the following outline. Not all items listed would be included in every manual.

Personnel Policy Manual Outline

A. Office organization
   1. Statement of goals
   2. Legal organization
   3. Functional organization
   4. Human resources statement
   5. Staff positions
B. Employment policies
   1. Recruitment
   2. Employee referrals
   3. Employment application forms
   4. Employment interviews
   5. Affirmative action plan
   6. Handicapped employees
   7. Communication in office
   8. Personnel records
   9. Promotions
   10. Staff and firm evaluations
   11. Outside employment
   12. Transfers
   13. Part-time employees
   14. Temporary placement
   15. Alcohol and drug abuse
   16. Layoffs
   17. Resignation
   18. Termination
C. Office procedures
   1. Pay period
   2. Hours
   3. Time sheets
   4. Overtime
   5. Employee-supplied equipment
   6. Office equipment
   7. Telephone
   8. Meetings
   9. Vendors/sales representatives
   10. Correspondence
   11. Reimbursable expenses
   12. Confidential information
   13. Public relations
   14. Smoking
   15. Personal property
   16. Music
   17. Collections and solicitations
D. Salary and benefits
   1. Salary
   2. Statutory benefits
   3. Insurance
   4. Holidays
   5. Vacation
   6. Sick leave
   7. Bonuses
   8. Profit sharing
   9. Personal leave
   10. Jury duty
   11. Military duty
   12. Maternity leave
   13. Funeral leave
   14. Medical/dental appointments
   15. Leave of absence
   16. Retirement plan
   17. Automobiles
   18. Professional dues
   19. Moving allowance
   20. Legal and financial counseling

E. Professional development
  1. In-house education
  2. Continuing education
  3. Seminars/conventions
  4. Intern program
  5. Licensing
  6. Writing for publication
  7. Speaking engagements
  8. Teaching
  9. Professional activities
  10. Civic activities

In-House Education Programs

Providing in-house education makes sense in several ways. Consider the following:

1. Since every office operates a little differently, it is required to orient experienced employees to particular procedures and train recent graduates in areas that they did not cover sufficiently in school.
2. It is one way of contributing to the continuing education every professional must have to stay current with new developments in the field. It should be considered an adjunct to outside classes and seminars, however, not a substitute. Office educational efforts can include such things as one- or two-hour seminars given by consultants or other experts in particular fields or noon-time talks by vendors showing new product lines.
3. Special programs may be necessary to educate the entire staff in new techniques or procedures such as computer-aided drafting.
4. Offering work-study programs for promising students of nearby design schools is an excellent way of finding and recruiting employees who can step in after graduation and be productive members of the office.

Evaluations

Although personnel evaluations are one of the most uncomfortable parts of running an architectural practice for most professionals, they are also one of the most crucial. On a personal level all of us want to know how we are doing compared with others in the same position. On a business level, evaluation is necessary for the growth of both the firm and the individual. Periodically, performance needs to be measured against goals to determine if any corrective action is required.

Since most design professionals are not trained in human resource management or personnel administration, evaluations often become simply a discussion of the employee's past mistakes and a basis for salary adjustment. There are a few fundamentals to keep in mind to make best use of time spent with evaluations.

1. Assessments should be made of the firm as well as the employee. It should be a time when the firm evaluates the employee and the employee evaluates the firm to review how successfully they are each performing to reach stated goals.

2. The goal of the evaluation is to improve both the firm and the employee, not simply to criticize past actions.

3. The reviews should be result-oriented; it is more important to study how well the intended effects of actions have been achieved than the specific actions themselves. There are many ways to achieve a given outcome and they should be established as a result of on-going management and project decisions rather than on the basis of two or three evaluations per year.

4. A productive evaluation can be made only if there is something to measure it against. It is therefore mandatory that employees have a clear understanding of their expected roles and that these roles have been formalized in some way for use during the evaluation. It is likewise necessary that the firm have goals and objectives that have been communicated to the staff so that evaluation of the office can be made.

5. Any objectives set should be measurable. It is not enough to simply say to an employee that his or her performance during the past six months has been poor. If, for example, an objective for a designer was to reduce the average time for designing projects of a given size and complexity by two weeks and he did not do that, then there is something definite to be discussed. You can then talk about poor performance or the reasons why that goal was not reached and take steps to improve on it.

The type of evaluation, timing, forms used, procedures and other aspects will vary among firms, depending on their operating philosophies, size, services offered and commitment to a program. Certain guidelines, however, should be included in almost any evaluation process. Compare yours to the following list.

1. Make sure the kind of performance you expect is known by the employee. Everyone needs to know what the ground rules are before any calls are made. This is why clear job descriptions or similar statements are important. It also helps eliminate any personal bias in the review process.
2. Evaluations should be made at least twice a year. Some firms schedule fixed dates related to bonus time. Others schedule them based on when each staff member started working. This has the advantage of spreading out the evaluation work load.
3. Have more than one person evaluate if possible. This eliminates a one-sided judgment that could possibly be based on personality differences or something else not related to job performance.
4. Both the employee and firm representative should evaluate themselves

first as objectively as possible. Their evaluations can then be compared by the other person to start a constructive dialog based on individual perceptions.

5. List strengths as well as weaknesses.

6. Suggest *how* weaknesses could be corrected in addition to simply pointing them out.

7. Try to eliminate unusual incidents as the only basis for evaluation. Consider performance over the entire time period, not just the highs and lows.

8. A thorough evaluation consists of many individual parts. Consider each one individually without letting opinions on one affect another. A staff member may be doing great in every area except one and this should not unevenly weight the entire review.

9. Use forms. These allow you to develop consistency from one session to another and focus attention on those areas that are most important to your office. Forms should not be overly complicated or lengthy; that will simply defeat the purpose. Written documentation is useful as an on-going record, too, so progress can be checked over the long term.

10. Try to keep review of salary adjustments separate from the preliminary performance review. Salary is based on other items in addition to performance, such as length of service, job categories, cost-of-living increases, comparison with other professionals in similar positions, and other factors. Financial rewards may be a result of good performance but not dependent on it.

11. Complete the evaluation with definite steps to be taken to improve weaknesses during the next review period. Also include any new objectives or expectations that will be looked at next time.

SOURCES FOR MORE INFORMATION

Books

Class, Robert Allan & Koehler, Robert E. *Current Techniques in Architectural Practice.* Washington: The American Institute of Architects, 1976.

Erickson, John R., McGovern, Katherine Savers, Sampson, Richard T., eds. *Equal Employment Practice Guide.* Federal Bar Association, 1850 H Street N.W., Washington, DC, May 1980. Vol. I & II.

Koehler, Robert E., Ed. *AIA Personnel Practices Handbook.* Washington: The American Institute of Architects, 1978.

Mager, William J. *Performance Evaluation in Architectural, Engineering and Planning Firms.* Newington, CT: Professional Services Management Journal, 1979.

McConnell, John H. *Complying with EEO*. New York: AMACOM, A division of American Management Association, 1979.

McCulloch, Kenneth J. *Selecting Employees Safely Under the Law*. Englewood Cliffs, NJ 07632 : Prentice-Hall, Inc., 1981.

Miller, Ned A. *Complete Guide to Employee Benefit Plans*. Rockville Center, NY: Farnsworth Publishing Co., Inc., 1979.

Scheer, Wilbert E., ed. *The Dartnell Personnel Administration Handbook 2nd ed.* Chicago: Dartnell Press, 1979.

Newsletters

The Guidelines Letter. P. O. Box 456, Orinda, CA 94563.

Professional Services Management Journal. 126 Harvard Street, Brookline, MA 02146.

Periodicals

Personnel. AMACOM-P, Trudeau Road, Box 319, Saranac Lake, NY 12983.

Personnel Administrator. American Society for Personnel Administration, 30 Park Drive, Berea, OH 44017.

Personnel Journal. A.C. Croft, Inc., 866 West 18th Street, Costa Mesa, CA 92627.

Supervisory Management. AMACOM-S, Trudeau Road, Box 319, Saranac Lake, NY 12983.

Seminars and Workshops Contact each for current schedule and topics.

PSMJ Seminars, 45 Van Brunt Avenue, Dedham, MA 02026.

Building Design & Construction Conferences, P. O. Box 31108, Raleigh, NC 27622.

Associations

American Society for Personnel Administration, 30 Park Drive, Berea, OH 44017.

Employee Benefit Research Institute, 1800 M Street N.W., Washington, DC 20036.

Employee Stock Ownership Plan Association of America, 1725 DeSales Street N.W., Washington, DC 20036.

National Center for Employee Ownership, 4836 South 28th Street, Arlington, VA 22206.

Others

Equal Employment Opportunity Commission. 2401 E. Street N.W., Washington, DC 20506 (202) 634-6930.

The 1982 Firm Survey. The American Institute of Architects, 1735 New York Avenue N.W., Washington, DC 20006.

Quality Circles. Chicago: Dartnell Press, 4660 Ravenswood Avenue, Chicago, IL 60640.

Wage and Hour Division, U.S. Department of Labor. 200 Constitution Avenue N.W., Room S-3028, Washington, DC 20210. (202) 523-7640. Also contact regional offices.

CHAPTER 8
Financial Tips for Successful Practice

FINANCIAL MANAGEMENT IS A NECESSITY for every design firm. It is not a result of practicing architecture but a necessary condition for every other phase of providing professional services. Historically, many firms, especially young ones, have placed "design" goals before profit goals because a frequent motive for being in or starting an architectural practice is design-oriented. Profit must be on the same level as design. Profit allows design goals to be achieved by providing opportunities for growth, financial security, the ability to hire and keep highly qualified people, and maintain an environment in which creative design effort can take place.

In addition to providing the required accounting for legal and tax purposes, financial management provides the practicing professional with powerful tools to help make decisions concerning other areas of practice. Figure 8-1 illustrates the relationship between major components of a financial management system within the larger context of architectural and design firm operations. Each component affects or is affected by another and financial decisions are essential to the achievement of the firm's goals.

This chapter will show some of the ways to use financial information to help make management decisions to improve your profit. I have not included elements of bookkeeping or accounting since these topics have been well covered in other sources and since each practice needs the assistance of specialists in this area to tailor accounting systems to meet the unique requirements of each office. The professional should, however, know enough to be able to clearly define his or her needs to such a specialist.

I have also not differentiated between cash and accrual accounting methods (although the information shown assumes an accrual system) or between proprietorships, partnerships or corporations. (Refer to the sources listed at the end of this chapter for more information on these topics.) Instead, emphasis is placed on understanding the broad issues of planning, monitoring, controlling, and deciding on fiscal actions.

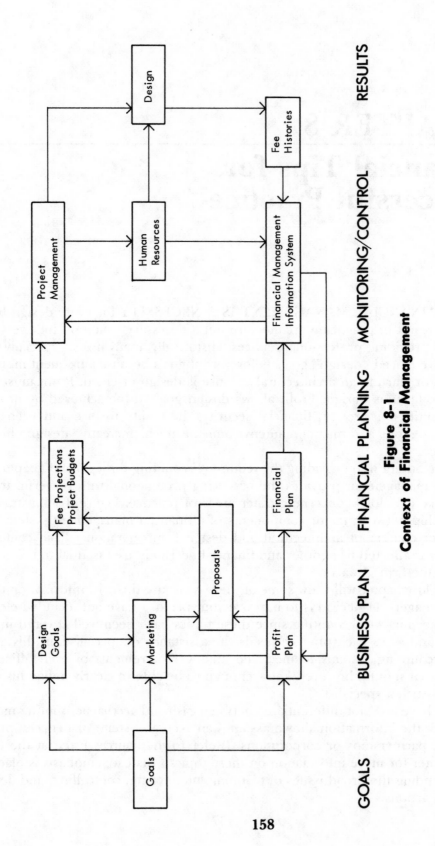

Figure 8-1
Context of Financial Management

GOALS   BUSINESS PLAN   FINANCIAL PLANNING   MONITORING/CONTROL   RESULTS

PLANNING YOUR OFFICE'S FINANCES

Architectural and design practice is different from many businesses in that there is a wide range of *value* placed on the "quality" of service sold in addition to the quantity. Design firms manipulate other aspects of their practice to reflect this value. It cannot show up on the balance sheet but does affect how a practice is run. For example, for personal or professional reasons one office may be willing to spend a portion of profit to offset some expenses in order to increase what they see as the quality of their design service. Another firm may choose to fix their profit margin and provide the best service they can for the revenue they are given. With this intangible aspect of value and quality in mind we can proceed with exploring financial planning.

The most fundamental equation for financial planning in any profit-oriented business is:

$$\text{Profit} + \text{Expenses} = \text{Revenues}$$

Usually this is shown in the form: Revenues − Expenses = Profit. Although the two equations are mathematically equal they imply very different ways of viewing the business world. Professional design firms too often conduct their practice based on the second equation. They try to market and set fees to produce as much revenue as possible, keep expenses as low as possible and hope that something will be left over for profit.

The first equation, on the other hand, assumes that the business *will* make a set profit and will incur certain expenses to provide the type and quality of service it plans for. The cost of these two items will then have to be offset with a certain level of revenue. It is the difference in attitude that sets the stage for either failure or success in a professional design practice.

Expanding the equation a little you have the following major components:

PROFIT
> Tax
> Profit after tax

EXPENSES
> Direct
> Indirect
> Reimbursable

REVENUES
> Project revenues
> Reimbursable

I have excluded any nonoperating revenues or expenses to simplify the outline. These include such items as interest from investments, real estate income and the like; anything not directly related to providing professional services.

In order to begin planning for the fiscal health of your office you need to identify those portions of the components listed above which most affect *your* bottom line. Knowing what percentage of your total budget is devoted to each item and comparing them with general averages in the profession may give you an idea of where improvements might be made.

Remember that the best source of financial information is from your own records. This is why complete and accurate record keeping is important to the fiscal health of your firm. Very little planning and monitoring can take place without a good base of data.

The following charts in this section are intended to give you an idea of the approximate average operating statistics of other design firms current at the time of writing. List your numbers alongside the averages to see how you compare. Keep in mind, however, that many design firms vary from the average for good reasons. Also remember that there are a variety of accounting and reporting methods in use in the design professions so the figures shown may be derived by slightly different formulas than those you use.

Figure 8-2 shows how a typical revenue dollar is spent. It is a further expansion of the various kinds of expenses listed above. While direct labor constitutes a large portion of the total, indirect labor and other overhead items together account for an even larger percentage. It is in these areas that you can make the greatest strides in improving your profit picture. Specific suggestions on ways to do this are given later in this chapter. Note that this chart was derived from information from one source. Others may result in slightly different percentages, but those shown are generally representative. The actual survey figures have been rounded off for simplicity.

Figure 8-3 lists in more detail some of the key overhead items. Amounts are shown both as a percent of total annual revenues (as in Figure 8-2) and as a percent of direct labor costs. Plainly, indirect labor (that is, labor not chargeable to jobs) is the single largest overhead burden. Controlling this is important to increased profitability. Note that due to the data collection methods some overhead line items are not included so those shown do not add up to the totals.

Figure 8-4 is in balance sheet format, showing typical percentages of assets, liabilities and net worth. This kind of figuring gives you a better idea of the overall financial status of your firm and can point out deficiencies that need corrective action. To give you a broader picture of various data collected, two sources of statistics are given.

Figure 8-5 contains some of the financial measures that bankers, analysts and others use to study the fiscal status of a design business. There are dozens of these kinds of ratios and you could spend most of your time calculating numbers

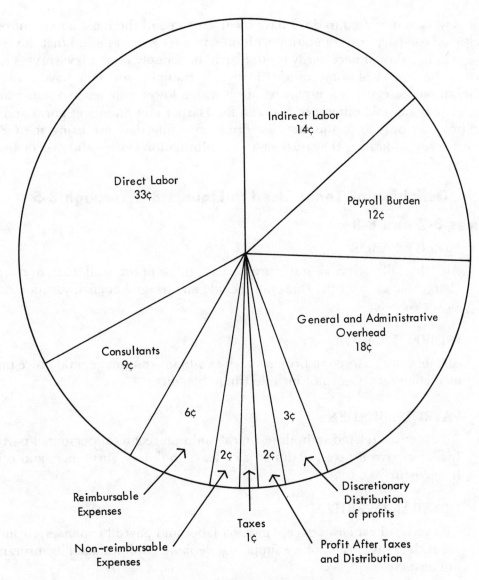

Figure 8-2
Distribution of the Total Revenue Dollar

Chart based on data from the *1982 Financial Statistics Survey for Professional Service Firms* conducted by Birnberg & Associates for the Professional Services Management Journal and Professional Services Management Association.

Values given are median values based on total revenues including consultants and reimbursables for the total survey sample of architectural, engineering, and planning firms. Figures are approximate and rounded to the nearest cent.

if that is what you wanted to do. I have included some of the most important ones to help you compare your operation with the average. Keep in mind that these are not figures you should necessarily try to match, but simply what a few surveys have shown to be typical of some other firms. For example, you may have a higher number in one category but it may be offset with a lower number in another area.

The noticeable difference between the Harper and Shuman figures and the other two may be due to the fact that firms providing data are using the CFMS system already, indicating they track financial information closely and may be better managed.

Definition of Terms Used in Figures 8-2 Through 8-5

Figures 8-2 and 8-3

DIRECT LABOR

All labor of technical staff, principals, and support staff that is directly chargeable to projects. Does not include any fringe benefits, vacation time, sick leave, etc.

INDIRECT LABOR

All labor not charged to projects such as administration, general office time, marketing, etc. Does not include fringe benefits.

PAYROLL BURDEN

All expenses related to both technical and non-technical personnel payroll. Includes payroll taxes, vacation, sick leave, holidays, insurance, and other fringe benefits.

GENERAL OVERHEAD

All overhead expenses except indirect labor and payroll expenses. Included are such items as rent, office supplies, telephone, utilities, liability insurance, interest, etc.

DISCRETIONARY DISTRIBUTION

Voluntary distribution of profits to owners and non-owners such as performance bonuses, profit sharing, incentive compensation and the like. The Birnberg survey separated this item since many firms see this as a necessary "expense" in order to be competitive in attracting qualified personnel. Other firms still view it as a profit item.

PROFIT AFTER TAX AND DISTRIBUTION

Includes gross profit based on total earnings of the firm, including revenues generated through consultants' efforts and reimbursables.

	Based on total annual revenues	Based on direct labor
PAYROLL BURDEN		
Mandatory payroll taxes	3.3	11.1
Vacation, sick leave, holiday	4.3	14.2
Group insurance	1.8	5.8
Annual pension expense	1.1	4.0
Bonus, incentive payments, profit sharing[1]	3.2	10.8
Other fringe benefits	.4	1.4
Total payroll burden[2]	14.5	44.9
GENERAL AND ADMINISTRATIVE (G & A)		
Indirect labor	13.7	44.9
Cost of space	3.6	11.4
Telephone	1.0	3.5
Liability insurance	1.2	3.8
Interest	.8	2.5
Bad debt expense	1.3	1.0
Other G & A	9.3	31.5
Total G & A[2,3]	31.9	105.9
TOTAL OVERHEAD[2]	46.3%	154.7%

[1] Discretionary distribution of profits shown here as a payroll burden expense. Figure 8-2 shows it as a separate item.

[2] Due to methods of analyzing data, individual items are not precisely additive.

[3] Median value for marketing expenses (including salaries) was found to be 5% of total revenues.

Percentages based on data from the *1982 Financial Statistics Survey for Professional Service Firms* conducted by Birnberg & Associates for the Professional Services Management Journal and Professional Services Management Association. Values shown are median figures.

Figure 8-3
Key Overhead Items

Figure 8-4

CURRENT ASSETS

All assets that can be quickly converted into cash such as accounts receivable or cash in the bank.

FIXED ASSETS AND NON-CURRENT ASSETS

Includes all items that cannot be converted into cash quickly such as furniture, fixtures, and real estate, less depreciation. Fixed assets may also include copyrights, patents and other intangibles.

CURRENT LIABILITIES

All short-term monies owed to vendors, consultants, short-term notes, taxes due, long-term obligations due within the fiscal year and the like.

NON-CURRENT LIABILITIES

These liabilities are any obligations in addition to long-term debts that are not due within the next year.

NET WORTH

Difference between total assets and total liabilities.

Figure 8-5

NET PROFIT BEFORE TAX

The percentage of profit based on net revenue; that is, total annual revenue less consultant's fees and reimbursable expenses.

OVERHEAD RATE

The ratio of total office overhead to total direct labor. When used to figure fees, the ratio is multiplied by the estimated cost of direct labor (no fringe benefits, taxes, etc.) and the resulting product is added to the direct labor amount.

NET MULTIPLIER

The figure derived by dividing net revenue (no consultants or reimbursables) by direct labor. This multiple is most often used to set fees when the cost of direct labor is known. The figure is multiplied by direct labor and the resulting number combined with consultant and reimbursable costs to get total fee. It covers fringe benefits, indirect labor, overhead, and profit. It should not be confused with the multiplier or direct personnel expense (DPE) which is slightly less since the cost of providing mandatory and optional fringe benefits is included in the DPE. For budgeting purposes you can establish an income goal for the year (at whatever profit level you want) and divide by the estimated cost of direct billable time that will be available to earn revenues. The resulting multiple will be what you must charge to

	Birnberg & Associates		Robert Morris Associates	
ASSETS				
Cash	4.4		10.3	
Accounts receivable	46.3		44.5	
Work in progress	14.7			
Other current assets	3.9		12.6[1]	
Total current assets		76.2[2]		67.4
Fixed assets		12.0[3]		20.6
Other non-current assets		5.5		11.9[5]
Total assets		100.0[2]		100.0
LIABILITIES				
Accounts payable	8.5		10.8	
Other current liabilities	26.7		32.5[4]	
Total current liabilities		40.6[2]		43.2[4]
Long-term debt		7.0		10.2
All other non-current liabilities		3.9		5.2
Net worth		42.6		41.3
Total liabilities and net worth		100.0[2]		100.0
Figures shown are based on percent of total				

[1]Addition of "Inventory" and "All other current" line items as reported in the Robert Morris Survey.

[2]Due to methods of reporting and analysis, individual line items are not additive to total.

[3]Addition of furniture, fixture & equipment, net real estate, and leasehold improvements.

[4]Addition of several line items in the Robert Morris survey.

[5] Includes intangibles (net).

Figure 8-4
Balance Sheet

Birnberg & Associates column based on data from the *1982 Financial Statistics Survey for Professional Service Firms* conducted by Birnberg & Associates, Chicago, IL, for the Professional Services Management Journal and Professional Services Management Association. Values shown are median figures.

Robert Morris Associates column based on data from *1982 Annual Statement Studies*, Robert Morris Associates, Philadelphia, PA. Copyright, 1982. Used with permission. See page 188 for interpretation of statement study figures.

Figure 8-5 (continued)

achieve your goals. If it is higher than the prevailing rate in your area, you may have to make adjustments somewhere to be competitive.

CHARGEABLE RATIO

The percentage of time, or dollars, spent on direct labor divided by the total time or dollars spent on direct and indirect labor in addition to vacation, holiday and sick leave time. A figure of 65 percent for the average of the firm is generally thought to be about the "break-even" point for most design firms. This is one of the most important measures to monitor.

AVERAGE COLLECTION PERIOD

The number of days from billing a client to receiving payment. Generally, the shorter the period, the better the cash flow and the less likely accounts will be delinquent.

REVENUES PER TOTAL STAFF

The amount of net revenue produced per staff member per year including part-time people and principals.

REVENUES PER TECHNICAL STAFF

The amount of net revenue produced per technical staff member, those most directly involved with charging direct time and producing jobs.

CURRENT RATIO

The current ratio is total current assets divided by total current liabilities. It is a measure of a firm's ability to meet current obligations. The higher the ratio, the better.

QUICK RATIO

The quick ratio is a refinement of the current ratio and includes only cash and equivalents, plus accounts receivable, divided by total current liabilities. It includes only those assets that are the most liquid and therefore is a more conservative measure than the current ratio. Since most current assets of professional design firms are tied up in accounts receivable and cash and little in inventory or non-current assets, the two ratios will often be about the same.

CAPITAL INVESTMENT PER EMPLOYEE

Total assets divided by the number of full-time equivalent personnel.

	A Birnberg & Assoc.	B Robert Morris	C Harper and Shuman
Net profit before taxes	3.61%[1]	4.9%	3.44%
Overhead rate	155%[2]	—	168.5%
Net multiplier	2.70[3]	—	3.07
Chargeable ratio (overall)	63%	—	61%
Average collection period (days)	69	68	70
Net revenues per total staff	$40,115	—	$43,220
Net revenues per technical staff	$51,805	—	$53,160
Current ratio	1.75	1.7	—
Quick ratio	—	1.4	—
Capital investment per employee	—	—	$22,020

[1] Based on net revenues after discretionary distribution of profits (bonuses, profit sharing, etc.)

[2] After discretionary distribution of profits

[3] Birnberg & Associates net multiplier reflects nonreimbursable expenses included as part of net revenues

A From *1982 Financial Statistics Survey for Professional Service Firms* conducted by Birnberg & Associates, Chicago, IL, for the Professional Services Management Journal and Professional Services Management Association. Values shown are median figures.

B From *1982 Annual Statement Studies*, Robert Morris Associates, Philadelphia, PA. Copyright, 1982. Used with permission. See page 188 for interpretation of statement study figures.

C From *1982 Operating Statistics for Professional Firms* taken from the Computer-based Financial Management System (CFMS) developed and administered by Harper and Shuman, Inc., 68 Moulton Street, Cambridge, MA, for the American Institute of Architects and the National Society of Professional Engineers. Values shown are median figures.

Figure 8-5
Key Financial Measures

MONITORING YOUR OFFICE'S FINANCES

Regular monitoring of the financial status of your firm and individual projects is necessary to help you meet your financial goals, to alert you to problems in time to take corrective action, and to satisfy legal and accounting requirements. Specifically, this monitoring should be a tool to help you accomplish the following tasks:

- Maintain the overall financial health of the firm by tracking assets and liabilities, profit and loss and pinpointing where problems are occurring.

- Keep track of individual job progress as part of an overall project management system.
- Assist in developing marketing strategies early enough so that workload projections are maintained and projected revenue goals are met.
- Provide information for making decisions regarding human resources: staffing needs, productivity, salary adjustments, bonuses, and benefits.
- Identify your month-to-month cash position so that current obligations can be met or money borrowed to compensate for short-term needs.
- Highlight problems with accounts receivable to maintain adequate cash flow and reduce potential bad debts.
- Provide historical data that can be used to accurately estimate fees.

These should be the fundamental goals of any financial management system, whether it is done by hand on a pocket calculator for a three-person office or with a sophisticated computer program for a giant A/E firm. Keep in mind that these goals are for the management of a firm and do not include the daily bookkeeping chores and accounting methods required for any business. The ledger sheets and journals, however, provide the raw data for a financial management system. Refer to the AIA's *Standardized Accounting for Architects* for a chart of accounts and more detail on bookkeeping methods. If your accountant cannot provide you with information to meet the goals outlined above, you should consider revising your system.

In order to provide management information many systems have been developed. Each provides a method for organizing data. Most are computer-based and generate a variety of reports in various formats. One danger is using a system that provides *too much* data. Piling a stack of computer printouts on someone's desk every two weeks will make the task overwhelming. A good system is one that can be selective in what information it outputs, and this must be backed up with management commitment not to be enamored with page after page of numbers. The Professional Services Management Journal periodically publishes a list of many of these commercially available systems. Write to them for a current list: PSMJ, P.O. Box 11316, Newington, CT 06111.

The best known system developed to date is the Computerized Financial Management System (CFMS) developed jointly by Harper and Shuman, Inc. in Cambridge, Massachusetts, and the American Institute of Architects as part of the AIA's Financial Management System. It was developed especially for architectural and engineering firms and offers a complete system for financial management from data input to check printing to various management reports. It is available as a service bureau format, on a time-sharing basis, and recently, as a stand-alone system with some brands of microcomputers. Service is provided for large firms as well as small firms.

Figures 8-6 through 8-11 are typical examples of some of the reports generated by the CFMS program. They are similar to many of the reports produced by other systems, giving most of the information necessary to accomplish the monitoring tasks listed above.

PROFIT PLANNING MONITOR
FOR THE PERIOD   3/01/81 - 3/31/81

ACCOUNT NUMBER NAME	CURRENT PERIOD ACTUAL	PLAN	VARIANCE	PCT	YEAR TO DATE ACTUAL	PLAN	VARIANCE	PCT	ANNUAL PLAN
─────────── I N C O M E ───────────									
401.00 BILLED REVENUE	60,000	65,000	5,000-	8-%	210,000	185,000	25,000	14 %	800,000
404.00 UNBILLED REVENUE	6,211	7,400	1,189-	16-%	2,053	24,400	22,347-	92-%	50,000
GROUP SUBTOTAL	66,211	72,400	6,189-	9-%	212,053	209,400	2,653	1 %	850,000
499.00 REIMBURSABLE REVENUE	300	833	533-	64-%	1,400	2,500	1,100-	44-%	10,000
TOTAL INCOME	66,511	73,233	6,722-	9-%	213,453	211,900	1,553	1 %	860,000
──────── R E I M B U R S A B L E S ────────									
516.00 TRAVEL	100	167	67-	40-%	500	500		0 %	2,000
517.00 REPRODUCTIONS	200	500	300-	60-%	1,000	1,500	500-	33-%	6,000
518.00 MODELS & PHOTOGRAPHS									
GROUP SUBTOTAL	300	667	367-	55-%	1,500	2,000	500-	25-%	8,000
520.00 OTHER REIMBURSABLES									
TOTAL REIMBURSABLES	300	667	367-	55-%	1,500	2,000	500-	25-%	8,000
INCOME LESS REIMBURSABLES	66,211	72,567	6,356-	9-%	211,953	209,900	2,053	1 %	852,000
─────── D I R E C T E X P E N S E S ──────									
602.00 DIRECT SALARIES	19,996	18,333	1,662	9 %	58,345	55,000	3,345	6 %	220,000
604.00 TEMPORARY HELP	39	83	44-	53-%	333	250	83	33 %	1,000
GROUP SUBTOTAL	20,035	18,417	1,618	9 %	58,678	55,250	3,428	6 %	221,000
611.00 STRUCTURAL CONSULTANTS	3,000	3,333	333-	10-%	9,000	10,000	1,000-	10-%	40,000
612.00 MECHANICAL CONSULTANTS		3,833	3,833-	100-%	16,000	11,500	4,500	39 %	46,000
615.00 OTHER CONSULTANTS	18,287	5,833	12,454	213 %	20,000	17,500	2,500	14 %	70,000
616.00 TRAVEL		500	500-	100-%	1,500	1,500		0 %	6,000
617.00 REPRODUCTIONS		1,667	1,667-	100-%	10,000	5,000	5,000	100 %	20,000
619.00 TELEPHONE		667	667-	100-%	2,100	2,000	100	5 %	8,000
GROUP SUBTOTAL	21,287	15,833	5,454	34 %	58,600	47,500	11,100	23 %	190,000
620.00 OTHER DIRECT		417	417-	100-%	916	1,250	334-	27-%	5,000
TOTAL DIRECT EXPENSES	41,322	34,667	6,656	19 %	118,194	104,000	14,194	14 %	416,000
INCOME LESS REIMBURSABLES AND DIRECT EXPENSES	24,889	37,900	13,011-	34-%	93,759	105,900	12,141-	11-%	436,000
───── I N D I R E C T E X P E N S E S ────									
702.00 INDIRECT SALARIES	9,819	10,000	181-	2-%	29,335	30,000	665-	2-%	120,000
703.00 JOB COST VARIANCE	293	333	41-	12-%	963	1,000	37-	4-%	4,000
GROUP SUBTOTAL	10,111	10,333	222-	2-%	30,298	31,000	702-	2-%	124,000
711.00 EMPLOYER'S FICA	5,400	6,000	600-	10-%	18,000	18,000		0 %	50,000
721.00 HOSPITALIZATION INSUR		625	625-	100-%	2,000	1,875	125	7 %	7,500
731.00 RENT	1,000	1,000		0 %	3,000	3,000		0 %	12,000
734.00 TELEPHONE	500	1,000	500-	50-%	2,875	3,000	125-	4-%	12,000
739.00 OTHER OFFICE EXPENSE	250	625	375-	60-%	1,438	1,875	437-	23-%	7,500
GROUP SUBTOTAL	1,750	2,625	875-	33-%	7,313	7,875	562-	7-%	31,500
743.00 DATA PROCESSING	1,736	1,667	69	4 %	4,500	5,000	500-	10-%	20,000
744.00 INTEREST	625	500	125	25 %	1,875	1,500	375	25 %	6,000
745.00 PROFESSIONAL LIABILITY		833	833-	100-%	2,500	2,500		0 %	10,000
GROUP SUBTOTAL	2,361	3,000	639-	21-%	8,875	9,000	125-	1-%	36,000
761.00 DEPRECIATION-FURN & FIX	1,042	1,250	208-	17-%	3,125	3,750	625-	17-%	15,000
TOTAL INDIRECT EXPENSES	20,664	23,833	3,170-	13-%	69,611	71,500	1,889-	3-%	264,000
TOTAL EXPENSES	62,286	59,167	3,119	5 %	189,305	177,500	11,805	7 %	688,000
PROFIT / LOSS (-)	4,225	14,067	9,842-	70-%	24,148	34,400	10,252-	30-%	172,000

Figure 8-6
Profit Planning Monitor

Statistics and reports shown in Figures 8-6 through 8-11 have been taken from the Computer-based Financial Management System (CFMS) developed and administered by Harper and Shuman, Inc., 68 Moulton Street, Cambridge, Ma., for the American Institute of Architects and the National Society of Professional Engineers. Used with permission.

APPLE AND BARTLETT
ARCHITECTS AND ENGINEERS

PROJECT PROGRESS REPORT
FOR THE PERIOD 3/01/81 - 3/28/81

PROJECT CITY HALL
NUMBER 08005.00

PRINCIPAL APPLE
PROJ MGR GRAY

DESCRIPTION	SPENT THIS PERIOD HOURS	DOLLARS	SPENT TO DATE HOURS	DOLLARS	TOTAL BUDGET HOURS	DOLLARS	PCT COMPLETE EXP	RPT	RATES BUDGT	EFFEC	BALANCE DOLLARS	HOURS @ BUDG	HOURS @ EFFEC
ARCHITECTURAL DEPT													
SCHEMATIC DESIGN	170.0	2230.00	470	6310	600	8300	76	78	13.83	13.43	1990	144	148
DESIGN DEVELOPMENT	40.0	530.00	160	1980	1100	10000	20	19	9.09	12.38	8020	882	648
CONSTRUCTION DOCUMENTS	220.0	1940.00	700	6300	3500	32000	20	16	9.14	9.00	25700	2812	2856
TOTAL ARCH	430.0	4700.00	1330	14590	5200	50300	29	27	9.67	10.97	35710	3693	3255
INTERIORS DEPT													
SCHEMATIC DESIGN	40.0	440.00	350	2750	300	4000	69	65	13.33	7.86	1250	94	159
CONSTRUCTION DOCUMENTS	20.0	300.00	80	1200	2000	16000	8	5	8.00	15.00	14800	1850	987
TOTAL INTERIORS	60.0	740.00	430	3950	2300	20000	20	17	8.70	9.19	16050	1845	1746
TOTAL LABOR	490.0	5440.00	1760	18540	7500	70300	26	24	9.37	10.53	51760	5524	4915
OVERHEAD ALLOCATION	490.0	7072.00	1760	23175		84360	27	24			61185		
TOTAL LABOR AND OVERHEAD	490.0	12512.00	1760	41715	7500	154660	27	24			112945		
DIRECT COSTS													
611.00 STRUCTURAL CONSULTAN		3000.00		9000		36000	25	25			27000		
612.00 MECHANICAL CONSULTAN				16000		64000	25	25			48000		
TOTAL DIRECTS		3000.00		25000		100000	25	25			75000		
TOTAL LABOR, OH, AND DIRECT	490.0	15512.00	1760	66715	7500	254660	26	24			187945		
REIMBURSABLE EXPENSES													
516.00 TRAVEL		100.00		1500		4000	38	50			2500		
517.00 REPRODUCTIONS		200.00		686		6000	11	10			5314		
518.00 MODELS & PHOTOGRAPHS				8000		8000	100						
TOTAL REIMBURSABLES		300.00		10186		18000	57	14			7814		
TOTAL LABOR, OH, DIR, & REIMB	490.0	15812.00	1760	76901	7500	272660	28	24			195759		

FINANCIAL ANALYSIS

	TOTAL COMP	SERVICES BILLED	EXPENSES BILLED	TOTAL BILLED	A/R	EARNED INCOME	SPENT	PROFIT (LOSS)	PCT PROFIT
CURRENT		4195.87		4195.87		4195.87	15812.00	11616.13-	276.8-
YEAR-TO-DATE		49309.87	886.00	50195.87		46000.00	40000.00	6000.00	13.0
JOB-TO-DATE	336325.00	79881.00	9886.00	89767.00	16423.87	89767.00	76901.00	12866.00	14.3

Figure 8-7
Project Progress Report

170

APPLE AND BARTLETT
ARCHITECTS AND ENGINEERS

TIME ANALYSIS
FOR THE PERIOD 3/01/81 - 3/31/81

CL	EMPLOYEE		TOTAL HRS WKD	TOTAL DIRECT	TOTAL INDRCT	A	B	C	D	VACATN	SICK	HOLDAY	PROMTN	CIVIC	MGT	PROF	STAND	GENRL	COMP	OTHER
02	GRAY	C	100	62	38	62	91	78	70	24	8	8						39		6
		Y	550	385	165	70	78	74	70	40	8	8	40							30
02	STONE	C	110	80	30	73	73	100	75				30							
		Y	580	464	116	80	80	89	75				100	16						
02	LAMBERT	C	80	40	40	50	67	50	65	20						12		40	8	
		Y	480	288	192	60	69	60	65	40	12	8			104	12			24-	
	CLASS SUBTOTALS	C	290	182	108	63	76	76	70	44	8	8	30			12		79	8	6
		Y	1610	1137	473	71	76	75	70	80	20	16	140	16	104	12			24-	30
	FIRMWIDE TOTALS	C	290	182	108	63	76	76	70	44	8	8	30			12		79	8	6
		Y	1610	1137	473	71	76	75	70	80	20	16	140	16	104	12			24-	30

EXPLANATION OF CHARGEABLE RATIOS:

A = TOTAL DIRECT/TOTAL HRS WKD

B = TOTAL DIRECT/(TOTAL WKD - BENEFIT HOURS)

C = TOTAL DIRECT/STANDARD HOURS

D = TARGET RATIO

Figure 8-8
Time Analysis

171

APPLE AND BARTLETT
ARCHITECTS AND ENGINEERS

OFFICE EARNINGS REPORT

FOR THE PERIOD 3/01/81 - 3/31/81

PROJECT NUMBER	PROJECT NAME	COMP	PCT COMPL	I	T	EARNED INCOME	BILLED	UNBILLED SERVICES	RECEIVED	A/R	SPENT	PROFIT (LOSS)	EARNED	SPENT	PROFIT (LOSS)
08000.00	COMPLETED PROJECTS	140000			4	140000	140000		140000		61000	79000	5000	4386	614
08005.00	CITY HALL	336325	25		4	89767	89767		73343	16424	76901	12866	46000	40000	6000
08015.00	BALBOA	175000	25	E		150263	136877	13386		136877	90000	60263	13386	6579	6807
08101.00	UNIV LIB	30000	36		4	11067	11067			11067	9529	1538	11067	9529	1538
08102.00	GOVT CENTER	150000	42		4	90000	90000		13362	76638	85729	4271	90000	85729	4271
08104.00	GNH MUSIC HALL	75000	50		4	42000	42000			42000	31702	10298	42000	36502	5498
08107.00	KLH OFFICE	10000	55		4	6000	6000		1104	4896	4386	1614	6000	4386	1614
08109.00	ABC PLAZA STUDY	7500	18		4						1097	1097-		1097	1097-
08110.00	DANCE CENTER	28000	5		4						658	658-		658	658-
08113.00	W GLEN ELE ADDN	2500	20		4						439	439-		439	439-
	FINAL TOTALS	954325				529097	515711	13386	227809	287902	361441	167656	213453	189305	24148

Figure 8-9
Office Earnings Report

172

APPLE AND BARTLETT
ARCHITECTS AND ENGINEERS

AGED ACCOUNTS RECEIVABLE
AS OF 3/31/81

PROJECT NUMBER	NAME/PRINCIPAL	INVOICE NUMBER	DATE	TOTAL	CURRENT	30-60	60-90	90-120	120-150	OVER 150
08005.00	CITY HALL	00111	09/30/80	1,063.53						1,063.53
	APPLE	00132	11/30/80	5,998.72					5,998.72	
		00166	01/31/81	5,165.75			5,165.75			
		00187	03/28/81	4,195.87	4,195.87					
			TOTALS	16,423.87	4,195.87		5,165.75		5,998.72	1,063.53
08015.00	BALBOA	00122	10/31/80	21,877.36						21,877.36
	BARTLETT	00133	11/30/80	40,000.00					40,000.00	
		00145	12/31/80	63,666.53				63,666.53		
		00173	02/28/81	11,333.27		11,333.27				
			TOTALS	136,877.16		11,333.27		63,666.53	40,000.00	21,877.36
08101.00	UNIV LIB	00168	01/31/81	11,066.73			11,066.73			
	APPLE									
08102.00	GOVT CENTER	00174	02/28/81	36,638.38		36,638.38				
	BARTLETT	00188	03/28/81	40,000.00	40,000.00					
			TOTALS	76,638.38	40,000.00	36,638.38				
08104.00	GNH MUSIC HALL	00167	01/31/81	27,000.00			27,000.00			
	APPLE	00189	03/28/81	15,000.00	15,000.00					
			TOTALS	42,000.00	15,000.00		27,000.00			
08107.00	KLH OFFICE	00175	02/28/81	3,791.94		3,791.94				
	BARTLETT	00187	03/28/81	1,104.13	1,104.13					
			TOTALS	4,896.07	1,104.13	3,791.94				
	FINAL TOTALS			287,902.21	60,300.00	51,763.59	43,232.48	63,666.53	45,998.72	22,940.89

**Figure 8-10
Aged Accounts Receivable**

173

```
          APPLE AND BARTLETT                              PAGE   1
          ARCHITECTS AND ENGINEERS               RUN DATE: 04/28/81
                                                           09:03:30
               BALANCE SHEET
               AS OF  3/31/81


          ------------------ ASSETS ------------------

     ACCOUNT
     NUMBER  ACCOUNT NAME                     AMOUNT

     101.00  CHECKING ACCOUNT               54,059.67
     102.00  SAVINGS ACCOUNT                 4,340.85
     103.00  PETTY CASH                         50.00
             SUBTOTAL                       58,450.52

     111.00  ACCTS RECEIVABLE-CLIENTS      287,902.21
     113.00  ACCTS RECEIVABLE-OTHER          1,171.90
     115.00  TRAVEL ADVANCES                 2,453.98
             SUBTOTAL                      291,528.09

     121.00  UNBILLED SERVICES              13,386.00

     131.00  FURNITURE AND FIXTURES         50,000.00
     132.00  DEPRECIATION-FURN & FIX         8,951.46-
             SUBTOTAL                       41,048.54

             TOTAL ASSETS                  404,413.15


     ---------------- LIABILITIES -----------------

     ACCOUNT
     NUMBER  ACCOUNT NAME                     AMOUNT

     201.00  NOTES PAYABLE-CURRENT          50,000.00

     211.00  ACCOUNTS PAYABLE-CONSULT       58,477.30

     231.00  SALARIES PAYABLE
     232.00  FICA WITHHOLDING
     233.00  FEDERAL WITHHOLDING
     234.00  STATE WITHHOLDING
     235.00  OTHER WITHHOLDING
             SUBTOTAL

             TOTAL LIABILITIES             108,477.30


     ----------------- NET WORTH ------------------

     ACCOUNT
     NUMBER  ACCOUNT NAME                     AMOUNT

     300.00  CAPITAL STOCK                  67,595.00
     301.00  PAID IN SURPLUS               110,925.00
     302.00  RETAINED EARNINGS-CURR         24,147.72
     303.00  RETAINED EARNINGS-PRIOR        93,268.13
             SUBTOTAL                      295,935.85

             TOTAL NET WORTH               295,935.85

             TOTAL LIABILITIES
             AND NET WORTH                 404,413.15
```

Figure 8-11
Balance Sheet Example

In addition to reports like these, you may want to summarize projected cash flow to assist in making decisions concerning short-term borrowing, investments, or capital improvements. Figure 8-12 is one form you can use for this. Estimating revenues from backlog, that is, work you have under contract but which has not been earned yet, and comparing it to your revenue goals is also important for developing marketing efforts necessary to bring in enough work to make up the difference between target revenues and backlog.

Item	Month					
	1	2	3	4	5	6
Cash on hand--beginning of month						
Cash Receipts						
Projected collections at 100%						
Possible collections at less than 100%						
Other cash receipts						
Cash disbursements						
Direct labor						
Indirect labor						
Direct costs						
Overhead costs						
Other costs						
Cash on hand-- end of month						

Figure 8-12
Cash Flow Projection Worksheet

175

BUDGETING AND MONITORING
PROJECT STATUS

Since the largest single factor in the overall profitability of a firm is individual project progress, an accurate system of setting fees and monitoring the expenditure of those fees is necessary. Such a system is a subset of effective project management procedures. (Refer to Chapter 9 for a more complete discussion of project management and how it coordinates with financial planning.) In this section, however, I will touch on two of the fundamental components of a financially successful project: setting the right fee and working within that fee.

There are many ways to set fees from "guestimating" a percentage of construction cost to detailing every individual work task required and setting a time and cost factor to it. One system that is being used more lately is the cost-based compensation method promoted by the AIA. The concept is simple. Fees are based on what it will actually cost to do the job plus a factor for profit. This is in lieu of a percentage of construction cost, cost per square foot, billing rate, or other pricing methods.

A cost-based method of setting fees is probably the best way to *begin* the fee-setting process; to establish accurately what the minimum level of compensation is that you need to break even. From there you can set your desired profit level and adjust your fee quote to the client up or down as required. This adjustment may be desirable to take into account the variables of the marketplace: what the competition is charging, what clients may be willing to pay, extra value that may be placed on your reputation or special expertise, a better time schedule that you can offer, and similar intangible factors.

For a double-check, you can compare the cost-based fee with other methods for which you have historical information such as fee per square foot, or percentage of construction cost.

Figure 8-13 illustrates one form you can use to begin estimating your in-house direct labor costs for a project. Individual staff members are listed down the left side and the spaces along the top can be used for whatever portion you are estimating. For example, you may make a very detailed list of every work task you can think of and assign estimated hours to complete them or you may use the form to summarize time and cost by phases. Totaling in both directions gives information by staff member or by work task that you can later use for monitoring progress. Depending on your system of including overhead factors, the "rate" for each person can be either direct cost (with an overhead factor to be added later) or an hourly charge based on your office's multiplier. However, I think the better system is to figure only direct labor cost at this point because this leads to a better budget figure that can be used later to manage the project.

The grand total of the direct cost worksheets is then noted on the first line of the Fee Calculation Summary, Figure 8-14. To this you can add overhead expenses by using your multipliers for direct personnel expenses and indirect expenses or

Project

Project no.

Date

Phase

Completed by

Personnel	Rate	Item of Work or Phase																			TOTAL	
		Hrs.	Cost	Hrs.	Cost	Hrs.	Cost	Hrs.	Cost	Hrs.	Cost	Hrs.	Cost	Hrs.	Cost	Hrs.	Cost	Hrs.	Cost	Hrs.	Cost
Total Hours																						
Total Cost																						

**Figure 8-13
Direct Cost Calculation Worksheet**

Project _____

Prepared by _____ Date _____

Direct payroll budget   _____

A ⌈ Direct personnel expense   _____

  ⌊ Indirect expenses   _____

or

B ⌈ Overhead allocation at _____%   _____

Non-reimbursable direct expenses   _____

Total Office Cost   [   ]

Consultants and outside services   _____

Contingency (if any)   _____

Profit   _____

Total Project Budget (Fee)   [   ]

Estimated reimbursable expenses   _____

Figure 8-14
Fee Calculation Summary

the overhead factor for your firm. Additional non-reimbursable direct expenses, consultants and profit are added on to arrive at the total project budget that is the minimum fee you should get to help you achieve your overall financial goals. From this point you can begin to evaluate whether you can or should negotiate your fee up or down or revise your proposed scope of services to match the client's fee budget.

Most computerized financial management systems show budgeted expenses for direct labor and other items. These will be shown on one or more of the report forms and will be compared to actual hours and dollars as reported through time cards. If you are not using a computer or would like a more compact summary, use a form similar to Figure 8-15 to monitor progress of each job. The budgeted

Project _____														
Phase/People/Departments		1	2	3	4	5	6	7	8	9	10	11	12	TOTAL
	Budgeted													
	Actual													
	Budgeted													
	Actual													
	Budgeted													
	Actual													
	Budgeted													
	Actual													
	Budgeted													
	Actual													
	Budgeted													
	Actual													
	Budgeted													
	Actual													
	Budgeted													
Total	Actual													

Time

Fee dollars

% complete — 100, 80, 60, 40, 20

At beginning of job plot budgeted total dollars (or hours) on graph.
Plot actual expended dollars (or hours) as job progresses.
Also plot estimated percentage complete as job progresses.

Figure 8-15
Fee and Progress Monitoring Worksheet

hours and dollars that are finally set in the contract are spread out over the time period for the job and listed by phase, staff member, department or any group that is most useful for you. The total for each time period (one-week periods for small jobs, one-month periods for very large jobs) is calculated and transferred to a chart on the lower portion of the page that provides a simple way to graphically depict the budgeted fees versus the actual fees so corrective action can be taken before it is too late.

A vital part of this graph is another plot line showing the estimated percent of completion of work as reported by the project manager or director of the job. Actual fees spent may be exactly on target with budgeted fees but task completion may be way behind. This is a simple method to compare the three measures.

For more detailed planning and monitoring of project progress refer to the chapter on project management. This system, however, quickly summarizes the broad view of project progress as it relates to financial planning and control.

GETTING PAID—MANAGING ACCOUNTS RECEIVABLE

Getting paid promptly for services rendered is basic to an architect's financial success. This has historically been a problem area for many professionals and at today's interest rates and high cost of doing business not solving the problem can spell disaster. Design professionals need to take a "get tough" attitude and realize that going after payment due is not unprofessional, but simply a fact of business life. If you are afraid of offending your client or losing the commission, realize that the client that does not pay or pays when it is convenient is one that you probably do not want.

There are four basic steps to collecting your accounts receivable: contract terms, timely billing, complete invoices, and regular procedures for following accounts.

Spell Out All Terms of Fee Collection in the Contract

Having a clear understanding with the client, before you start work, of the fee and how it will be paid is basic to avoiding misunderstandings later. If problems do develop, you have little procedural or legal recourse if everything is not itemized in your agreement with the client. Provisions should include the basis for the fee, when invoices will be sent and in what form, when payment is due, and any penalties for late payment such as interest charges after 45 days or some reasonable period of time. Check with your attorney for specifics in this area and the contract language to use.

You might also consider stating that after a certain period of time, work will stop on the client's project until payment is made and that no work will be given to the client or any presentations made until the problem is resolved.

Submit Invoices Promptly

Send out your bills as soon after the payroll period as possible. Every day you delay is one more day until you get paid. If possible, maintain a minimum monthly billing cycle. Some firms bill twice a month to keep cash coming in more regularly. Avoid lump-sum payment at the end of phase completion—this can sometimes delay any cash inflow for months on a large project. Quicker billing also makes it easier for the client to associate the invoice with work actually performed during the billing cycle and may lessen the chance for questioning the invoice amount.

Make Each Invoice Complete

Every invoice should be easy to read and understand. Of course, the name and address of the client, project name and number and reference to a contract are standard. In addition, the actual amount due should be backed up by a detailed breakdown of the work performed and the billing associated with each item. The exact format will depend on your method of operating and keeping track of professional time and the conditions of the contract, but may include a breakdown of time each team member spent on the job, their billing rate and total cost. Or you might itemize by the phase or work task that was outlined in your contract. Whatever form you choose, do not just submit a lump-sum amount due. That is an open invitation for the client to question (and rightly so!) and delay payment.

Also include reimbursable expenses with backup documentation and any amount past due. Keep a consistent format from invoice to invoice so that the client always knows what to expect and where to look for the information.

Regular Procedures for Tracking Accounts

Establish a policy for how each account receivable is to be treated by the people responsible for collecting. A good idea is to check with the person receiving the invoice about two weeks after it is sent to verify if it was received and if there are any questions. This lets the client know you are closely following the account and often catches simple problems early such as a lost invoice or a question that can be easily answered.

Additional procedures may be to send a past-due notice after thirty days, personal calls and visits after an additional amount of time and finally legal action if the account becomes too overdue. Any procedure you follow should be consistent with your contract provisions, and these procedures should be known to your client before work is started. If every policy is not stated in the contract, you may consider printing a standard policy statement that is given to every client at the start of a project or that is attached to the contract.

Keep a written record of all your office's actions in regard to trying to collect money owed. It might be useful later if legal problems develop.

Additional Tips

1. Always use the personal approach in collecting fees. Send a cover letter with your invoices explaining the progress on the client's job and what efforts the billing represents. Have the project architect or project manager sign the invoices to let the client know they have been reviewed and do not come just from the accounting department. When problems develop, make a phone call or personal visit, not a threatening letter. A face-to-face approach is always more successful than impersonal bills.

2. Have a system that produces aged accounts receivable reports so you know exactly what client is delinquent and for how long. The report should show 30-, 60-, 90- and 120-day outstanding accounts. Figure 8-10 shows the report produced by the Harper and Shuman system. Work on the oldest accounts first since these are the most likely not to be collected unless immediate action is taken.

3. Know what your client's payment procedures are. Often, an invoice must travel a tortuous route through a large organization with multiple approvals before a check is issued. Know how long the process should take and whom to contact with questions if there is a delay.

4. Plan your cash flow. Figure 8-12 illustrates one simple way of doing this. When you can anticipate what your cash position is likely to be in a month or two it becomes very clear how important collecting fees is. In the same way, you can use the cash flow projection to evaluate whether or not to press for collection on an unusual project where timely payment is a problem.

5. On your invoices, print the name and telephone number of the person to contact if the client has any questions. It is better to encourage the resolution of problems than to create distance between each firm's accounting departments.

6. Consider offering a 1 percent or 2 percent discount for payment made within two weeks or some other specified period of time. Encouraging prompt payment this way may actually cost less than borrowing short-term money to cover a weak cash position, lost interest on short-term investments, or legal assistance with late collections.

7. Require a retainer before work starts. This may be anywhere between 10 percent to 20 percent of the fee or based on an average anticipated monthly billing amount. Most projects require some up-front money and there is no reason why the architect should not receive some of it. Explain to your client the amount of time and money your office must expend before a normal billing payment is made. A client who has objections to this approach may be worth further investigation to verify his financial solvency.

8. If you expect the project to be a long one (over a year's involvement of your firm), include contract provisions for renegotiating terms, billing rates and other financial considerations that may change within the time of the original contract.

9. Offer to work with the client who is having unusual financial problems that may be temporary. This will be a judgement call on your part, but the goodwill it provides may be well worth the cost and wait to you. It should, however, happen only in special cases. Doing it too often will give you a reputation you do not want.

10. Watch out for delay tricks of delinquent clients. They often send a letter of dissatisfaction to justify not paying you. As long as you have fulfilled your contractual obligations, don't let this dissuade you from agressively pressing for payment. Occasionally, the client may send a check with the note written on it: "payment in full for all obligations due." No matter how much you need the money do not cash this kind of check. It may preclude your right to demand additional money that may be due you. Return it and request another check without that stipulation. Also beware of the check that is improperly filled out. Sending it to the bank will only delay payment. Return it personally to your client and ask for another.

11. Be prepared to file a lien against the client's project. Lien laws vary from state to state, so check with your attorney.

HOW TO MAKE BETTER USE OF YOUR PAYROLL BUDGET

Even though direct and indirect payroll costs are the largest portion of your expense budget and usually more or less fixed there are ways to lower them without sacrificing productivity. Consider the following ideas.

1. Analyze existing productivity and methods of production. Can they be streamlined? Refer to the section on time management in Chapter 4 and also to Chapter 5.

2. Have the proper tools and equipment available for your staff. Saving a few dollars on useful equipment may cost you many times the amount in lost productivity.

3. Analyze your office space. Replan if necessary for maximum efficiency. Does it correspond to your workflow? Are necessary resources at hand? Does it hinder communication? Does it encourage *too much* communication?

4. Is everyone doing the appropriate task for his or her job level? Is the best use being made of everyone's skills and talents for the maximum amount of time? Should you hire additional administrative or clerical help to take over jobs that people are doing instead of billing at their maximum rate?

5. Set reasonable goals for percent of billable time for every technical level person in the office. Review them periodically and take action immediately if the actual varies too much from the projected.

6. Make sure any time spent on projects by support staff is recorded and

billed to that job. Do not let legitimate direct time get lost because of job classi-fication.

7. Use consultants and contract labor when necessary instead of putting more people on your payroll. Benefits and overhead costs are expensive for extra staff. Many firms, for example, use drafting services for much of their production work. Properly organized and controlled, farmed out work can save unnecessary costs.

8. Resist the temptation to do other people's work. Do not take on the tasks that sales reps, subcontractors, vendors and others should be doing for you as part of their normal services.

9. Consider developing an incentive program that ties bonuses or other rewards to job productivity.

10. Be sensitive to the general morale of the office. Bad feelings mean low productivity. Find out what is wrong and take steps to correct any problem.

11. Insist on clearly defined and planned task assignments for all staff. No one should ever be sitting around waiting for a decision to be made before he can start work.

12. Maintain all the up-to-date reference material required for your office's project types. Have it organized so minimal time is required to get the information required to do a job.

13. Maintain a rigorous system of filling in and checking time sheets. Collect them at least weekly and have project managers or other supervisory personnel check to make sure they are accurate and that no legitimate direct time has been missed. This includes checking the principal's time sheets as well.

14. Establish and maintain agreements with other offices on loaning and borrowing staff as a way of retaining good people during slow periods and avoiding the need to hire additional people during a short-lived crunch.

CONTROLLING OVERHEAD

1. The single largest overhead expense is non-billable labor. Every office's first priority in reducing overhead should be to minimize this component. The first step is to tighten up on time card reporting. Much of the legitimate time spent on a project often ends up listed as "office" time or some other non-chargeable category. This usually results when staff fills in their time cards at the last minute, trying to remember an entire week or two weeks of work late on a Friday afternoon. Principals are often the worst offenders, listing their efforts as general coordination, marketing, or administration when they were actually working on a specific job. Some offices require time cards to be turned in daily, others have task sheets that can be filled in during the day as jobs are worked on, then later summarized on the time card. This is especially useful for project managers or others who may be

involved on several projects every day. All time cards should also be checked by the project coordinator or project manager to verify that all legitimate time is being charged. Don't forget about support staff, too. If a secretary, office boy or other non-technical person spends time on a specific job, charge it as billable labor. Include this provision in your contract so there are no questions.

2. Record all significant non-labor direct expenses. The costs for project-related travel, construction document printing and the like are usually included in every office's billing, but there are often many expenses left out that are considered to be general overhead. Keep accurate records of the following kinds of project-related expenses and charge them to the client:

> Progress prints made during the course of the job
> All copy machine reproduction
> Paper, acetate and other drawing media
> Model supplies for a specific job
> Postage and delivery
> All local travel expenses
> Presentation supplies used for the project

Some of these may seem small at first, but for many jobs over a year's period they can amount to a substantial sum—money that should be reimbursed to you.

3. Shop around for the best telephone service deals. With the recent break up of the A T & T system and agressive marketing by private long-distance telephone companies, there is money to be saved in this area. Of course, strict record-keeping of chargeable, long distance calls is a must. You might investigate the automatic, electronic systems that are available to record calls, duration, destination, and job number to be charged. These are more accurate and complete than having everyone fill out phone slips as calls are made and such a system may more than pay for itself in a short time.

4. Review your office location. With lease rates increasing rapidly in many parts of the country, you may be paying more and more for a location that really does nothing for your business. Go through a site selection process as you would for any client to find the best location for your money. Also, review your utilization of the space you do have. Is it efficient? Could some storage be located elsewhere at a lower square foot rate?

5. For general office supplies, order less frequently and in larger quantities. Many stores give discounts when they have to make fewer delivery trips and sell in quantity.

6. Double up with other offices on continuing education costs. Instead of three offices sending three people to a trade show or seminar, send one person who then shares what was learned with all three offices. Work out a system of alternating people from each office so everyone has a chance to attend at some time.

7. Evaluate your budget for subscriptions to professional journals, newspapers, and similar expenses. Are they being read? Are they useful for the office? Can the needed information be extracted from indexes or individually researched on an as-needed basis?

8. Study your insurance policies to see if you have too much coverage or overlapping coverage. Consider raising the deductible on health care coverage to lower premiums. Shop around for insurance, too, to get the lowest possible price. Also consider low base coverage and then project insurance as needed. The project insurance may then be billed as a reimbursable expense to the client.

9. Make sure you get the lowest possible rate with hotels and rental car companies. For non-chargeable travel this money can be better spent elsewhere.

SOURCES FOR MORE INFORMATION

Books

The first four documents listed comprise the essential elements of the American Institute of Architects' Financial Management System.

Mattox, Robert F. *Financial Management for Architects: A Guide to Understanding, Planning and Controlling the Firm's Finances* (Washington: The American Institute of Architects, 1980.)

Standardized Accounting for Architects. Washington: The American Institute of Architects, 1978.

CFMS: An Introduction to the Computer-based Financial Management Service. Washington: The American Institute of Architects, 1981.

Compensation Guidelines for Architectural and Engineering Services, 2nd ed., revised. Washington: The American Institute of Architects, 1978.

Birnberg & Associates. *Texas Society of Architects; Professional Financial Management Workbook.* Austin, Texas: Texas Society of Architects, 1981.

Hayes, Rick Stephan, Baker, C. Richard. *Simplified Accounting for Engineering and Technical Consultants.* New York: John Wiley & Sons, 1980.

Walker, Ernest W., Petty, J. Willian II. *Financial Management of the Small Firm.* Englewood Cliffs, NJ: Prentice-Hall, Inc., 1978.

Surveys and Reports

1982 Financial Statistics Survey for Professional Service Firms. Birnberg & Associates, 1905 North Halsted Street, Chicago, IL 60614. Sponsored by the Professional Services Management Journal and the Professional Services Management Association.

1982 Operating Statistics for Professional Firms. Harper & Shuman, Inc., 68 Moulton Street, Cambridge, MA 02138.

Annual Statement Studies. Robert Morris Associates, P.O. Box 8500, S-1140, Philadelphia, PA 19178.

1980 Financial Statistics Survey. MRH Associates, Inc., P.O. Box 11316, Newington, CT 06111.

The 1981 AIA Firm Survey. Washington: The American Institute of Architects, 1982.

Seminars Contact each for current schedule and topics

Financial Management for Architects. Professional Development, The American Institute of Architects, 1735 New York Avenue, N.W., Washington, DC 20006.

PSMJ Seminars. 126 Harvard Street, Brookline, MA 02146.

Professional Services Management Association. 1700 East Dyer Road, Suite 165, Santa Ana, CA 92705.

Harvard Graduate School of Design/Continuing Education. 48 Quincy Street, Cambridge, MA 02138.

Don Thompson Associates. 3247 Embry Hills Drive, Atlanta, GA.

Birnberg & Associates. 1905 North Halsted Street, Chicago, IL 60614. 60605.

Newsletters

The AE Manager. Birnberg & Associates. See address above.

Two newsletters mentioned in previous chapters often contain items pertaining to financial management although it is not their only topic.

Guidelines Letter. Box 456, Orinda, CA 94563.

Professional Services Management Journal. MRH Associates, Inc., P.O. Box 11316, Newington, CT 06111.

Interpretation of Statement Studies in Figures 8-4 and 8-5

RMA recommends that Statement Studies data be regarded only as general guidelines and not as absolute industry norms. There are several reasons why the data may not be fully representative of a given industry:

(1)   The financial statements used in the *Statement Studies* are not selected by any random or statistically reliable method. RMA member banks voluntarily submit the raw data they have available each year, with these being the only constraints: (a) The fiscal year-ends of the companies reported may not be from April 1 through June 29, and (b) their total assets must be less than $100 million.

(2)   Many companies have varied product lines; however, the *Statement Studies* categorize them by their primary product Standard Industrial Classification (SIC) number only.

(3)   Some of our industry samples are rather small in relation to the total number of firms in a given industry. A relatively small sample can increase the chances that some of our composites do not fully represent an industry.

(4)   There is the chance that an extreme statement can be present in a sample, causing a disproportionate influence on the industry composite. This is particularly true in a relatively small sample.

(5)   Companies within the same industry may differ in their method of operations which in turn can directly influence their financial statements. Since they are included in our sample, too, these statements can significantly affect our composite calculations.

(6)   Other considerations that can result in variations among different companies engaged in the same general line of business are different labor markets; geographical location; different accounting methods; quality of products handled; sources and methods of financing; and terms of sale.

For these reasons, RMA does not recommend the Statement Studies *in figures be considered as absolute norms for a given industry. Rather the figures should be used only as general guidelines and in addition to the other methods of financial analysis. RMA makes no claim as to the representativeness of the figures printed in this book.*

CHAPTER 9
Techniques for Improved Project Management

SOME OF THE GREATEST GAINS IN THE EFFICIENCY, QUALITY, AND PROFIT of your office can be accomplished through improved project management. Stiffer competition, more demanding clients and the need to coordinate teams of specialists to solve design problems require firms of all sizes to take a closer look at their efforts in this often neglected area of office practice. Even on small projects the amount of planning and coordination necessary to successfully complete a job today requires a concentrated management effort in addition to the traditional needs of design and production.

Project management is not just for the large firms. Small offices also need a system. The primary difference is that one person in the small office will probably be handling the project management functions as well as other tasks such as design or production or managing more than one job. The important thing to remember is that project management is a discipline and is dependent on an attitude and process, not on size.

Figure 9-1 shows the ideal position of the project manager in relation to others involved with a job. He or she should be the one person coordinating all members of the design and construction team as far as they relate to the activities of the architect's office. In this central role the project manager may have some or all of the following responsibilities.

1. To be part of any team marketing efforts.
2. To help write proposals and fee estimates.
3. To help prepare the owner-architect agreement.
4. To schedule the project.
5. To prepare the man-hour estimate for work to be done.
6. To assist in hiring consultants and coordinating their activities.

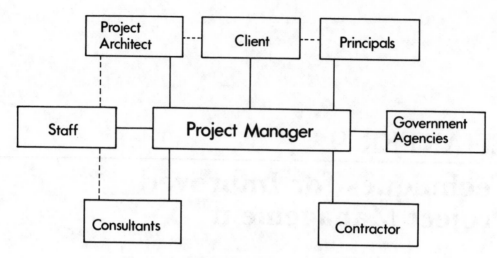

Figure 9-1
Central Role of Project Manager

7. To organize and coordinate all activities necessary for the completion of the job.
8. To keep the entire project on track toward the original goals laid out by the client and the design team.
9. To schedule meetings and coordinate progress among all people on the team.
10. To manage the personnel assigned to the project.
11. To act as the primary link between the principals and the project team and to provide status reports to the principals.
12. To act as the office contact with governmental agencies and other regulatory groups.
13. To attend client presentations.
14. To obtain client approvals at critical job milestones.
15. To help resolve conflicts among team members.
16. To see that all aspects of the job are documented.
17. To process all change orders, certificates for payment, work authorizations and similar documents.
18. To verify that the office is meeting all of its contractual obligations.
19. To review all invoices to the client.
20. To review all consultant's billings for payment.
21. To check man-hours spent on the job against the original estimate and take corrective action if necessary.
22. To check construction cost estimates against the client's budget as design and production proceed.
23. To coordinate construction document production.
24. To assist in bidding or negotiation procedures.
25. To see that proper contract administration and construction observation are carried out.

26. To assist in collecting overdue billings.
27. To work with the client during and after move-in with construction-related problems.
28. To complete all job close-out activities.
29. To conduct periodic follow-up with the client after move-in.
30. To coordinate with other project managers in maintaining overall office workload scheduling.

These responsibilities only outline hundreds of activities that a manager must complete during the course of a typical project (a more detailed task checklist is outlined later in this chapter). While they may seem extensive to someone who does not currently have a strong project manager system they are all activities that must happen in order for a job to be completed. Centralizing control of these responsibilities in one person makes it much more likely that the client's project will be completed on time and on budget and that the design goals will be met in a profitable manner.

SCHEDULING AND MAN-HOUR PROJECTIONS

There are many systems for scheduling and allocating fees. Whatever method you use, it should meet the following criteria.

1. Be coordinated with the office's methods of estimating fees, keeping time sheets, billing, estimating man-hours and other parts of the accounting system.
2. Provide for easy monitoring on a relatively "fine-grain" basis—weekly on most projects, monthly on very large projects—so corrective action can be taken in time.
3. Give information on personnel required per week for overall office man-power planning.
4. Provide an easy way to make specific work task assignments to individual staff members.
5. Show *actual* compared to *budgeted* data to develop a historical reference for future estimating.
6. Be complete, but minimize paperwork and time required.

Scheduling

There are three basic levels of scheduling in an office and the project manager plays a central role in developing all three. There is the overall office schedule used by the principals or office management to track long-range commitments, staffing needs, and backlog. There is the individual project summary schedule that shows each project broken down by phase of service used to develop proposals, project staff needs for each job, and detailed job task schedules. Finally, there is the fine-grain schedule for each project that shows on a weekly basis, and often a daily basis, who should be doing what task in what sequence to complete the job. This is used to make work assignments, monitor progress of each staff member, and assist in determining deadlines to avoid last minute rushes.

All job scheduling should begin with the project manager. Since this person will ultimately be responsible for producing the work he or she should be involved with deciding if the office should go after a job in the first place, writing the proposal, and be a part of the marketing team to discuss scheduling with the potential client.

Project scheduling is an iterative process. It is continually refined as new information is presented. The first pass at a project begins with the project summary schedule where only broad categories of work are listed, usually the major phases of a job. As this is fine-tuned, the information is added to and coordinated with the overall office schedule. It is also broken down into more detail by the project manager in preparation for scheduling personnel and tasks on a week-by-week basis.

Usually the overall project schedule is determined by outside forces. These serve as the starting point for the schedule. They may include such things as,

- The client's lease expiration in his present building.
- Financing limitations.
- Need to mesh with other master plan activities.
- Estimated delivery time of long lead items.
- Requirements of a building landlord for move-in date.

These criteria may establish the completion date or some other part of the process.

Adding estimated time requirements to those given during the preparation of the proposal should allow you to determine the feasibility of the *client's* schedule, the ability of your office to do the job within the time given and personnel available, and the need to establish critical constraints from the beginning such as fast-track, pre-purchasing of material, "quick-ship" furniture ordering and similar techniques. Do not promise more than you (or any office) can deliver. Adding temporary personnel, working overtime or collaborating with another office are possible ways of trying to accommodate a client's tight schedule, but there is a limit beyond which unreasonable time demands will only result in mistakes, an improperly designed project and an unhappy client. Tell the client this if necessary.

Since fees are usually one of the major constraints on the in-house schedule, the initial time estimate should also include this information. Either the tasks required or a client's fixed budget will determine the fees and the time frame, so the project summary schedule should allow the project manager to work back and forth between these two factors under the direction of the office principals. If there are conflicts between the client's fee budget, tasks required to do the job, and schedule (and there usually are) then this initial schedule can be used to help resolve them early.

Figure 9-2 illustrates one way of starting the project scheduling procedure. The phases or broad task categories you are using for the proposal or for billing

Project _____   Project no. _____   Date _____

Completed by _____   Project manager _____   Total fee _____

Phase or Task	Period / Date													% of total fee	Fee allocation by phase or task	Man-hrs. est.

Budgeted fees per period														100%		
Person–weeks or hours																
Staff assigned																
Actual fees expended																

Figure 9-2
Summary Project Schedule

purposes can be listed in the left column. These may be the standard phases outlined in the AIA's *Compensation Guidelines for Architectural and Engineering Services* or any other listing that may be appropriate for your individual project. The time frame is listed at the top of the form. One-month periods are usually used for long projects at this stage of scheduling although weekly periods may be used for shorter jobs. Make your best estimate on the total amount of time each phase will require working within the fixed dates you may already know.

At this point you do not necessarily know how many people will be working on a job at any one time, but only that particular phases of work need to be completed within beginning and end points and that these phases will have particular fees associated with them. The project summary schedule should be reviewed with any consultants to verify that they can work within the time limits or to solicit their opinions. It should also be reviewed by other directors or department heads in the office to check for any possible conflicts. For example, the specification writer may see that you have scheduled specifications to be done when four other jobs are simultaneously timed for specs and when he will be out of town attending a seminar. A quick check will avoid these obvious problems and put the responsibility for a schedule where it belongs—with the people who have to meet it.

After any revisions are made, man-hour projections can be calculated, a detailed project schedule drawn up, and the project time and personnel requirements added to the office scheduling board. These are discussed in more detail in the following sections.

Man-Hour Projections

When you are ready to begin man-hour projections you should have estimated the amount of calendar time each phase will take. Fees are usually set at this time and they now need to be allocated to each phase. One method of doing this is first to take the total fee quote given the client or agreed to in your contract and subtract consultant fees, non-reimbursable direct expenses, and a contingency, if any. Remember, if you added a contingency in figuring your fee (see Chapter 8), deducting something here will be a double contingency. The result is the "working fee" that the project manager must use to produce the job. At this point you can either work with billing rates that take into account the office multiplier for overhead and profit or subtract the "overhead allocation" and profit figure if you are working with direct labor costs. Refer to Figure 8-14.

List the percent of the total fee that each phase will be allocated in the appropriate column in Figure 9-2. This percent may be based on rules of thumb your office has developed (one of the reasons for keeping accurate time records) or from the initial estimate you did when working up the fee proposal. Multiply each percentage by the total working fee to arrive at a dollar amount for each phase. Dividing by the estimated phase duration in weeks gives you a fee amount per week (or month). This figure may be transfered to a form similar to that shown in Figure 8-15 to monitor budgeted fees with fees actually spent.

Translate the weekly budgeted fee into person-weeks by dividing the average billing rate per week into the fee. For example, if you have budgeted $4,000 per week in fees and your average billing rate is $40 per hour, or $1,600 per week, then you can allocate 2.5 people that week. Of course, things are not that simple. The average billing rate will vary from phase to phase depending on who are working on the project at any one time and what their billing rate is. Early in the project, for example, there may be heavy principal and marketing involvement at higher rates than later when production personnel are charging at lower billing rates. The *average* billing rate you use to estimate man-hours will, therefore, be higher during that initial phase and this will in turn affect your estimated man-hours.

This problem can be solved by weighting the billing rates of each person involved according to the percentage of involvement he or she will have. Figure 9-3 shows an example of this (using billing rates rather than direct labor costs). The straight average of billing rate is different from the weighted average. On large projects, or where there are wide variations among billing rates, this difference can become significant when estimating time allocations.

Of course, this is just one way of determining man-hours. It is also possible to use direct labor time instead of billing rates and to calculate man-hours rather than man-weeks. The results are the same: to determine the exact staffing requirements for a project and to integrate those requirements into the overall office staffing projections.

When you get to the point where you need to enumerate individual staff

Phase _Schematic design_

Staff	% involvement	Billing rate	Hourly rate for average
Principal	5%	$60.00	$3.00
Project manager	20	50.00	10.00
Designer	60	37.50	22.50
Draftsperson	15	25.00	3.75
Total		$43.75	$39.25

Figure 9-3
Weighted Average Billing Rates

assignments, you can also use the form shown in Figure 9-2. Simply place each staff member's name in the column where the project phases are. Hours to be devoted to a particular project can then be listed for each week for each person.

Detailed Project Schedules

Once the project manager, firm principals, consultants, and others are satisfied with the preliminary schedule and it represents a reasonably accurate projection of the required man-hours per week, the manager needs to expand it to a greater level of detail. This is necessary to assist in making individual staff work assignments on a weekly basis and to provide a clearly stated plan against which to measure progress. If man-hours are exceeded or tasks not accomplished within the given time frame, corrective action can be taken before it is too late. A detailed schedule is vital to make sure intermediate deadlines are met.

The bar chart is the most common technique of scheduling for the typical design office. It is quick, easy to understand, easy to construct, shows durations of tasks graphically and can be simple or complex to suit the circumstances. Its primary disadvantages for design scheduling are that it is limited in the complexity it can show, cannot show dependencies of one task on another in much detail, or the sequences of many tasks.

If the job is of short duration or is fairly simple, bar charts work perfectly well. As shown in Figure 9-2, phases, individual tasks, or staff members can be listed vertically in the left column and time plotted horizontally. Critical dates can be graphically depicted as well as the times required for client involvement. Total budgeted hours and actual expended hours can also be summarized at the bottom of the chart to relate task accomplishment with fee expenditure.

For more complex projects where many people are involved or where there are many tasks to be coordinated a network schedule is useful. The most well-known of these is the Critical Path Method or CPM chart. This graphically depicts all of the tasks required to complete a project, the sequence in which they must occur, their duration, earliest or latest possible starting time, earliest or latest possible finishing time, and defines the sequence of tasks that are "critical" or that must be started and finished exactly on time if the total schedule is to be met.

Most CPM schedules are very complicated and are supported by computer programs that either generate them or keep track of all the starting, finishing times and durations. While this level of detail is beyond the needs of most design projects, a CPM chart can be useful for project managers in a design office. Even in a simplified form it requires team members to think through the job before committing time to it and to study the complex sequences of tasks that must be performed. It is a way of graphically showing how everyone, including the client and consultants, must work together to achieve the desired results.

Figure 9-4 shows a portion of a CPM chart that might be developed for part of the schematic design phase of a small architectural project. Each arrow represents

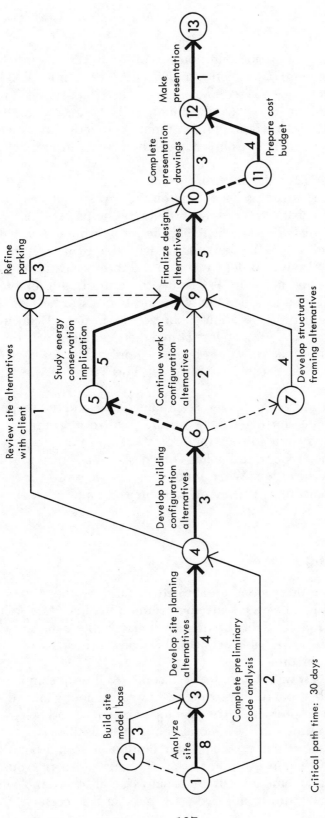

**Figure 9-4
CPM Network**

Critical path time: 30 days

197

an activity with a beginning and end point (represented by the numbered circles). No activity can begin until all activities (indicated by arrows) leading into the circle have been completed. The dashed lines indicate dependency relationships but not activities themselves and thus have no duration. They are called "dummies" and are used to give each activity a unique beginning and ending number and to allow establishment of dependency relationships without tying in non-dependent activities.

In the example, a dummy from event 8 to event 9 is used to show that "finalize design alternatives" is dependent on "review site alternatives with client" as well as all other activities preceding it while "refine parking" is dependent only on "review site alternatives with client." If the arrow from 4 to 8 led directly into event 9 instead, and the "refine parking" activity started with 9, this would imply that "refine parking" was also dependent on the three activities between 6 and 9.

The heavier line in Figure 9-4 shows the critical path, or the sequence of events that must happen as scheduled if the deadline is to be met. The numbers under the activities give the duration of the activity in days. Delaying the starting time of any of these activities or increasing their duration will delay the whole project. The non-critical activities can begin or finish earlier or later (within limits) without affecting the final completition date. This is called the "float" of each activity.

A complete discussion of CPM scheduling is beyond the scope of this book, but the basic concepts illustrated here can be used to help the project manager develop a detailed schedule to keep the project team working together in the most productive way. One of the typical failings of a design job is that it proceeds without clear and organized direction. When time or money begin to run out it is usually too late. Detailed scheduling provides a valuable communication and management tool to help avoid this problem.

Office Scheduling Board

As man-hour projections are firmed up and a schedule established, the information should be integrated into the overall office schedule. While this is not necessarily the responsibility of the project manager, the data he or she provides must be as accurate as possible to help the firm's principals or office manager schedule time and personnel.

One of the best ways to do this is to compile all project information on one large office scheduling board. It provides a way to see in a glance the status of all projects and potential problem areas needing correction, and it lets all staff know what is happening in the office—a morale booster in itself.

Figure 9-5 shows one possible configuration of such a board. Projects are listed down the left column and time period columns across the top. For this kind of broad view, monthly time periods are usually best although the columns may be large enough to break down into two-week periods if necessary. For long-range

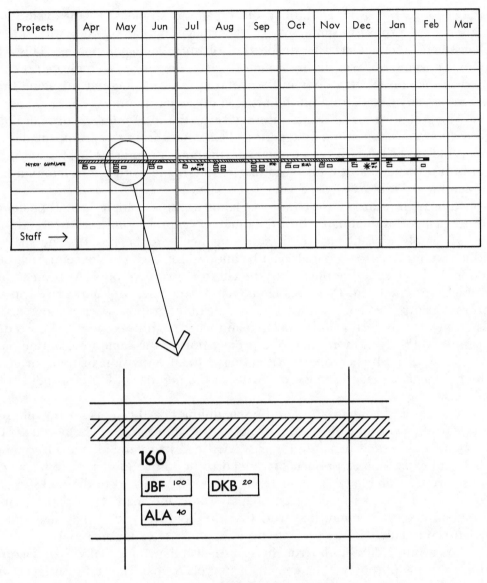

Figure 9-5
Office Scheduling Board

planning and staffing, the board should show at least a one-year period. The physical configuration of the board should allow one section of time, say two or three months, to be removed as that time period passes, then revised and placed at the far end of the board to accommodate a new period. This way, the full board does not have to be revised at once and there is always nine or ten months of current information visible.

The enlarged detail of the board shows the three essential elements of each time block for each project. First, the project manager should show the overall time schedule for the project in simple bar chart format. This can be done with colored tape or some other material to divide the job into its major phases. This way, groupings of similar phases during similar times in the office can indicate potential workload problems. Several jobs in the working drawing stage at the same time, for example, may put a strain on the production department.

The second piece of useful information is the total number of man-hours projected to be needed in the time period. This comes from the project manager's estimate and can be taken directly from the form shown in Figure 9-2. This succinctly shows firm management the likely staffing requirements with a long enough lead time plan for slowdowns or overloads.

In order to translate pure hours of labor to actual people or staff positions, the third element of the board consists of markers representing each person in the office (or simply a blank marker if someone needs to be hired). One marker, identified with the person's initials, can be allotted for each employee in each time period and all placed at the bottom of the chart in a reserve pool. As projects and personnel are scheduled, their marker is taken from the pool and placed in the appropriate slot. This becomes a very easy, flexible, graphic way to show who is working on what project, who is available and where extra people may be needed. For people working on more than one project during the same time period, split markers can be used, each one representing a smaller division of time, or space can be left on each person's marker to write in the number of hours scheduled for that project.

The physical configuration of the scheduling board can take many different forms depending on your office size, project types, and budget. The board should be as large as possible to allow for easy viewing, space for all the information needed, and expansion as projects are added to the office job list. The board can be constructed of simple tackable material set in rails attached to the wall if cost is a problem. Lines can be made of graphic arts tape and markers of paper pinned to the board. Keep in mind, however, that the board is useful only if it can be modified continually, so take this into account when selecting materials.

For a more durable board, there are several commercially manufactured products for this purpose. They consist of porcelain enamel writing surfaces with colored, magnetic markers, grooved boards, boards with pegs and any number of accessories. Some of the major manufacturers are listed below. Write to them for catalogs and more detailed information.

Caddylak Systems, Inc.
201 Montrose Road
Westbury, NY 11590

Magna Visual, Inc.
1200 N. Rock Hill Road
St. Louis, MO 63124

Methods Research Corporation
Asbury Avenue
Farmingdale, NJ 07727

Oravisual
Box 11150
St. Petersburg, FL 33733

Pryor Charting Products, Inc.
1006 S. Michigan Avenue
Chicago, IL 60605

Rol-A-Chart
Division of Wm. A. Steward Company
P.O. Box 367
Diamond Springs, CA 95619

PROVEN TECHNIQUES FOR
DAY-TO-DAY MANAGEMENT

Project Notebook

One of the best tools for project management is the project notebook. For immediate, day-to-day reference this record gives the project manager finger-tip access to the information for planning, coordinating, and monitoring the job. It can be taken to meetings and the job site as well as used in the office.

The notebook should contain most of the following items. You may want to modify the list somewhat to suit the unique requirements of your projects.

1. General reference

    a. Index of the notebook
    b. Project directory—names, addresses and telephone numbers of the client, consultants, contractors, regulatory agencies, major vendors and others
    c. Filing index—names and code numbers of office filing system for the job

2. Contracts

    a. Owner/Architect agreement
    b. Work authorizations
    c. Lease provisions (if an interior design project)

3. Fees and schedules

    a. Preliminary schedule and detailed schedule
    b. Man-hour projections and fee budgets
    c. Task assignments
    d. Financial management report summaries

4. Programming

    a. Goal statements
    b. Program or program summary
    c. Code and zoning search
    d. Special equipment needs
    e. Other special needs
    f. Utility information

5. Budget

   a. Construction budget
   b. Furnishings budget
   c. Other special items
   d. Updates

6. Job communication

   a. Major correspondence
   b. Meeting minutes
   c. Telephone log
   d. Transmittal log
   e. Design review notes
   f. Written client approvals

7. Construction administration

   a. Shop drawing/sample log
   b. Bulletins
   c. Change orders
   d. Field orders
   e. Field reports
   f. Application and certificates for payment

8. Close-out and follow-up

   a. Punch list
   b. Certificate of substantial completion
   c. Summary of construction costs
   d. Summary of fee expenditures and other job-related costs
   e. Comments on completed job
   f. Consultant evaluations
   g. Notes on follow-up visits

Project Management Task Checklist

In defining the roles and responsibilities of project team members, each design office will have a slightly different approach depending on its organization, size and staff availability. If you choose to have a strong project manager system, however, you may want to compare the assigned duties of that person with the following checklist. The items listed should ideally be the responsibility of one person to maintain the overall control and communication that are vital to an efficiently run project. If the job is large or the project manager is running several other jobs, some of the tasks may need to be delegated, but with overall supervision still the responsibility of the manager.

Project Management Task Checklist

Pre-Contract

1. Assist in development of proposal.
2. Estimate time and fees required for project proposal.
3. Develop preliminary schedule.
4. Contact consultants to establish their fees and time proposals.
5. Make tentative selection of project team with input from principals or office manager.
6. Assist with compilation of final contract if necessary.
7. Verify with firm principals if additional project insurance may be needed.

Post-Contract

8. Set up project files.
9. Start project notebook.
10. Develop detailed schedule.
11. Complete detailed man-hour projections.
12. Finalize goals of office and client goals—in writing.
13. Hold orientation meeting with in-house team to discuss project goals, project scope, schedule, design problem, fees, working procedures, and similar concerns.
14. Finalize consultant's contracts.
15. Hold orientation meeting with consultants to discuss schedule, project scope, methods of coordination, goals, and design concepts (if any at this point).
16. Hold meeting with client to introduce project team and discuss schedule, project scope, critical dates, responsibilities of the client and team, consultant involvement, design problems, procedures of communication and coordination with client contacts.

Programming and Pre-Design

17. Organize programming effort.
18. Prepare staff task assignments for programming work.
19. Refine client's project budget.
20. Complete code search and zoning study.
21. Contact and coordinate with utilities, governmental agencies and other regulatory bodies as required.
22. Schedule and coordinate programming interviews and meetings with client.
23. Assist in or supervise completion of programming.
24. Coordinate consultant involvement (if any).

25. Present final program and obtain client's *written* approval.
26. Monitor fees expended and conformance of work to schedule.
27. Review invoicing to client.

Schematic Design

28. Meet with the project team to discuss program, client's goals and direction of schematic design work.
29. Monitor work by the project team for conformance to contract requirements, program statements and other client needs.
30. Coordinate consultant's work.
31. Prepare probable project budget.
32. Record and maintain all documentation of this phase: client decisions, changes in scope of project, minutes of design meetings, etc.
33. Write work authorizations if client changes scope of work.
34. Hold in-house design reviews as concept alternatives are developed.
35. Hold schematic design presentation and obtain client's *written* approval.
36. Monitor fees expended and conformance to schedule.
37. Review invoicing to client.
38. Review and approve consultant's billings.

Design Development

39. Meet with project team to discuss direction of design development work.
40. Monitor work by team for conformance to contract requirements and project goals.
41. Coordinate work by consultants.
42. Revise project budget as required, notify client of any changes.
43. Initiate work on outline specification.
44. Hold progress meetings with client as required.
45. Hold in-house design reviews.
46. Maintain all documentation of this phase.
47. Write work authorizations if client changes scope of work.
48. Hold final design development presentation and obtain *written* approval of client.
49. Monitor fees expended and conformance to schedule.
50. Review invoicing to client.
51. Review and approve consultant's billings.

Construction Documentation

52. Organize drawing mock-ups and document production methods with project architect, production team or others responsible for this phase.
53. Organize task assignments and monitor progress of work.
54. Submit base sheets to consultants—coordinate their work as documents are produced.

55. Review drawings with client at intermediate completion points.
56. Obtain owner's requirements on bonds, insurance, allowances, alternates, etc. for inclusion in project manual.
57. Initiate work on specifications and project manual.
58. Review documents with building department and other regulatory agencies as required.
59. Schedule a check of working drawings and specifications by an experienced person in the office who has not worked on the project.
60. Recheck drawings against building code search developed in the programming phase.
61. Have documents printed.
62. Monitor fees expended and conformance to schedule.
63. Review invoicing to client.
64. Review and approve consultant's billings.

Bidding or Negotiation

65. Prepare bid documents with client.
66. Prepare list of contractors if bid is by invitation.
67. Advertise for bids, if required, in local newspapers and trade publications.
68. Submit documents to local plan room.
69. Distribute bid packages to contractors—maintain distribution log and bid deposits.
70. Hold pre-bid conference.
71. Issue addenda.
72. Receive and tabulate bids.
73. Assist client in review of bids.
74. Write letter of thanks to unsuccessful bidders.
75. Assist in contract negotiation if not a bid job.
76. Monitor fees expended and conformance to schedule.
77. Review invoicing to client.

Contract Administration

78. Verify that owner has received required performance bonds and labor and material payment bonds.
79. Verify that contractor issue certificates of insurance to client.
80. Hold pre-construction conference.
81. Set up schedule of weekly construction meetings with contractor, consultants, subcontractors, and client.
82. Establish site visit schedule based on contract requirements.
83. Review work tasks with construction administration coordinator if this job is not done by the project manager.
84. Review shop drawings and samples and keep shop drawing log—maintain reasonable turn-around time through consultant's offices.

85. Receive construction schedule from contractor.
86. Review delivery schedules of furniture and accessories if project is an interior design job.
87. Conduct regular site visits and make comprehensive field reports on each visit.
88. Issue change orders as required.
89. Issue field orders as required.
90. Receive field reports from consultants and forward copy to client.
91. Attend weekly job meetings.
92. Review test reports and forward to client.
93. Monitor progress against construction schedule and notify client of any problems.
94. Review and process certificates and applications for payment.
95. Conduct punch list with contractor and client.
96. Verify correction of punch list items.
97. Issue certificate of substantial completion.
98. Verify issuance of certificate of occupancy.
99. Maintain all documentation of this phase.
100. Monitor fees expended and conformance to schedule.
101. Review invoicing to client.
102. Review and approve consultant's billings.

Project Close-out and Follow-up

103. Verify that all operating instructions, guarantees, maintenance procedures, etc. are forwarded to client.
104. Verify owner has received all lien waivers.
105. Process final application and certificate for payment.
106. Assist with move-in if project is an interior job.
107. Prepare maintenance manual for client if an interiors job.
108. Respond to owner's questions and problems during "shake-down" period immediately after move-in.
109. Send gift to client for open house.
110. Compile information on fees and construction costs for in-house records.
111. Have project photographed.
112. Hold in-house review of project.
113. Evaluate consultant performance for future work.
114. Complete job history for office records and marketing staff.
115. Maintain contact with client for at least one year after move-in to review problems, maintenance, expansion ideas and other potential work.

Project Data Filing and Records Management

For efficient project management as well as productive office management, a system of classifying, storing, retrieving and utilizing the thousands of pieces of paper passing through a design office is essential. Most offices, even some of the giants, are buried under this mountain of paper. The results are inaccessible documentation of important decisions and information, wasted time in filing and retrieving records, lost opportunities for making use of historical data, and the inability to find support material when legal or billing problems arise.

Project filing should be an integral part of an overall records management system. Figure 9-6 illustrates this relationship. As a record is generated in the office or comes in from an outside source it can generally be classified into one of three groups: accounting, general office, or project-related. The project management notebook duplicates some of the project files for the convenience and use of the project manager. As information in accounting and the project files is used and reformed, some of it will be transferred to the general office files. Technical evaluations and fee histories, for example, on one particular job should be added to the office pool of information for future use and not be buried with the project file when it is put in storage.

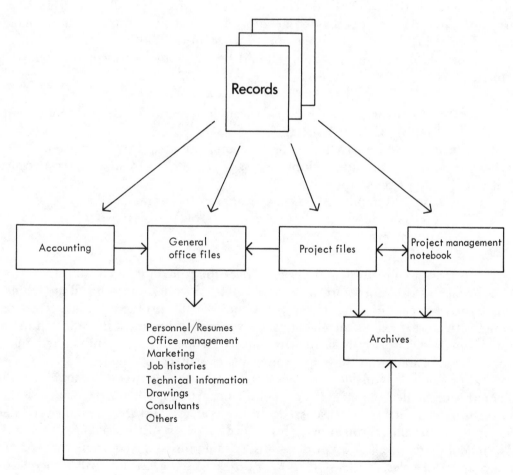

Figure 9-6
Records Management Structure

Some of the difficulties with records management and project filing in design offices are caused by the following:

- The variety of physical types of records from financial information to large drawings.
- The various people who need to access the records.
- The fact that many individual documents contain information on several different subjects.
- Inconsistency in format of records.
- Lack of a clearly stated, uniform classification system.
- Variations in interpretation of what a filing category may mean or how to classify a particular record.

Some of these problems can be partially solved by delegating the responsibility of maintaining records to one person. However, there are problems with such an approach: that work position may be filled by several people due to employee turnover, emergency access may be needed when that person is sick, and smaller offices cannot justify a separate position to perform the job.

Instead, an organized system should be developed to meet the following criteria.

1. It should assure retrieval of the required record or all pertinent records if more than one is needed.
2. It should be easy to use and minimize time and cost required.
3. It should provide multiple access points such as by subject, date, record type or person involved.
4. It should minimize the space required for storage.
5. It should allow the "reconstruction" of a project when required for legal or evaluation purposes.

In most architectural and design offices the functions of classification, storage, and access of records are usually combined in one area—the filing cabinet. This basic approach in itself accounts for most of the problems. The record determines to a great extent the classification which, in turn, must be reflected in the storage method. Both of these then require someone trying to find something to access the information in the same way it was classified and filed.

For example, consider the minutes of a meeting between the architect, the client, the mechanical engineer and a building department official to resolve a design problem. Certain items are discussed, decisions made and the meeting recorded on a meeting minutes form. How is this record filed? An office may have a category for "meeting minutes," "design decisions," "building code requirements," or any of a number of titles. If it is put in one of these categories, how will someone on the production team find it for detailed information it may contain on changes to make for the mechanical system? How will accounting find it for back-up on possible additional billing for increased scope of work? If the design is found to be in violation of code requirements four months later, can the record be found to use as proof that a building official gave an earlier approval?

These are just a few of the problems all designers have encountered at one time or another in trying to file and retrieve records. In spite of these recurring difficulties most offices make little progress in improving the situation.

The first step in solving the problem is understanding how records can be classified. In the professional design office they can be filed in several different ways.

1. By record type such as transmittals, letters, contracts, budgets and the like.
2. By subject such as programming information, specification data, roofing products, etc.
3. By date, usually the most recent first.
4. By phase of service such as schematic design, contract documents, bidding, and contract administration. These are usually subdivided into record types or by subject.
5. By people involved, although this is seldom used.
6. By an identification number assigned to each document. This is also seldom used in design offices.
7. By some combination of the above.

Most offices use some combination of record type, subject, and phase of service. If a chronological record is needed, a copy is made and placed in a separate file. The most prevalent problem is that a mixture of subject and record type usually results in problems similar to the one discussed above. Is a letter outlining the solutions to a roofing problem filed with correspondence during the design development phase, with design decisions, or with product information on building systems? When someone eles needs the record later, where do they look for it? What interpretations do they place on the information and how it is probably filed?

No one system is right for every office. The method best suited for your office will depend on the kind of work you do, the size of your firm, the amount of money you want to spend, and the priorities you place on having easy, accurate access to your records. If yours is a medium-to-large-size firm you may want to hire a records management consultant to set up a system that is tailored to your office's operations and unique needs. The following five levels of records management can be used in a design firm. They are listed in increasing order of sophistication. Determine which is right for you and start making the necessary reorganization to your project filing system and your office files. You can consider starting at one level and progressing up as you need to.

LEVEL 1

Classification, storage, and retrieval are all the same. This is the standard system used by most design offices and usually the most disorganized. Each document is placed in a labeled file folder according to some "master list" of labels. If a different indexing is needed, a copy of the document is made and placed in a separate file drawer in a different order. A work authorization for extra compensation, for example, may be placed with the project files and a copy given to accounting for their files indexed by project number.

This system takes up the most space, is usually the most inaccurate and requires the most time to use. Its advantages are that it is quick to set up and low in *initial* cost.

LEVEL 2

This is the same as Level 1, but with tab coding and other refinements to the physical filing system. Various commercial products are available that utilize colored tab systems with numbers and letters that make it possible to add a limited second level of indexing on the primary set of files. For instance, records could be filed according to subject with colored or numbered tabs placed along the edge to identify the document as being a particular record type. For instance, a quick glance would tell the searcher what records within the entire file were transmittals if the searcher was looking for documentation that something had been sent.

This system eliminates the need for duplicating records if the secondary access method required is not too complicated. Tabbing documents and file folders this way is laborious and requires more clerical time.

LEVEL 3

Only one record is stored in a given order with additional indexes being maintained on $3'' \times 5''$ cards. This is the standard library card catalog approach, but very useful if multiple access points are needed at a relatively low cost. As with a library, each record can be filed according to some classification system, but also needs a unique identifying number that can be used on the cards and the record for quick searching.

With this system, project files could be arranged according to phase of service and record type for the majority of day-to-day reference. A card file could be set up by subject matter so that if the roof leaked a week after move-in, all the records for the entire job that pertained to roofing could quickly and accurately be retrieved to examine how the problem developed and possibly to serve as legal defense.

LEVEL 4

This is the same as Level 3 in concept, but uses a microcomputer to provide the classification and indexing records. File management systems for micros are plentiful and simple to set up. Any office that already has a computer for other tasks can probably get a program to do this job as well. The actual storage system becomes less of a concern with a computerized system since multiple indexes are easy to maintain. As long as each record is uniquely identified with a number it can be filed according to that number. The document search is made on the computer and the numbered record then retrieved.

LEVEL 5

This is the most advanced system to date for both text and pictorial records management. It carries Level 4 one step further and substitutes storage of microfilmed records for the actual document. As records are generated, they are microfilmed and indexed by computer. When a document is needed, the required index is used. The roll and frame number of the microfilm are identified and brought up on a viewing screen. If required, a hard copy can be made.

This system is probably not needed by the majority of design firms today, but with the increasing amount of information that must be managed, rising costs for office space, and decreasing costs for the equipment, it will be used more in the years ahead.

If you are starting a new project filing system or reorganizing an existing one based on one of the first three levels discussed above, check your filing categories against the following list. Add or modify as required to suit your needs, but try to keep the number of divisions to a minimum. In the following list, try to limit yourself to the first subdivision under each phase. Use the second subdivision only if the job is very large. Too many slots for project information simply make it more difficult to classify each record and figure out where to retrieve it later.

Project Filing Categories

1.0 General administration
  1.1 Initial correspondence and meetings
  1.2 Filing index for job
  1.3 Project directory
  1.4 Contracts

  1.4.1 Owner-Architect
  1.4.2 Architect-Consultant agreements
  1.4.3 Supplemental work authorizations
  1.4.4 Construction contract
  1.4.5 Owner leases and work letters

1.5 Fees

    1.5.1 Fee projections and allocations
    1.5.2 Financial management reports
    1.5.3 Invoices
    1.5.4 Time sheets
    1.5.5 Consultant invoices

1.6 Schedules
1.7 Cost budgets and cost information
1.8 Marketing

    1.8.1 Copies of marketing reports
    1.8.2 Reprints, clippings, publicity
    1.8.3 Future client needs

1.9 Client information

2.0 Programming and pre-design

2.1 General correspondence/meeting notes
2.2 Programming information

    2.2.1 Questionnaires
    2.2.2 Existing facility survey
    2.2.3 Program document
    2.2.4 Special equipment needs
    2.2.5 Goal statements for design
    2.2.6 Owner-furnished data

2.3 Feasibility studies/economic analysis
2.4 Lease analysis
2.5 Regulatory agency requirements

    2.5.1 Code and zoning searches
    2.5.2 Submittal and approval log

2.6 Utility and soils information
2.7 Regulatory agency requirements

3.0 Schematic design and design development

3.1 General correspondence/meeting notes
3.2 Design notes

    3.2.1 General concepts, sketches, notes
    3.2.2 Design standards
    3.2.3 Client input

3.3 Research information

    3.3.1 Building systems
    3.3.2 Products—analysis and selection

3.3.3 Behavioral research
3.3.4 Historical research

3.4 Furniture and accessories
3.5 Outline specifications
3.6 Consultant information

3.6.1 Structural
3.6.2 Mechanical
3.6.3 Electrical
3.6.4 Other

4.0 Construction documents

4.1 General correspondence/meeting notes
4.2 Drawings
4.3 Project manual

4.3.1 Bidding and contract requirements
4.3.2 General and supplemental conditions
4.3.3 Technical specification sections

4.4 Consultant information

4.4.1 Structural
4.4.2 Mechanical
4.4.3 Electrical
4.4.4 Other

4.5 Furniture and accessories specifications

5.0 Bidding or negotiation

5.1 General correspondence/meeting notes
5.2 Addenda and approvals
5.3 Bids

5.3.1 Submitted bids
5.3.2 Bid tabulation and evaluation
5.3.3 Bid bonds
5.3.4 Bidding document deposits

5.4 Certificates of insurance and bonds
5.5 Furniture bids and quotes

6.0 Contract administration

6.1 General correspondence/meeting notes

6.1.1 Architect-contractor
6.1.2 Architect-owner
6.1.3 Architect-consultant
6.1.4 Other

Meeting Notes

Documentation of all meetings is vital to a properly managed project. The human memory is short and usually inaccurate. Trying to reconstruct what happened in the past from remembered events will only lead to disagreements. Minutes of every meeting should be taken and distributed to the participants. These minutes will serve to improve communication, avoid misunderstandings, and provide a written record should disputes or legal problems arise.

The best technique for taking meeting minutes is to have a preprinted form. There should be a place for the project name and number, date, place of the meeting, time, people attending and the subjects covered. You may also want a column for follow-up: who is to do a task and by what date.

Taking good notes requires a little practice. You must be complete, accurate, unbiased, and to the point. The document may have legal implications later on. Immediately after the meeting, have the notes typed up and distributed to all people attending as well as to the client and other necessary people on the project team if they did not attend but need to know what happened. At the end of the form include a statement such as "If there are any additions or corrections to these minutes, please notify this office within five days." This gives everyone a chance to set the record straight when it is fresh in their minds and is protection against someone's disagreeing later on when it may be to his advantage to do so.

Telephone Log

Telephone conversations also can become sources of misunderstandings. Recording telephone calls is a tedious task, especially when a project is at its peak of activity. With a little self-discipline and preprinted forms, however, it is possible to do so and it adds a great deal to project documentation and communication.

Each member of the project team should have his own forms next to the telephone with a place for date, person talked with, subject, and decision reached, if any. A single date can be entered at the beginning of the day and only last names used to simplify the recording. One or two words to state the subject and a brief description of the conversation are all that is needed to complete the record. Long conversations, of course, will require some effort but most can be handled in a line or two. An added benefit is that this procedure focuses your attention on how much of a typical phone call is really productive and how much is a waste of your time. It may turn out that you will be talking less and freeing up more time for other tasks.

Project Perfection Syndrome

In their efforts to complete a job or some portion of it the project team spends time working toward some established or idealized level of quality. Initially, time expended results in a rapid progression toward this goal. As the job is worked on and refined, however, more and more time is required to get closer to this "perfect" level of quality. This is illustrated schematically in Figure 9-7. There is a point at which a great deal of additional time (and therefore fees) is required to make marginal progress toward "perfection." The desire to do so is the "excess perfection syndrome." In the diagram, for example, an increase of 10 percent in project perfection from 80 percent to 90 percent requires half again as much time as was expended to reach the 80 percent level.

The question for the project manager is whether the additional time and money are justified. If fees are available and the time had been originally planned for, it may be a simple decision to proceed. If fees have been spent or are close to running out and more work should be done but may not absolutely *have* to be done, the choice is more difficult. A joint decision by the project manager, project designer, firm principals and others would have to be made.

The most common situation with the project perfection syndrome occurs when contractual and office quality standards have been met, but the designers or

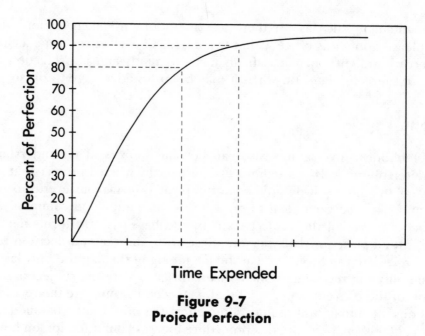

Figure 9-7
Project Perfection

production staff want to keep changing and refining the design in an attempt to improve it. Although this is a natural tendency, if allowed to happen it can mean the difference between a profit and a loss on the job with no real improvement to show for the extra time expended.

Every office has its unique project perfection curve similar to the one shown in Figure 9-7. Its form depends on the skill and talent of the people involved and how efficiently design and production are managed. For some the curve may not level out so quickly; for others it may not rise so steeply in the initial stages of work. The project manager must know the special characteristics of the office's project perfection curve and be prepared to judge how far to go before stopping work.

DEVELOPING THE ART OF TEAM COORDINATION

Project management is fundamentally people-oriented. Its ultimate success depends on the project manager's ability to understand interpersonal relationships within the context of a business environment and apply this knowledge to all of the people involved with the project. All of the techniques, forms, and procedures in the world are of limited value if this human aspect is not respected. Of course, people being the complex creatures they are makes this the most complex and difficult part of project management. Volumes have been written on the subject and research continues to expand knowledge of the art and science of management. The following list highlights some of the actions you can take as a project manager to add the necessary personal dimension to your everyday direction of team coordination.

1. Since communication is one of the most important aspects of project management be aware that there are four basic kinds of communication in a design office: work assignments, instructional, reward and punishment, and social. For the greatest impact, deal with each separately. For example, chatting with a draftsman about yesterday's football game and then mentioning that he is doing a good job does not have the same emphasis and effect as telling him directly that he is valuable to the team, that his efforts are appreciated, and so on. A single purpose message is more likely to be communicated.

2. Always clarify your expectations of people on the project team. Make sure they know exactly what you want, when you want it and at what level of detail or quality. Telling an engineering consultant to "look into" a problem is too ambiguous—you will have to be prepared to get something that might not be useful to you. Instead, define the problem, outline some of your thoughts, tell him or her you want a specific number of different concept approaches, specify a time limit, and suggest an approximate maximum fee limit. Do the same for in-house staff. Outline the task, time allowed and results expected.

3. Never give responsibility without the appropriate amount of authority to make decisions and carry out actions. The two must work together.

4. Be sensitive to the manager-subordinate relationship. Recognize how the different points of view may affect work output. The subordinate may be concerned with moving up in the organization, wanting due credit for his or her efforts on the project, protecting position, wondering what kind of job he is doing and whether the manager is a partner or a competitor. The manager may be wondering if the subordinate wants his job, if the manager's work is as important as the subordinate's, and how to advance himself in the organization. These various points of view will affect communication, work assignments, quality of work, and general enthusiasm for the project. The effective project manager must recognize these feelings and work within their limitations or take steps to minimize their negative effects.

5. Provide for ways staff members can grow and advance. Some of these opportunities may be determined by office policy and general personnel practices, but on the project management level, each person can be challenged with work assignments and encouraged to expand his or her knowledge and skill levels.

6. Every person needs to be stroked. Provide recognition when it is due and encourage self-esteem. When praise is given, do it publicly.

7. Evaluate performance of the staff members on the project team. People like to know what kind of jobs they are doing, so this evaluation should be on a continuing basis, not the formal six-month office evaluation. If criticism is needed,

do it constructively; suggest techniques for improvement and offer to help if required. Remember, too, when criticism is given, do it privately.

8. Encourage general discussions of the broad issues involved in a project at appropriate times. It is too easy for everyone to get so involved in the pressures of completing a job that the overall view is lost. Take time at in-house seminars, retreats, or social gatherings to review what everyone is doing, why, and ways to improve.

9. Do not be alarmed when people get angry. All of us do it and it is a necessary part of living. Don't let it be negative, however; make it work for you. A good project manager will recognize anger as a signal of something significant, not just a personality trait of some hothead. The manager should analyze the anger, what may be causing it and work with the person to solve the problem the anger represents—not simply dismiss it or get angry in return. It may be pointing out a problem on the project that would not come to the surface any other way until it was too late.

10. Commit yourself to resolve conflicts as they occur. The natural tendency for most people is to avoid a problem and hope it will go away. It seldom does; it usually just gets worse. Solve the problem as soon as possible.

11. Open up communication among the project team. This must start at the top. Keep everyone informed of job progress, problems, schedules, goals and general status. Encourage participation in decision making to the extent possible and listen to gripes and suggestions on ways the project can be improved.

12. Recognize that most clients want to be involved with the design of their building or space in some way. Don't adopt the attitude that the design team knows best and shut the client out. Direct the client's interests in the areas where it will do the most good. Some clients are more analytical and are interested in defining the needs of their organization (programming) while some focus only on the broad view. For these clients more involvement in design reviews and presentations may be appropriate. Do not expect much client interest in evaluating mechanical systems if what they really want to do is select colors.

13. Bring in consultants at the earliest possible time. As with everyone, consultants like to feel they are an integral part of the team and not just an afterthought. Their early input will prove valuable in developing design concepts and avoiding misdirected design efforts. A few basic assumptions laid out by the mechanical engineer, for example, may save weeks of design time exploring an inappropriate scheme.

14. Establish an environment in which initiative will be encouraged. Design is a creative business and an atmosphere that stifles fresh thinking and a willingness to explore is simply counterproductive. The project manager is in the best position on a day-to-day basis to perform this function. The results will be better morale and a better project.

THE FORGOTTEN INGREDIENT—FOLLOW-UP

A job should never be over when the client moves in. Changing buildings or spaces is a difficult experience for a client since both operational processes and personnel must adapt to a new situation. Even if the new building is much better than the old one, people find it hard to make changes and get used to a new environment. Problems and complaints will be common during the first few weeks of occupancy. The architect or designer should be available to assist with minor problems: having the contractor correct any defects which were not caught on the punch list, advising on minor adjustments to furniture, building controls, and the like, explaining maintenance procedures, and generally answering questions of the occupants.

Maintaining a strong follow-up program has several advantages for the design firm:

1. Helping a client through this difficult period creates a good impression of the firm. Satisfied clients are good references and one of the most important components of any firm's marketing program.
2. Continuing follow-up makes it possible to maintain contacts within the client's organization for future business development, either for expansion of the client's space or for referrals to other organizations.
3. Follow-up provides the opportunity for in-use evaluation of a completed design. The knowledge gained should be recycled for future projects to continually upgrade the quality of your firm's service.

In addition to closing out project files, contracts and other administrative matters, the follow-up tasks should include the following:

1. After the move-in, set up regular meetings with the client during the "shake-down" period. They may be several times a week initially if the project is a large one or once a week if the project is small. At these meetings, questions should be answered, problems discussed, and action plans set up for any additional work that is needed. These meetings may last for several weeks and should be budgeted for by the project manager in his or her initial fee allocations.

2. Make sure that the client has a manual of all operating instructions, maintenance procedures, guarantees, names and phone numbers of people to call for help with major building components, where to reorder expendable items, and similar schedules. The contractor should be responsible for a majority of these items, but you are in a better position to compile all of it in an organized, easy-to-use manual. Give two sets to your client and keep one for your records.

3. Send the client copies of the professional photographs you have taken of the building or interiors.

4. Establish brief monthly or bi-monthly meetings with the client for long-term follow-up. These may run for six months or more depending on the complexity of the job and the needs of the client. At the meetings you may want to discuss maintenance problems, use of the building or interior as originally designed, general problem areas, mechanical system operation, defects covered by guarantees, and additional design work involving expansion or modification to the building.

Establishing a rigorous follow-up program for all clients as a matter of office policy will pay big dividends in the long run. It should be as much a part of project management procedures as monitoring fee expenditures or attending job meetings.

SOURCES FOR MORE INFORMATION

Books

Antill, James M., and Woodhead, Ronald W. *Critical Path Methods in Construction Practice*, 3rd. Ed. New York: John Wiley & Sons, 1982.

Dellinger, Susan, and Deane, Barbara. *Communicating Effectively: A Complete Guide for Better Managing.* Radnor, PA: Chilton Book Co., 1980.

Gill, Suzanne L. *File Management and Information Retrieval Systems.* Littleton, CO: Libraries Unlimited, 1981.

Haviland, David. *Managing Architectural Projects: Case Studies.* Washington: The American Institute of Architects, 1981.

Haviland, David. *Managing Architectural Projects: The Effective Project Manager.* Washington: The American Institute of Architects, 1981.

Haviland, David. *Managing Architectural Projects: The Process.* Washington: The American Institute of Architects, 1981.

Kerzner, Harold. *Project Management: A Systems Approach to Planning, Scheduling and Controlling.* New York: Van Nostrand Reinhold, 1979.

Stasiowski, Frank, Ed. *Project Scheduling and Budgeting.* Professional Services Management Journal, 126 Harvard Street, Brookline, MA 02146.

Stuckenbruck, Linn C., Ed. *The Implementation of Project Management: The Professional's Handbook.* Reading, MA: Addison-Wesley Publishing Company, 1981.

Reports and Manuals

Project Management. Professional Services Management Journal, 1978, 126 Harvard Street, Brookline MA 02146.

Means Scheduling Manual. R.S. Means Co, Inc., 501 Construction Plaza, Kingston, MA 02364.

Seminars and Workshops Contact each for current schedule and topics

PSMJ Seminars, 126 Harvard Street, Brookline MA 02146.

Professional Services Management Association, 1700 East Dyer Road, Suite 165, Santa Ana, CA 92705.

American Institute of Architects, 1735 New York Avenue N.W., Washington, DC 20006.

Center for Conferences and Management/Technical Programs, University of Colorado, Boulder, CO 80302.

Harvard Graduate School of Design/Continuing Education, Gund Hall, Cambridge, MA 02138.

Fred Pryor Seminars, 2000 Johnson Drive, Shawnee Mission, KS 66201.

Rensselaer Polytechnic Institute, School of Management, Troy, NY 12181.

University of Wisconsin Extension, Department of Engineering and Applied Science, 432 N. Lake Street, Madison, WI 53706.

American Management Association, 135 W. 50th Street, New York, NY 10020.

Guidelines, P.O. Box 456, Orinda, CA 94563. Guidelines also publishes five volumes of material specifically related to Project Management: *The Guidelines Working Drawing Planning and Management Manual, The Guidelines Master Notation and Keynote Manual, The Guidelines Predesign and Planning Manual, The Guidelines Project Management Task Module Manual,* and *The Guidelines Construction Administration Manual.*

Associations

Professional Services Management Association, 1700 E. Dyer Road, Suite 165, Santa Ana, CA 92705

Newsletters

Professional Services Management Journal, 126 Harvard Street, Brookline, MA 02146

The Guidelines Letter, Box 456, Orinda, CA 94563

CHAPTER 10
A Graphic Program That Pays Big Dividends

A WELL-DESIGNED GRAPHIC PROGRAM can strengthen and support your marketing effort and improve your in-house efficiency and productivity. Your graphic identity can be more than just something to look pretty; it can be a potent tool you can use in many areas of your practice. A properly planned graphic system can:

1. Visually communicate the philosophy of your firm to your clients.
2. Present a strong, visible identity to support your marketing efforts, distinct from your competition.
3. Improve the *communication* of your message to potential clients and others.
4. Give your firm a visual coherence and consistency.
5. Provide you with a framework in which to place new graphic items as they are developed as well as existing components of the system.
6. Organize and improve your internal office procedures and project documentation.
7. Streamline your production process.

The benefits that a graphic program can provide fall into two general categories. These are marketing efforts and in-house paper flow and working procedures.

Anything related to the image you want to project, your marketing message or "identity" must be *client* based. It must be planned to appeal to the market segment you want to attract and be designed based on your potential client's perceptions, not yours. Too often, an architectural firm will design in-house or lead a graphic designer toward a solution that appeals to the principals involved rather than what the market would want or expect. The final product may look great and be graphically correct, but solve the wrong problem.

The way in which the design is organized on paper used for in-house work should be based on the requirements of the *office*. Although this part of the design should be consistent in format (type face, color, mark design, proportions, etc.) with the rest of the graphic system, it serves a different purpose and needs to be designed accordingly. Forms, scheduling worksheets, and the like are examples that make up this part of the graphic system.

In order to establish a coherent graphic system that solves both marketing and in-house workflow problems while remaining consistent in format and design within the constraints of budget, time, and technology available in the printing industry a graphics specialist is required. Like all good design, it looks easy when it is finished but the process and knowledge required are complex. Any architect not trained and experienced in graphics can make a serious mistake thinking that he or she can do it and hand it over to a printer for implementation.

This chapter will discuss the various elements of a complete graphic system, tips on how to select a graphic design consultant, outline the process involved if you decide to undertake the implementation of a graphic identity program, including cost and phasing implications, and conclude with a case study highlighting a typical process.

HOW TO STRENGTHEN YOUR MARKETING WITH GRAPHICS

One of the primary goals of a professional service organization's graphic system is to help implement marketing strategies. What a design firm has to offer, how it is unique among the competition, what its philosophy is, in short, its "image," can be enhanced or damaged by the various visual means through which the firm represents itself to potential clients, others in the industry and to the general public.

A graphic design concept begins to emerge based on the initial elements of the marketing plan: goals, analysis of the firm, and market analysis. These were discussed in Chapter 2 and should be considered vital to the graphic design effort. With a clear understanding of these elements, you can identify the specific graphic items that your firm will need in order to complete its marketing objectives. These fall into three broad groups: those that state your qualifications and experience, those that support your primary marketing effort, and those that serve as secondary reinforcement to your image.

Qualifications/Experience Items

Brochure(s)
Job lists
Staff member resumes
Photograph files
Slides and slide show systems
Newspaper and magazine reprints

Primary Marketing Items

Proposals
Newsletters
Direct mail
Presentation packages
Office "scrapbook"
Project signs
Advertising
Project updates
Annual reports
Government qualification forms

Secondary Marketing Items

Announcements, invitations, Christmas cards
Office decoration, signs, plaques, nameplates, etc.
Hard hats
Vehicle identification
Posters
Calendars
Pencils/pads
T-shirts

Of course, not all firms will have all of these as part of their graphic system. The list illustrates the wide range of possible graphic tools an office can use as part of its marketing plan.

One of your first tasks when beginning to work with a graphic designer is to determine which of these items you will need as part of your program. If money is a problem, you may decide to develop those that are the most critical, such as a brochure, proposal format, job lists, and staff resumes within a master plan that will accommodate other parts of the system when they are needed and as your budget allows. However, the more items that carry your graphic image, the more memorable will be your firm in the marketplace. Visibility and repetition are important considerations.

Remember that whatever parts of the system you have, the graphic design must be uniformly applied and the overall message it communicates must be consistent with the image you want your publics to perceive. If you are starting small with just a few pieces such as a letterhead and brochure, make sure the entire system is designed before trying to place any one piece into it. This way it will be effective as other parts are added.

STREAMLINE IN-HOUSE PAPER FLOW

An often overlooked benefit of graphic design in the design professional's office is the potential improvement in operating efficiency. In this case, management decisions and procedures are closely related to graphic systems. Making a decision about how a particular task is to be organized (setting and monitoring project schedules, for example) is only part of the problem. It then needs to be implemented in a clear, organized, efficient way. A good graphic designer should be able to understand your office procedures and suggest ways to design forms and other graphic tools to manage and record the information you require.

Office systems can be divided into four major groups: business systems, forms, secondary items and construction documents. The following list indicates some of the possible components you can consider including in your program.

Business systems

Letterhead
Envelopes
Business cards
Mailing labels
Invoices
Checks
Large envelopes

Forms

Memos
Meeting notes
Time sheets
Transmittals
Purchase orders
Interview sheets for programming
Change orders
Work authorizations
Field reports
Field orders
Expense reports
Fee calculation worksheets
Project scheduling forms
Accounting forms
Shop drawing and sample log

Secondary items

Executive stationery
Employee manual
Pocket cards
Rubber stamps
Sample tags
In-house newsletter
Working drawing checklist
Other types of checklists

Employee interview form/Application for employment
Contractor qualification form
Consultant's qualification form
Proposal request
Other project forms
Project status reports
Engineering calculation pads
Telephone logs
Job histories
Library forms
Bid tabulation forms
Binders

Construction documents
Title blocks
Project manual format and binder covers
Standard detail file format
Sketch pads
Maintenance manual format and covers

Guidelines on Forms

Forms can be either time savers or time wasters. The primary purpose of forms in the professional office is to collect and record information required for administrative, management and legal purposes in the most accurate, efficient way possible. They should be designed to save staff time while encouraging the documentation of necessary data and serving as a tool in office and project administration.

Most forms turn out to be time wasters because they are poorly designed and not part of an overall management system. Too often, someone decides a form is needed and quickly lays one out for reproduction on the office copier or the local instant-print shop. After a period of time, more and more forms appear. There is no coordination, information is duplicated, some are unnecessary, and soon resentment builds among the employees that the office is being turned into a vast bureaucracy. Resentment eventually leads to haphazard use of the forms, or they are completely ignored. The information the forms were intended to collect becomes lost or at the very best, incomplete. For those forms that the client sees, consistency of image and visibility are also lost—a mistake from a marketing standpoint.

Standard forms, such as those published by the AIA, are often used as a quick, inexpensive way around these problems. A great deal of work is applied to designing and publishing such standard forms and they are useful for many situations and many firms. However, as with any "standard" form, they may not apply to a particular office's method of working. It is also impossible for them to be consistent with a firm's graphic image. While this is not crucial for many of the purely in-house forms never seen by the client, a graphic program is most successful when *all* graphic images the client sees are consistent. A transmittal form sent to the client becomes an important adjunct to the brochure, letterhead and all other identity devices that graphically portray the firm.

Every office needs to carefully assess its form requirements in relation to both its management methods and its graphic image. In making this assessment, ask yourself the following questions.

1. What process is used to complete a particular task or satisfy a management function? How do forms help (or hinder) the process? Could a new or redesigned form improve the process?
2. Who needs the form? Why?
3. What information must the form contain?
4. Who originates the form?
5. How and when is the form referenced? By whom?
6. What is the final destination of the form? How is it filed?
7. Is the form completed manually, by typewriter, word processor or by computer?
8. Does it have legal implications?
9. Can several forms be combined into one?
10. Can the form be completed by one person in one writing?
11. Can the information be collected and stored electronically? Should it?
12. Does the client or a potential client see the form?
13. Is the form worth the cost of printing, filling out, handling, and storing?
14. How many forms of each type are required?
15. How will the form be bound and filed?

Form analysis and design is a management science in itself, but to get you started with improving your paper flow, list the forms you think you need to custom-design after considering the questions listed above. Use the outline in Figure 10-1 to summarize your analysis. Some of the standard content items needed in many architectural and design office forms are listed across the top of the chart. Use the blank spaces to add those you may need. As you check off the content items needed on your form list, a pattern will begin to emerge. Your graphic design consultant can use this as a guide for blocking out zones of data and maintaining visual consistency. This will make it easier to file and retrieve and thus save time and money.

As you review your existing forms and help develop new ones, keep these basics in mind:

1. Your name and graphic mark should be consistent on all forms.
2. Each form should have a title, clearly legible and stating what the form *is* or what it *does.*
3. Information requested should be arranged logically so that the person filling it out can start at the top and complete it without having to jump

	Signature line													
	"Page__of__pages"													
	Space for 3rd party approval													
	"Copies to"													
	Document sequence no.													
	Body (ruled lines)													
	Body (check boxes)													
	Body (no lines–blank)													
	"To" (addressee)													
	Employee number													
	Employee name													
	File number line													
	Date line													
	Job number													
	Job name													
Copies to														
Prepared by														
	Computer processed													
	Typed													
	Handwritten													
	Job communication													
	In-house form													
Form Title														

**Figure 10-1
Form Analysis Summary**

back and forth. Space for optional information should be placed after mandatory information.

4. Similar or identical information is best placed in a consistent location so that users of the forms always know where to look for particular data. For example, a consistent location for file numbers on all forms makes it easier and quicker for a file clerk.

5. Combine related information into "zones" on the form. This makes it easier to read and find the needed data. It also aids in completing and filing the form.

6. Consider spacing of lines. If the form is to be filled out by hand, provide enough room for usually large human writing. Machine-processed forms require their own spacing. Line spacing that does not match the office typewriter or word processor is frustrating, sloppy and results in wasted time.

7. Review the use of color to aid in identifying, sorting and filing the forms.

8. If possible, make the form as self-explanatory as possible so that new employees or people using the form for the first time will find it easier. Overall, you are more likely to get the kind of information you want if it is clear exactly what is needed without having to refer to a manual or to ask someone.

9. Captions should be small enough not to conflict with or compete with the information. You can place captions under the line, within a "box" where the information is to be placed, or in front of the blank line. Whatever system you choose, be consistent and place the caption so there is no confusion.

10. Keep lines, boxes, borders and other graphic "support" simple and unobtrusive. The essence of a form should be the information it helps collect, not the form itself. It is only a means to an end.

SELECTING A GRAPHIC DESIGN CONSULTANT

Selecting a graphic designer is very similar to the way most clients select an architect. Initial contacts are made through referrals, inquiries, or direct marketing approaches. If the designer contacted is interested, the process of interviewing, reviewing qualifications, and evaluating proposals is initiated, ultimately leading to the selection of one consultant. You can begin by asking other professionals for referrals, finding out who did work that you liked for others outside the profession, or requesting statements of qualification from all the graphic designers in your area if you are willing to review the amount of submittals you may receive. From the initial list you can eliminate many who obviously are not qualified. From this reduced list of possibilities, begin the final selection through interviewing.

The following are some of the considerations you should use in your selection of graphic designers.

1. *Experience.* Review their portfolios. Have they done the kind of work you need? Ask about the background of each piece they show you. How did it solve the client's problem? What were the constraints? If the designer is a free-lancer or new firm, what has been his or her experience with other firms and types of projects?

2. *Problem orientation.* Are they interested in solving *your* marketing and business problems or just designing a pretty mark? Do they have an understanding of the architectural profession and its requirements?

3. *Process.* How would the designers propose to proceed with the project? What is their design methodology?

4. *References.* What recent projects have they completed? Were they similar? Check with their client. Did the designer solve the problem? Did they know the market? Were they responsive to the client's needs? Did they work within the allotted time frame and within the budget? Did the designs bring results?

5. *Scheduling.* How do they schedule? What time frame would they estimate for your project? Good graphic design, like architectural design, takes time. Beware of anyone who estimates a time frame much shorter than other people you interview. What is their current workload and how would your job fit in?

6. *Their office.* What other project commitments do they have? What number and kind of staff do they have to accomplish your project?

7. *Fees.* How do they charge for their services? What is their billing method and cycle? How are expenses handled? Do they mark up printing charges? What are their hourly rates? You might ask for an estimate to do your job if it is defined enough. This is seldom the case, however, and the cost of doing your project depends on many variables, just as the fees required to design a building vary. One of the first tasks of the designer selected may be to assist you in defining a budget for your graphic program.

8. *Contract.* What kind of contract for services do they propose? What are some of the major provisions?

9. *Printing.* How do they work with printers? How do they propose selecting a printer? Are they experienced in buying print and other sub-vendor services?

THE GRAPHIC DESIGN PROCESS

The ideal graphic design process in developing material for an architectural, engineering, or interior design firm is quite similar to the architectural design process: the problem is defined (programming), concepts generated and evaluated, the "best" solution selected for refinement, and then implemented. From analysis through synthesis each step of the process becomes more refined and detailed, with intermediate check points during which the design can be reviewed and evaluated against the original goals and objectives. If these objectives are not being met, the design can be modified before too much time and money have been spent.

The client must be an active member of the team making the development of the system a top management priority. The client must provide input to define goals, budget, time frame and scope of work. Client involvement must continue in review sessions while the design is being completed and through final sign-off of the press proofs before actual printing.

If you have not been through the process of developing an extensive graphic program, be prepared for more work and soul-searching than you might have expected. In addition to the technical and creative expertise the graphic consultant brings to the project, he or she also should act as a gadfly, asking you to analyze your philosophies of practice, marketing style, aspirations, purposes, and dreams that affect how you do business and how you will ultimately represent your firm through the medium of graphics.

Each designer is unique and follows his own design process, but generally you should expect to see five major phases to a graphic program, regardless of scope: problem definition; conceptual design development; refinement/application; production; and implementation.

Problem Definition

Many of the issues previously discussed in conjunction with the marketing plan apply equally to a graphic program. Setting goals and analyzing both your own firm and your market are essential to setting the proper direction for a visual image. Review the questions listed in Chapter 2 again, this time thinking of the possible implications they might have for graphic design. In the initial meetings with the graphic designer, use the following programming checklist as a starting point for your discussions. Record your responses both for the designer's use and for your review as the program develops.

Graphic Design Programming Checklist

1. What is your philosophy of practice?
2. What are your goals for the firm? Personally? For employees?
3. What kind of work do you want to be known for?
4. What is your present "image" in the marketplace? Think about clients, other professionals, contractors, manufacturers' representatives, and the public at large.
5. What kind of image do you *want*?
6. Define what you are offering to your clients. Some examples are full-service, business-oriented, small, personal firm, low cost, fast service, one specialty, etc.

7. Analyze your firm name. Do you want it to reflect the reputation of one or two key people or should it indicate that your firm is a collection of qualified people? Is it easy to apply to the various graphic devices you will be using: letterhead, forms, hardhats, project signs, mailings, and so forth? Is it consistent with the image you want? The naming or renaming of your firm is one of the most difficult jobs you and your graphic consultant will have.

8. Look at what your competition is doing with graphics. Do you want to be similar or entirely different? How much are you going to have to do to stay even or surpass your competition?

9. Who is your market going to be? What kind of image and style are they accustomed to? What would appeal to them? Remember, you are designing your visual image more for your market than for your own whims.

10. How are you going to market your firm? What techniques are you planning on using? Personal contacts, cold calls, direct mail, advertising, presentations? Place them in order of priority. Although a well-designed graphic concept will be applicable to any form, a heavy emphasis in one area may suggest certain approaches over others. For example, a firm planning extensive advertising and direct mail that will reach a great number of people may need a compact, easily identified mark to establish instant recognition.

11. What geographical areas do you plan to work in? This will have implications for quantities of printed material as well as style.

12. Are there any project types and markets you *do not* want?

13. Is a change in address or phone number likely? How soon?

14. What is your present forms use? How many letters per month do you send out? Invoices, transmittals, change orders, and others? What is your expected growth in forms? Have this information tabulated for easy reference by your graphic designer.

15. Analyze your present *system* for using forms and other methods of paper flow. Where are the problem areas? Are some functions being duplicated? Will you be converting some paper work to electronic media in the near future? Where and how could a change in graphic format improve your operating efficiency?

16. What type of forms do you need? Single sheets, carbonless, computer printout?

17. Do you want a phased program for development of graphics?

18. How do you want printed material to coordinate with slide shows and other presentation techniques?

19. What is your time frame for developing a graphics program? Is it related to other events in your overall business plan?

20. What is your budget? If you do not have one, your graphic consultant can help you establish a realistic range.

Conceptual Design Development

Once you have defined your graphic design problem, the consultant is ready to begin studying ways of translating your needs into visual form. He or she will begin by exploring all possible ideas though the use of small, quick sketches called thumbnails. See Figure 10-2. This is visual thinking much like what an architect does when he sketches notes and forms on the backs of envelopes or tracing paper

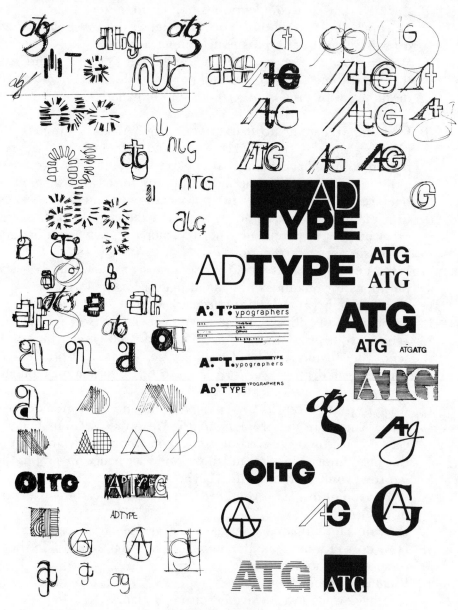

Figure 10-2
Thumbnail Sketches

for further study. You probably will not see the majority of thumbnails the designer tries. Those that offer the most potential for further development and seem to come closest to solving the problem are selected for further exploration. Then they are revised at a larger scale and in more detail for presentation to you. Depending on the designer and the scope of the program and your budget, these alternatives may be in sketch or finished mock-up form. The ideas can be discussed, evaluated against the original goals of the program, and one selected for complete refinement.

Refinement/Application

When one concept and direction has been decided, the graphic consultant will make refinements to achieve the best possible layout, proportions, color selection (if there is one), sizes; in short, everything that will appear in the final printed piece. He or she will also finalize how the design will be applied to the various parts of the system, such as letterheads, business cards, forms, report covers, brochures, signage, and anywhere else it is appropriate. Usually, the final product is an accurate, full-size mock-up of each part of the system including any special printing techniques such as embossing, die-cutting, or foil-stamping.

If photographs are being used and are available at this time, reproductions of them may be blocked in to give an accurate representation of how the finished design will look. At this point, type usually has not been set, but any text copy has been counted to determine approximately how much space it will occupy in the piece. These mock-ups will be presented to you for final review and signed approval before production. You can think of this step as being equivalent to the design development stage of an architectural design.

Production

After the mock-up, all that remains is the preparation of final, camera-ready art. At this stage, the graphic designer compiles all the final type-set copy, artwork, and photographs that will be part of the printed piece and puts then in a form that the printer can use to prepare printing plates. Printing specifications are also prepared, stating quantities, binding instructions, paper type and other pertinent data. See Figures 10-3 and 10-4.

Once the printer has prepared the plates, a blueline proof and/or color key will be made of each piece as a final check for alignment, "broken type," and other errors. Although this proof is essentially for the printer and graphic designer, you should also review them since it will be your last chance before printing. You are then responsible for any errors in spelling. Keep in mind, though, that this is *not* the time for making changes in design, text or layout unless you are willing to spend extra money—those kinds of changes should be made as the design proceeds and at the very latest, after seeing the final mock-up. You will probably also be requested to give your written approval of this proof before it goes to press.

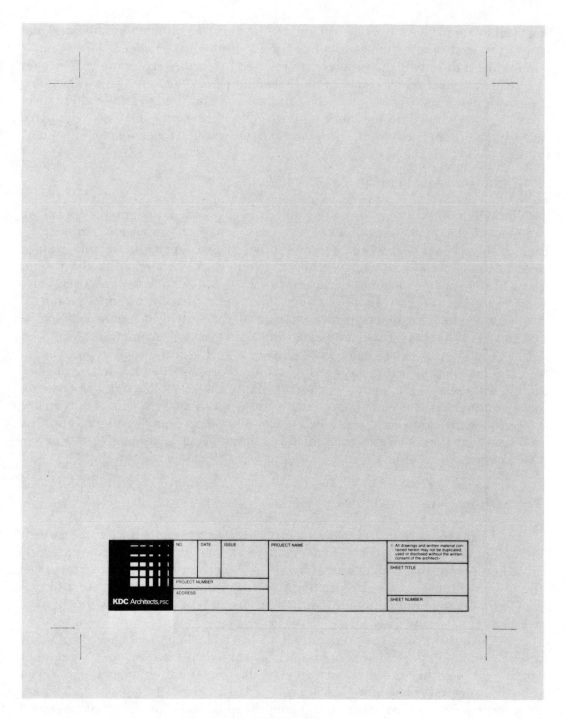

Figure 10-3
Camera-Ready Art

Printing Specifications

From: _____   Date: _____

Address: _____   Work Order No.: _____

Phone: _____

Description: _____

Quantity: _____

Size: _____

_____

Stock: _____

_____

Print: _____

_____

Inks: _____

Special: _____

Bindery: _____

_____

Delivery: _____

_____

_____

_____

_____

Samples: _____

Schedule: _____

☐ Request For Bid   Purchase Order _____

Agreed Price: _____   By: _____

Figure 10-4
Printing Specifications

Implementation

Printing and delivery are the fastest parts of the process. Depending on the quantities, binding, and special treatment such as die-cutting, you should have your work delivered in about ten days to two weeks after camera-ready art goes to the printer for one or two-color work. For four-color pieces it may take four to six weeks. When it arrives, check to see that you have the quantities and types of material you ordered. Check also for any errors in the printing itself. Most graphic designers should do this for you, however. Notify the graphic consultant and the printer immediately if any printing mistakes are discovered.

GRAPHIC DESIGN COSTS

Asking what a graphic design program will cost you is like one of your clients asking what a building costs. It depends on many variables. Remember, too, that just as with architecture, a high budget does not necessarily mean good design—that depends on the person doing the work and how creative he or she is in solving the problem within the given constraints.

Budgeting

Before you decide to undertake a new graphics program, try to establish at least a budget range within which you can operate. You may find that you will need to allocate anywhere from 10 percent to 20 percent of your total marketing budget for printing and graphic design fees. If you are a small firm and just developing a brochure, business system, and forms, the percentage may be much higher the first year. Your accountant should be able to offer advice on cash flow you will have available for a special program or how you can finance unusual first costs.

In preparing your budget, divide expected costs into three areas: graphic design consultant, printing, and in-house costs. Figure 10-5 shows one way of organizing this budget. Remember that the first try is rough and may only be a high-low range. As you begin to define the scope of your program, numbers can be revised.

Graphic consultant costs include professional fees and reimbursable expenses for out-of-pocket items such as typesetting, photostats, special art materials, long-distance telephone, travel, and similar costs directly related to your project. If your job requires it, photography may also be included in this category if it is coordinated by the consultant. If you are spending money on a brochure or other promotional piece, don't skimp on photography. A bad photograph can ruin an otherwise compelling and effective graphic piece. Find the best architectural photographer you can and have your projects shot in black and white and color negatives in a 4″ × 5″ format (do not accept any smaller format) and color transparencies in a standard 35mm slide format. Since the greatest cost of a photographer is his

Budget Items	Initial Estimate	Revision	Revision
Dates of estimates			
GRAPHIC CONSULTANT			
Fees			
Design			
Layout			
Production			
Print coordination			
Expenses			
Special photography			
Copywriting			
Sub-Total			
PRINTING			
Sub-Total			
IN-HOUSE COSTS			
Principal's involvement			
Marketing coordinator			
Sub-Total			
Total			

Figure 10-5
Graphic Program Budget Worksheet

or her time, spending a little extra money on film to get the three different formats is worth the cost. Once a shot is set up, changing film takes little time.

You may also find that you need help with words. Writing good, succinct, commanding copy for a brochure or other promotional piece requires an excellent grasp of the language, an understanding of style and grammar, and the ability to avoid professional jargon. You also want the words to be saying the same thing the graphic images are saying. It is difficult for an architect or other designer to write about his firm's work in an objective way. Hire a copywriter if you are having problems in this area or have your graphic designer suggest one.

Printing costs are self-explanatory. If you have not been through the process before, you may not be able to budget anything the first time around except perhaps for a maximum amount you feel you can spend. Once you retain a graphic consultant, you can establish at least an educated guess before the entire scope of work is known.

It is impossible to state standard rates for printing since there are so many variables. Printing costs are affected not only by the type, complexity, and quantity of the piece, but also by such things as local market conditions, suitability of the print shop for the job, and the competitive atmosphere in which the printer is quoting a job. Material prices, especially paper, fluctuate too, so any estimate is quickly out of date. Once the scope of the project begins to emerge, your consultant can help you balance all of the variables to arrive at the best possible solution within your budget.

Keeping Graphic Costs Low

If your budget is especially tight, but you still feel you need to initiate or upgrade a graphic program, consider the following tips. Remember that the creativity of the designer is more important than misdirected money lavished on the actual printing.

1. Design around standard paper sizes. Since paper is one of the big material cost factors in printing, use every bit of paper you have to buy without waste. $8\frac{1}{2}'' \times 11''$ is one standard modular size. If the same paper stock is being used for several pieces, one press run can be planned so that all pieces are printed on one large sheet of standard-sized paper and then trimmed out.

2. Design for the printing shops and equipment available in your area. Taking a small quantity, two-color job to a plant that specializes in large run, four-color printing will result in a hefty premium (if they take the job at all).

3. Get double duty out of what you do print. One large run of a cover can be used as a brochure cover, presentation folder, and proposal binder if it is designed with that thought in mind. For example, a large quantity of stock can be printed on one side that would be the same for all pieces. Only a portion of that quantity would then be turned over and printed on the other side for the brochure cover.

The presentation folder and proposal binder would be blank on the back side. This way, the larger printing run would result in lower unit costs.

4. Consider using inserts in brochures instead of a fixed binding. Not only is this more flexible, it is less costly to update and you save on expensive binding charges.

5. Instead of a brochure, print progressive reports on your projects, people, client list, and services. They can be combined to form a custom "brochure," issued with press releases, and used with a direct mail effort. This method also spreads out the cost of printing over a longer period of time to ease cash flow problems.

6. Do not feel you must use four-color printing for your photographs. There are many design and printing techniques available with a less expensive two-color process that can make your printing stand above the competition. Check with your graphic designer for possible ideas consistent with your needs.

CASE STUDY—KDC ARCHITECTS

The development of a graphic program for KCD Architects in Denver, Colorado, represents a typical process in designing a system for a medium-size architectural office. At the time the firm decided to revise their graphics, they were experiencing the growing pains of any newly organized business—building a client base, refining their business structure, constructing a sound financial foundation and honing their in-house production processes. Their graphic identity and corresponding printed pieces had simply "evolved" to solve the immediate problems as they arose. There was little consistency in print and viable marketing tools were practically non-existent.

At the time the graphic design program was begun several needs were identified:

1. A new graphic image was necessary to reflect the character and style of the firm as well as to respond to the expectations of the targeted client base. The firm wanted to project their emphasis on *process* (based on a comprehensive design system they had developed) and on *technology* exemplified by their use of computers, in-house engineering and other services. They also wanted to project a fairly conservative, efficient image for their primary client base of developers and business people.

2. A new name was desired. As with many young firms, the name had incorporated the full name of the principal who founded the office. As the firm was growing and adding new principals there needed to be less of an identification with any one person and more of an office identification.

3. There were two separate companies, one architectural/interiors and another that provided engineering services. Both needed unique iden-

tities because of different marketing needs, but the firm wanted some consistency in mark design and layout so the same forms and other graphic pieces could be used by both companies to reduce the cost of designing and printing entirely different base forms.

4. Cost and growth were both important concerns, so the system had to get the most out of a limited budget and be designed to accommodate planned additions to the system.

5. A flexible brochure was needed that would have immediate impact on clients using the completed projects available at the time the brochure was printed, but which could be expanded as new jobs were photographed.

Phase one of the project involved selecting a new name and new mark for both the architectural firm and the engineering firm. This was done after extensive review of the goals of the firm, the desired image they wanted to project, and how the graphic system would support their marketing efforts. Hundreds of names and marks were explored for each firm. At first, the engineering principals wanted a conservative image, reflecting their nature while the architectural principals wanted a more unique, "flashy" image, reflecting their interests.

It was finally decided, however, that just the opposite was needed. Since the architects marketed primarily to conservative business clients, it was decided to use that kind of simple, businesslike approach. The engineering firm, on the other hand, marketed a great deal to other architectural firms—clients who would respond to something less conservative. The marks were designed accordingly. Subsequently, the work for the engineering firm was postponed.

The architectural firm name was established as a simple, straightforward approach, one that would not become quickly dated, would make the transition from the old name easy, and be applicable to a variety of graphic pieces. The accompanying mark was selected as a simple, bold graphic image that reflected the technical, process-oriented structure of the firm's design methods. Additionally, it is utilized in different ways on other pieces as a basis for tabbing systems, column marks and the like (Figure 10-6). It is used in both a printed and embossed form.

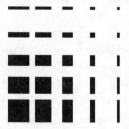

KDC Architects, PSC

Figure 10-6
Final Mark Design

The brochure was the key marketing tool to be developed. In order to keep costs as low as possible and provide for expansion, the contents of the brochure are spiral-bound but attached to the cover in such a way that when closed, the binding is not visible, providing an appearance not normally associated with binding of this kind (Figure 10-7). The cover itself was delivered separately with the three folds. As brochures are needed, they are assembled with an in-house binding machine. This not only allows brochures to be "custom made" but reduces the overall printing costs since the print shop does not have to do the folding or binding. Additionally, if a cover is needed with an inside pocket, the rightmost flap is simply cut off. This gives an attractive folder for proposals, press kits and reports.

An integral part of the brochure system was a design for a newsletter that will begin publication at a later time. The newsletter was designed to serve as a continuous marketing tool *and* a way to keep the brochure up to date. As projects are completed and photographed, they will be featured in the newsletter as a separate insert sheet. During printing of this insert sheet, the photograph and project description will be printed on one side. A quantity of these will be held for use as brochure update sheets. The remaining quantity of the press sheets will be turned over and printed on the back with whatever additional material is going in the newsletter. Both the brochure and newsletter are designed so that the entire package is compatible when assembled. The same graphic piece gets double duty and better use is made of the marketing dollar.

Figure 10-7
KDC Architects Brochure

Forms, stationery and other components of the graphic system are designed to be consistent, so that a strong image is established in the minds of existing clients as well as new business prospects (Figure 10-8). As need and budget allow, additional pieces of the system can be added easily and without disruption.

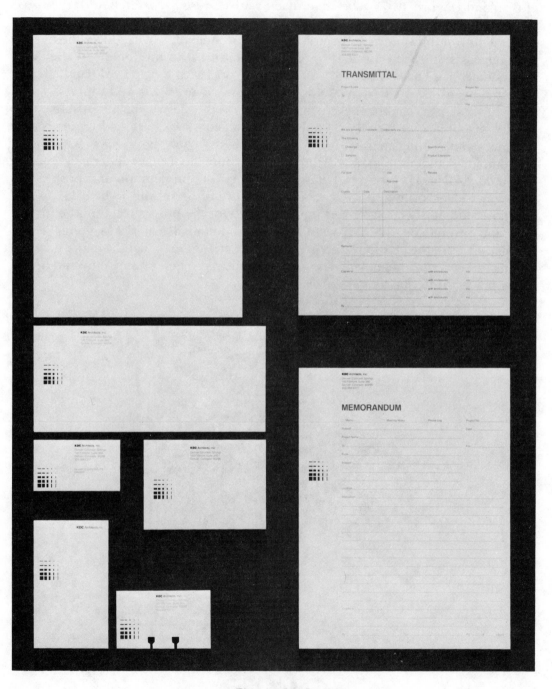

Figure 10-8
KDC Architects Graphic System

CHAPTER 11

Research and Information Management

In 1982, SWEET'S CATALOG, THE COLLECTIVE "BIBLE" of the architectural products industry, listed an estimated 10,000 products from 2,000 different manufacturers. In all, the 1982 Sweet's contained 44,000 pages, but still is nowhere near listing all the potential materials and products that are available today.

Spec-Data®/II, a joint effort by the Construction Specifications Institute and Information Handling Services that offers product information on microfilm, listed over 740,000 pages from 5,500 manufacturers in their 1982 collection. Spec-Data®/II is updated every sixty days to keep pace with the building products industry.

The American Institute of Architects library catalogues approximately 1,500 titles of books, reports and other items each year. Over 200 periodicals are published that offer relevant information to various parts of the design and construction industry in the United States alone.

Professional and trade associations number in the hundreds. These range from the very broad-based support organizations like the AIA to very specific groups like the Building Waterproofer's Association.

These statistics illustrate the staggering proportions of available data related to the architectural profession—part of the late twentieth century "information explosion" we hear so much about. In addition, there are university research groups, specialized libraries, consultants, directories, indexes and, more recently, computer data bases that offer an almost incomprehensible amount of information that changes and grows each day.

Generally speaking, the problems of research related to the design and construction process occur because of the fragmented and diverse nature of the industry and the wide variety of information needs of architects and designers. Each segment of the industry (manufacturers, contractors, code groups, etc.) has its own particular interests and develops its own data in a form that is best suited for that particular segment. Sometimes the results are usable and well-received by the architectural profession. The classic examples of this are Sweet's catalogues—they are conveniently packaged, fairly comprehensive, updated regularly, and generally contain information in a usable form.

In other cases, what may be valuable is effectively lost to architects. For example, many worthwhile government-sponsored research project reports are too lengthy, not graphic enough for architects, or are not publicized in the usual architectural channels, so they go unnoticed.

Figure 11-1 illustrates the complexity of many of the sources and the diversity of information needs of the architectural profession they must meet.

To date, no one information source or organization has been able to provide access to all the possible sources to meet all the research and information needs of the architectural profession. For the practicing architect this is a frustrating situation, at best. Faced with the pressures of running an office and producing work profitably, architects generally turn to the convenient, familiar, and low-cost approaches. Recent studies have indicated that the professionals rely on traditional means such as trade magazines, telephone and personal contact with representatives, personal advice from colleagues, books and reference material in the office, and personal observations for most of their information, even when other sources may be more appropriate.

It is clear that practicing architects are going to have to do a better job of research and information management. Here are some of the challenges we face.

1. The complexity of building problems today demands better information. In order to keep pace with the industry and rapidly changing technology the architect must improve his or her access to appropriate information.

2. Increasing liability claims against architects demand that they practice at least with the degree of skill and judgment that can reasonably be expected from other professionals placed in the same position and that they not be negligent (unaware of current standards of practice). When new products or building techniques are tried, it is even more imperative that accurate, comprehensive information be brought to bear on the design problem at hand.

3. Better research and information management are needed to preserve and expand the profession. The marketplace is continually demanding better delivery of services at the lowest possible cost. Architects who do not keep up to date with technologies and methods will find themselves left far behind. The homebuilding industry, for example, offers the majority of planning and design services for single-family housing completely outside the mainstream of standard architectural services because it can deliver the product faster and at less cost than the architectural profession.

4. In order to remain competitive, architects need to apply the best, most current information to the delivery of design services. Professionals who cannot do this will find their clients knocking at some other architect's door.

INFORMATION SOURCES

INFORMATION AND RESEARCH NEEDS	Magazines	Newsletters	Books	Product catalogues	Libraries	Trade associations	Government agencies	Sales representatives	Professional colleagues	Conferences/Seminars	Private information vendors	University research groups	Code and standards groups	Testing laboratories	Directories/indexes	Computer data bases	Professional consultants	Personal observation
Business activity	●	●				●	●		●		●				●	●	●	●
Marketing techniques	●	●	●						●	●							●	
Space and equipment data	●		●	●				●					●					
Programming procedures	●		●		●				●	●							●	●
Project financing evaluation	●		●						●						●	●	●	
Building products and systems	●		●	●		●	●	●	●	●	●		●	●	●	●		●
Cost data	●	●	●	●		●			●	●	●				●	●	●	●
Life cycle costing	●		●		●		●				●						●	
Zoning and building codes		●					●						●	●				
Energy conservation	●	●	●	●	●	●	●		●	●	●	●	●		●	●	●	●
Alternative energy sources	●	●	●	●	●	●	●		●	●	●	●			●	●	●	●
Fire and life safety	●		●				●				●		●	●	●	●	●	
Contractor qualifications						●		●	●						●			●
Consultant contacts						●		●	●	●					●		●	●
Statutory regulations	●	●	●				●			●	●		●	●			●	
Association standards	●	●		●		●					●		●	●	●	●		●
Specifications	●		●	●	●	●	●	●			●	●	●	●			●	●
Working drawing production	●	●	●						●	●								●
Construction detailing	●		●	●		●			●	●							●	●
Environmental psychology	●	●	●		●	●			●	●		●			●	●	●	●
Post occupancy evaluation	●		●		●	●			●				●		●	●	●	●
Office and project management	●	●	●			●			●	●					●	●	●	●
Information management	●		●		●	●						●					●	●
Computer use	●	●	●			●	●	●	●		●	●			●	●	●	
Office equipment	●			●		●		●	●		●				●			●

Figure 11-1
Information Needs and Sources

Faced with these challenges and the complexity of research and information management, the practicing architect needs to take two steps: 1) develop and improve in-house facilities and methods for research and, 2) develop contacts and working relationships with outside research consultants when specialized or extensive information gathering is needed.

This chapter will discuss some steps you can take to improve your office's research and information management capabilities and ways other firms have approached the problem. Also included are valuable source lists to show you where to go for more information for your own particular needs.

ACCESSING INFORMATION: IN-HOUSE FACILITIES

Before you can evaluate your current research processes and develop a plan for improving them, you need to define whether your needs are for data, information, research, or some combination of all three. For the purposes of research and information management related to architectural practice, I will use the following definitions.

Data: Organized or unorganized facts that may exist singularly, or in groups, that usually mean very little by themselves. Data may be numbers, words or graphic symbols.

Information: Organized data creating a concept in such a way that the data are applicable to one or more problems.

Research: The process of collecting, analyzing and organizing timely data and information to apply to a particular problem solution or knowledge field.

An example will illustrate the distinctions. The building code requirement for the handrail height is a given "fact." In the Uniform Building Code this piece of "data" is given in the form of words and numbers and exists as a range of from 30″ to 34″. The data are organized within the chapter on stairs, exits and occupant loads. This particular piece of data by itself does not mean much. Knowing only this fact is not enough to allow you to design a stairway that meets the code. However, if all you need for detailing is this fact, and you know where to find it, then the availability of data such as this will meet your needs.

If your office designs a great number of buildings with stairs in many different configurations and several people are responsible for these designs, you might find it useful to have all the building code requirements for stairs organized in one place in a summarized form available for ready reference by any designer at his or her work station. Not only would you have the facts (data) related to dimensions, but you also might have summarized the requirements for finish materials, minimum lighting levels, acceptable rise and run proportions, and so on. This "information" would be structured for your office's use related to a particular finite concept and would be applicable for almost any stairway problem you might have.

If you were designing a monumental stairway for a very important commission, the "information" you have on hand may not be enough. In addition to the code requirements, you might be interested in knowing more about a wider range of materials that could be used, new products on the market for special lighting of stairways, how people behave on stairways in panic situations and other aspects of the problem. Research would then have to be undertaken to collect information you didn't already have, it would have to be up to date, and you would have to analyze it to determine what was relevant to the specific requirements of your design.

GETTING STARTED—EVALUATING YOUR RESOURCES AND NEEDS

Every office has some form of research and information management capability. The only major differences are amount of information, number of people needing it, methods for storing and accessing it, procedures to make access possible, and the success with which it is used.

While some firms have made major efforts at organizing their research and information management procedures, the majority of offices have rather makeshift "libraries" where they keep the product catalogues, miscellaneous books, and files of loose material that have been collected over time. In addition, most of the architects in the office will have their "black book" of collected information that they have found useful over the years that each keeps at his or her desk for ready reference.

Regardless of office size, type of work, length of time in business or budget available, every firm should be able to have exactly *what* information and data it needs to practice more effectively, *when* it needs it, in the most *concise, accurate* form, gathered in a *cost-effective* way. The question is not *if* you should have an in-house center but what its scope should be. You need to decide roughly what percentage of questions you would like to be able to answer without going outside the office. This will help determine the size and extent of your in-house facility.

CASE IN POINT

Environmental Planning & Research, Inc., headquartered in San Francisco, has an excellent library, organized so that a question can be answered with an in-house source about 80 percent of the time. Their practice is about 70 percent interior design, 20 percent architectural, and 10 percent store planning work so much of their collection is product literature, either in binders or loose leaf format. This is categorized according to *Sweet's Guideline* numbering system and then alphabetically by manufacturer. The remainder of the material is grouped by format and content such as code books, government reports, construction guides and the like. In addition to the in-house collection, outside library sources are used as well as a very important informal network arrangement with other design firm librarians.

If you need to improve your library and research procedures (and most offices do) you should first assess your existing situation and define what your needs really are. You will find the following checklist of questions useful in making this evaluation. Later in this chapter I will outline some considerations in planning strategies to bring your office into the "information age."

Evaluation Checklist

- *Summarize existing resources.*
1. What kinds of information resources and collections do you have now? Books, catalogues, reports, magazines, directories, slides, samples, etc. How many of each do you have? How much space do they occupy? You can use the form in Figure 11-2 to collect this information.
2. How current are these resources? When was the last time a product catalogue was updated? Do you have the latest edition of major reference books?
3. How are your information resources and collections organized? How are they filed and shelved? How are they catalogued? Is the cataloguing useful? Can you find what you want when you want it without wasting time searching?
4. Do you have a system for ordering in-house reference materials? What method of selection is used? How is material evaluated as to its usefulness?

- *Review existing processes for research.*
5. What information sources do you refer to now? In what order of priority do you conduct a search? Is the search for material generally found in the office only or do you look elsewhere? What materials are referred to the most? What isn't useful? What do people think would be useful but isn't available? Depending on the size of your office, the level of detail you want, the time and money you have to spend in answering these questions and your level of desire to improve your research capabilities, you may want to conduct a formal survey of your staff.
6. When you have a special research project, who does it? How long does

	Number	Space occupied	Use					Currency	
			Very frequently	Frequently	Occasionally	Hardly ever	Not at all	Oldest in collection	Most recent
Technical reference books									
General books (history, etc.)									
Magazines									
Newsletters									
Technical reports									
Codes and ordinances									
Standard drawings (by size)									
Photographs									
Product data (loose leaf)									
Product catalogues									

Figure 11-2
Survey of Information Resources

it take? How is it accomplished? Is it billed separately to the client? Is the process recorded and filed for future use?

7. How much time is typically spent in obtaining necessary information to do your work? Consider the time for locating in-house material as

well as material from outside sources. Is time spent on research recorded on time sheets separately from other phases of a job?

- *Establish present and future needs*

8. From the information gained from Step 5, determine what *kind* of knowledge you seek the most often. Consider first whether it is data, information, or research, then break it down into generic types. For example, is it cost data, building activity in your marketing areas, standard detail drawings, or what?
9. What form does the data, information, or research have to be in? Hard copy, microform, drawings, formal for a presentation, quick answer, etc.
10. How many people in your office will need the material, now or in the future?
11. Will the material be needed in only one office or several locations?
12. How current does the material have to be in order to be accurate and useful to your practice? Weekly updates? Monthly, quarterly, semiannually, annually? Generally, the more frequent the updating, the more the information costs.

ACCESSING INFORMATION—RESEARCH CONSULTANTS

In many cases, obtaining information in-house or conducting special research is not feasible. The situation may be that you don't have the staff to devote to a project, you need outside objectivity, you lack the specialized knowledge of research procedures and sources, or that someone else could accomplish the same task at a lower, total effective cost.

Of course, for very special information or research needs, you can contact a consultant in a particular field, if one exists. A fire protection consultant, for example, can assist you with unusual problems you may have with a one-time building design, based on his or her expertise in the field. One disadvantage, however, is that you may need a broader view of your problem. You may want a consultant who can also understand your design process and needs, the space-planning needs of your problem that may suggest a reconfiguration of the building itself to solve fire and life-safety problems, what interior furnishings are available that meet your needs and don't pose a fire danger, and so on. Since architectural design is a synthesis of many variables, a research consultant who can provide this broad view *and* get the information needed for specific problems may be your best alternative.

For a listing of specialized consultants, you may want to review the *Consultants and Consulting Organizations Directory* published by Gale Research Company, Book Tower, Detroit, MI 48226. It is published biannually and includes individuals and firms active in consulting. A description of services is provided with each entry, along with names, addresses, telephone numbers and founding date. A subject index by geographical location is also included along with an alphabetical index of individuals.

Another possibility is to contract with a business research firm. There are many types of these firms ranging from specialized services such as market research to "information brokers," free-lance people who work for businesses needing special information help. They are listed in the phone directory under various titles such as "research," "library research service," or the specific type of research they conduct. These services can provide some help, but since they work within a very broad realm, they are many times unfamiliar with the special information sources in the building industry and what the unique needs of architects and designers are.

A third direction to take is with someone knowledgeable in architecture as well as research techniques and information sources. There are many architectural firms around the country that undertake research as one of many services they offer, but very few that specialize in the particular needs of the architectural profession and the building industry as their sole business. You may be more comfortable working with an independent research consultant than with another architectural firm.

Whatever direction you decide to take, the decision between doing your own research or hiring a consultant is basically one of quality and economics. This is where a reasonably accurate audit of the time and money spent on in-house information gathering and research previously discussed is especially useful.

The relationship between research (the quality of the product), cost, and time must be understood and evaluated. Figure 11-3 illustrates this relationship.

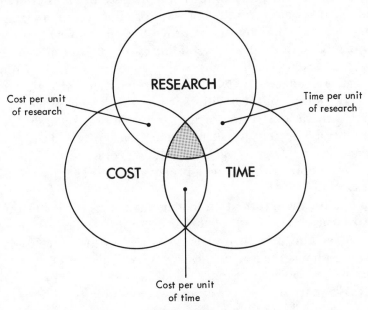

Figure 11-3
Balance of Architectural Research

There is an optimum *balance* that represents an efficient utilization of time and money to achieve a required amount and quality of research.

In comparing the cost of doing research with office staff against a consultant, keep in mind *all* the expenses associated with using available personnel. It is not a direct hourly charge comparison. In addition to the wage rate for the staff member, there are the usual direct personnel expenses of insurance, taxes, vacation pay, and so on. Additionally, there is the cost of support services for secretarial assistance and other overhead items that may be directly related to the research effort as well as special resources for a job that a consultant may amortize in his or her fee.

Another critical variable is the time required to do a particular task. A staff member not well versed in appropriate information sources or procedures of good research can waste a great deal of time (and money) trying to obtain the same result that a specialist might get in half the time.

SETTING UP AN INFORMATION MANAGEMENT SYSTEM

Information Management in Architectural Practices

For the purposes of this chapter, information management is the process of seeking, selecting, organizing, analyzing, presenting, storing, and updating knowledge and applying it to solve design problems or maintain a design practice. All architects must carry out these activities to one degree or another. This section will help you understand some of the many ways of effectively managing information and how you can set up a system or improve the one you have in order to apply the best information with the least expenditure of time and money.

Architectural, engineering, and interior design firms are unique in their information management needs. Not only are they deluged with data from many different types of sources and for different phases of their practice, but they also are challenged with various forms of that information. An architect or engineer must store and be able to retrieve such diverse items as rolled drawings, large, flat sheets, catalogues, books, periodicals, file folders, computer disks, samples, slides, reports, and photographs. Developing a process that works for your office is crucial to your success.

An outline for the information management process is illustrated in Figure 11-4. The two basic components of this process are 1) organizing and handling material that comes into the office or is generated in the office and, 2) obtaining information, not in-house, that is needed for a particular inquiry. The second part of this process will be covered in more detail in the next section.

Use this diagram to analyze your present situation or to set up a new system. The following steps will give you some ideas on how to improve information management in your office.

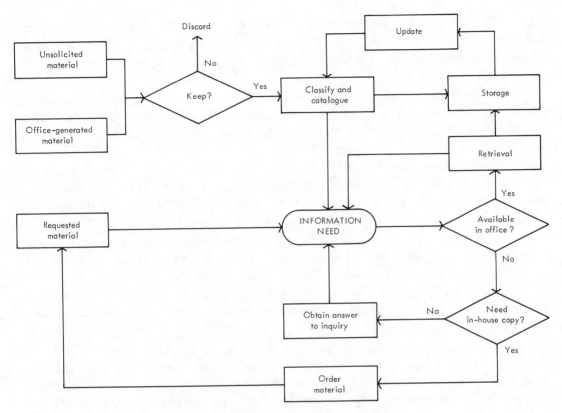

Figure 11-4
Information Management Process

1. Purge out-of-date material. Information that is not current is often more of a problem than having no information at all. This first step will not only give you more room for the right kinds of resources, but also give you an indication of what really is and is not useful.

2. Determine the kinds of resources you need. This information should follow directly from your identification of needs outlined in the previous section. You may find that a book or periodical needed infrequently can best be accessed through a directory or listing your office puts together rather than spending the money to have a copy in the office.

3. Determine how much space you will need to devote to a resource center. In addition to the usual bookshelf space, also consider vertical files for pamphlets and other loose material, workspace adjacent to the shelves and files for spreading out the material being reviewed, catalogue files, workspace for whoever is responsible for maintaining the resource center, space for a copy machine if one is used here, and sufficient space for the organized storage of samples.

4. Decide on the equipment needed. For most resource centers this will be minimal. Card catalogues, magazine racks, and files for odd-sized material may be

all that is required. For larger centers, you may need copy machines, microform readers, computer terminals, and other special equipment. Catalogues from local library supply houses can provide you with information on the various types of equipment available.

5. Establish a budget. This should be based on what you need to run *your* office most efficiently. If your budget is restricted you should have a very accurate idea of what kinds of resources you need the most so that the money you have is well-spent. In a report on current library practices published by the *Professional Services Management Journal* in 1982, William Van Erp found that approximately 33 percent of an office's library expenditure was for periodicals, 50 percent for books and 17 percent for technical reports, computer time and library administration. Use the form shown in Figure 11-5 for preparing your line item budget.

6. Set up a regular, consistent method for announcing to office staff the arrival of new material, services the resource center offers, and other information relative to the center. Letting people know what is going on increases the likelihood of the center being used and encourages everyone to keep up-to-date. The method can range from a simple hand-written note on the bulletin board to a monthly, printed announcement.

7. Formalize a method of ordering material. Regardless of office size, only one person should be responsible for ordering books, periodicals and other resources, to avoid duplication and to verify that the ordered material is really needed and fits within the general scope of the office's reference collection. Anyone should be able to suggest items to have in-house as long as the request is coordinated through one control point. Some type of standard form should be used so there is a record for the resource center, the bookkeeper (for obvious accounting and tax reasons), and, of course, one to be sent to the publisher or agency distributing the publication. Figure 11-6 suggests one possible format for a publication request and order form. You may want to modify the design somewhat to meet your own needs, but the one shown uses a carbonless, two-part format with perforated tear-offs so that only one form is necessary for requesting a publication, sending the order to the publisher, keeping a record in the resource center for follow-up, and providing a record for accounting purposes. It could also be used as a single sheet with photocopies made as required.

8. Determine how you will keep reference material updated. Each type of published information has its own renewal cycle; some books are never revised, in which case they should be replaced with new ones on the same subject while some cost information, for example, should be brought up-to-date monthly. Most periodicals send renewal notices, so those are not much of a problem. For material that is likely to be updated yearly or less, one method is to establish a system of colored tabs that can be slipped over the cards of each item in the collection. There can be twelve positions across the top of the card, one for each month. As you catalogue the item, position the tab in the month or year when you know or think

Personnel	Monthly budget
Librarian or other staff members coordinating and maintaining the resource center	_____
Consultants, other outside assistance	_____
Sub-total	_____

Equipment	
Furniture--include shelving if not built in	_____
Depreciable equipment	_____
Expendable items	_____
Sub-total	_____

Resources	
Standard periodicals	_____
Special periodical subscriptions	_____
Newspapers, Newsletters	_____
Books	_____
Directories and indexes	_____
Special technical reports	_____
Conferences and seminars	_____
Codes and standards	_____
Computer data base searches	_____
Sub-total	_____
Total	_____

Figure 11-5
Information Resource Center Budget

the updating should occur. Then, at a set time each month, a quick glance at the column for that month will tell you what items should be checked for updating.

9. Determine who will be responsible for organizing and maintaining the resource center. Regardless of the size of your firm there should be only one central control, whether a secretary, business manager, project architect, or full-time librarian. If your firm is small and the duties of maintaining the resource center are handled by a part-time person, you must budget for and devote a reasonable amount

Order Request

Title _____   Publication type

                                                            ☐ Book
Author _____   ☐ Periodical

                                                            ☐ Report
Publisher _____   ☐ _____

Publication date _____   No. copies _____   Reimbursable?

Order no. _____   Price _____   ☐ Yes   ☐ No

Ordered by _____   Date _____   Job _____

Approved by _____   Job # _____

Date ordered _____   Date received _____   Reorder date _____

Location _____   Index number assigned _____

Comments _____

_____

_____

_____

Publication Order

To: _____   P.O. # _____

_____   ☐ Payment enclosed

_____   Date _____

_____

Title	Author	ISBN	Copies	Price	

Ship to: _____   Bill to: _____

Figure 11-6
Publication Request

of time each month for the various activities required. Taking the position that "someone will get to it" when there is time will not work.

For a review of some of the functions and operating methods of design firm libraries, get a copy of *The Architecture/Interior Design/Engineering Library, A Report on Current Practices* by William Van Erp, published by the *Professional Services Management Journal,* 126 Harvard Street, Brookline, MA 02146.

If you think that you need a specialist to help organize and oversee maintenance, but still are not at the point where you need a full-time librarian, you might consider hiring a library consultant. There are several of these people who specialize in the needs of architectural and engineering firms (you can contact the Association of Architectural Librarians, AIA Library, 1735 New York Avenue N.W., Washington, DC 20006). You can also utilize the Special Libraries Association. They offer a one-day consultation visit that is free, with the exception of travel expenses. Direct your requests to the Executive Director, Special Libraries Association, 235 Park Avenue South, New York, NY 10003.

10. Set up a classification, indexing and storage system. This is the most difficult part of the process since *having* information is useless unless you have an easy, effective means for *accessing* it. In the following section I will review some existing classification schemes and some fundamentals you need to consider if you set up your own system. The decision flow chart shown in Figure 11-7 will give you an overview of one method of setting up an in-house classification system.

Setting Up an In-house Classification and Storage System

In the simplest system, classification, storage, and access are the same—visual. A small collection is put on the shelf arranged according to broad subject matter, and when something is needed a quick view tells if it is there and where it is. This system works fine for very small collections. As an architectural office and its information grow, however, it is necessary for the information management system to grow also.

Classification is the most important aspect of the process because it provides the basis for retrieval. Any storage system can be used (although some are better than others) as long as the indexing and cataloguing system allows you quick and easy access. The difficult thing about systems for an architectural office is that most practicing architects have neither the time nor the patience to use an overly complicated classification system. Even if a full-time librarian is employed, that person will soon become overburdened with information requests if the system is so complex that it cannot easily be used by the professional staff.

Before I discuss some classification systems that you might find useful, consider the following checklist of criteria that any classification and indexing system should meet. If you already have some type of system, use this checklist to evaluate how it is working for you. If you decide to establish your own system, use it in your planning.

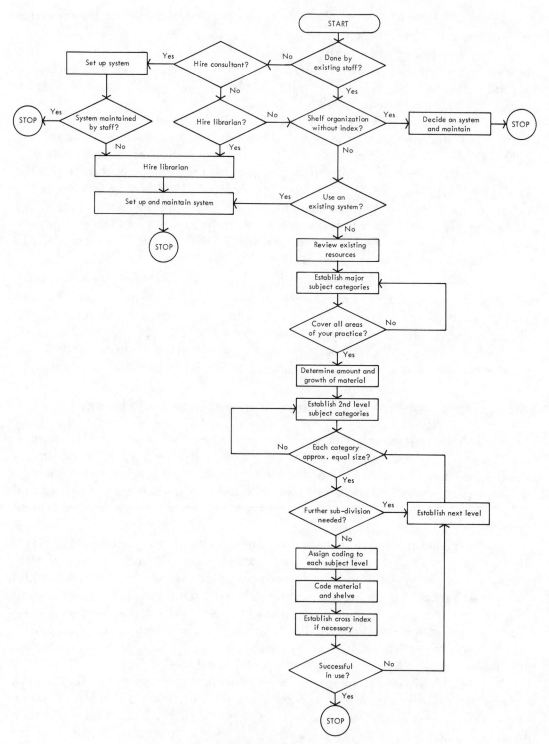

Figure 11-7
Classification System Decision Flow Chart

Criteria Checklist for Classification and Indexing System

1. Does it respond to the unique type of work your firm does and to the amount of information you have to manage? Is it easy to retrieve the data you have?
2. Is it flexible enough to allow for varying degrees of detail under different subject headings?
3. Can it be expanded to allow for new material in existing subject areas or entirely new subject areas?
4. Is it easy for anyone in the office to use? Some search assistance should be built into the system with such aids as "see" and "see also" references.
5. Does it permit a broad, general search as well as a detailed search depending on the needs of the user?
6. Is it systematic enough so that a single concept or piece of information can be retrieved as well as one concept in relation to other subjects?
7. Does it allow for the points of access you want, such as subject, author, title, etc.?
8. Does the index contain enough information to allow you to decide whether the document or other material is worth retrieving?
9. Is there alphabetic index in addition to any other type of index to allow effective use by someone unfamiliar with the system?
10. Does the system result in both an acceptable "recall ratio" and "precision ratio"? The recall ratio is the number of relevant items retrieved to the total number of items in the index and the precision ratio is the relevant items retrieved to the total number of items retrieved. Ideally, you want to retrieve the maximum number of items in the collection that relate to your need for information and to have all of them be of use to you. You should establish a system that comes as close to this ideal as you need, within your limits of time and money.
11. Does it allow for various forms of material to be classified (books, photographs, drawings, tear sheets, etc.) and allow for consistent shelving of this material?
12. Does it minimize search time?
13. Does it have an acceptable cost associated with its design, preparation, use, and maintenance?

There are, of course, the familiar types of classification schemes such as the Dewey Decimal System, Library of Congress (LC), Universal Decimal, and others that divide the entire universe of human knowledge into broad subject fields and further arrange that knowledge according to some hierarchy. Architecture and allied fields are only a small part of these systems. The PSMJ survey found that about two-thirds of the firms surveyed use either the Dewey Decimal System or the Library of Congress system. The offices that use these systems pick out those subject categories that apply to their practice. Generally speaking, however, these types of systems cover a broader range of subjects than is necessary and don't relate to the way architects practice or to the kinds of information they need.

With the widespread use of computers in the last decade there have been a number of indexing systems developed that have been applied to specialized fields of knowledge. With these, the attempt is not so much to develop an elaborate classification system as it is to use the computer's speed and storage ability to access a collection of material in many different ways and at many different levels to improve both the recall ratio and the precision ratio. Coordinate indexes, for example, assign key words to each document or item indexed. When one or more key words are entered into the computer, it searches for all the documents that have such key words assigned to it. By using various search techniques and computer commands, the search can be as broad or detailed as required. The displayed information usually includes bibliographic data as well as an abstract, so the searcher can decide if the item should be retrieved. Some attempts have been made to use such computer systems with architectural information, but to date none are in widespread use.

Many classification systems specifically designed for architecture, urban design, and the construction industry have been tried. Some have not been successful while some remain in use today. A few of the present systems include the CI/SfB, primarily used in the United Kingdom and other parts of Europe, the CIB Master List of Properties and, of course, Masterformat developed by the Construction Specifications Institute in the United States.

Each system has its advantages and disadvantages. Usually, the comprehensive systems are too involved and complex for most practicing architects to use and simpler systems don't provide the depth and flexibility needed for modest to large size libraries. As shown in the Decision Flow Chart in Figure 11-7, one of the early decisions you need to make is whether an existing system will work for you and to what degree you need to modify it.

Since most architects are familiar with the CSI Masterformat, this is usually the one selected. Its major drawback for general organization, however, is that it was developed mainly for *product* information filing, cost data organization and production of specifications. There are few provisions for the multitude of information categories outside the 16-division format. The *Uniform Construction Index* published by the CSI in 1972 (superseded by Masterformat in 1978 and 1983) did contain a data filing format outlined in Division 1 that could be used for information not classed in the product sections. The headings are reproduced in Figure 11-8.

For a small, general practice office, this data filing format along with the more detailed product divisions may be adequate with minor modifications.

If you decide to establish your own classification system here are some ideas on how to proceed.

1. Begin by reviewing the information you collected earlier using the Evaluation Checklist. This will establish the kinds of information your office needs and begin to suggest broad subject categories.

General information
Associations
Building industry relations
Building types
Codes/regulations
Computer applications
Construction equipment & tools
Consultants/Specialists/Services
Controls
Cost data
Design elements
Documents & forms
Ecology
Education
Energy conservation
History
Informations systems
Instruction manuals
Insurance
Legal aids
Maintenance/Operational equipment
Network systems
Office equipment
Office management
Office supplies
Planning
Preservation/Restoration/Remodeling
Programming
Project delivery methods
Project development
Project documentation
Project financing
Public relations
Safety
Standards, building
Standards, office
Tax aids
Temporary facilities

Figure 11-8
Data Filing Format—UCI

Reproduced with permission, The Construction Specifications Institute

2. Expand and refine these subject categories until you are satisfied that they cover all areas of your firm's practice. Be sure to include categories for business, financial and management related information. Although there are other ways to classify (by accession number, author, etc.) I would recommend sticking with subject divisions because this is more familiar to practicing professionals and allows for "directed" browsing when someone wants to casually review all the material on the shelf concerning a particular topic. Consider this first division a "level 1" classification and try to limit it to a small number, say from five to ten divisions. This allows a quick, first glance division for either cataloguing or searching and is easy to remember.

3. If these cover all your present and expected future classification needs, then proceed to establish a second level of division under each of the first level

categories. Although a very small office with a small collection might be able to use only the first division, chances are that at least a second subdivision is needed. In setting up the subdivisions, try to keep approximately equal amounts of material you are trying to classify and store in each. This is a good way to check yourself so that the subdivisions remain useful. It is also a good indication that the proposed system will be able to accommodate expansion in a logical way.

4. Continue to create additional levels of division as they are needed for *your* office's information needs. You may find that only a few subject areas need three or four levels of division while others need only two.

CASE IN POINT

The Washington, DC office of Skidmore, Owings & Merrill uses a color-coded system with a two-level division while the other SOM offices use a more detailed numerical system for their needs.

5. Separate general reference works that deal with a variety of subjects into one category. Books like *Architectural Graphic Standards* and *Time-Saver Standards* would be in this category. Since every architect knows what is in these types of references, no further indexing or classification is necessary.

6. Decide how the various formats of information will be grouped on the shelves. Most offices group by formats with books and catalogues on shelving, cut sheets in vertical files, drawings in flat files, samples in boxes, and so forth. This system can work well if your collection is small or your indexing system accurate. The problem is that some material on a desired subject is located while other material is often overlooked because it is out of sight, misfiled or not convenient to access.

If you decide not to get involved in a complex indexing system, and instead depend on the "browsing" method, it is important to group all material on the same subject together regardless of format, as much as this is practical. For example, loose sheets can be bound or put in boxes available from any library supply house. Drawings, likewise, can be reduced to fit in a binder that can be located on a shelf.

7. Catalogue the items you have in your collection. As a minimum you need a title list arranged alphabetically that also includes author (if any), publishing data, price, location, and a brief description of the item. $3'' \times 5''$ cards work fine for this. This is essentially the same as a card catalogue in any library although your listings don't have to be as complete. To provide better access to the collection, you might copy the original cards and arrange them by subject corresponding to your classification scheme, by author, or any other method that will be the most useful to you.

If you have a microcomputer, almost any data base management program will allow you to do this faster, more accurately and increase the number of ways you can search for material.

WAYS TO SPEED RESEARCH AND INFORMATION GATHERING

Establish a Process

Regardless of whether you have an extensive in-house library or go outside the office for your data, it is essential that you have a logical, efficient method to find the information you need. I have found the following outline of steps to be a useful way to approach the gathering of "information" or for more extensive applied research projects. For data collection, the process is slightly different and not usually so involved.

1. *Define the problem.* Just as defining a design problem precisely (programming) aids in the problem solution, so does clarifying the exact nature of a research problem help in gathering what information is needed quickly and efficiently. Some of the questions you need to answer include:

- What is the purpose of the research?
- Who needs the research? Will it be used by designers, marketing people, draftsmen, etc.?
- Is the information needed specific to one job only or will it be used for several similar jobs? To get the most from your research dollar, try to structure the effort so it *is* usable for as many jobs as possible.
- When are the research results needed?
- What money is available for the research?
- What degree of reliability is needed?
- What should the final form of the research information be? Will it be best to have it summarized in a drawing, report, list, etc.?
- How current must the information be? Generally, the cost of research increases in proportion to the timeliness of the information sought.

2. *Establish a strategy and schedule.* If the problem is complex, break it down into manageable units. Structure each part so that a specific information source can respond to it. Generally, it is best to divide according to what sources are available.

At the same time, determine what level of detail is needed for each part as well as for the whole problem. Finally, decide when you need to have information on the various parts in time for analysis and compilation. Establishing deadlines is critical in controlling research time.

3. *Determine appropriate sources.* This is probably one of the most difficult aspects of research since one "best" source for one problem may be useless for another, even one that is similar. This is why knowing exactly what you are looking for (although not always possible) is so important. Sources can be evaluated initially based on the likelihood that they will provide the kind and quality of information you need.

Consider first whether you need primary, secondary, or tertiary source material or whether you might need to do your own original research or have someone do it for you. Primary sources, for example, are such things as statistical data, interviews with people who are "experts" or are conducting on-going research. Secondary sources are journal articles reporting on current activities in a particular field, association literature compiling information on a product and the like. Tertiary material includes most books and reference sources. Generally, primary sources are more reliable but cost more to compile and coordinate with other primary source material to construct a usable set of information.

Some of the possible sources of information are listed in the matrix in Figure 11-9. The important thing to understand about each is the bias it may have. Even though the data are "packaged" in just the form you want, they may be arranged to favor a particular viewpoint. A classic example of this is the set of scaled, tracing details that many window manufacturers include in their catalogues. They make it very easy to use, but are based on one manufacturer that may or may not be the best for the job. The ratings indicated in the matrix in Figure 11-9 will give you a general idea of how the various types of sources usually rank, based on several criteria, on a scale of one to five. Use the blank spaces provided to evaluate your information sources on particular jobs you have to help direct your research efforts.

Concentrate on sources that have *practical* in-the-field experience as well as theoretical knowledge. Be careful not to assume that the results of a few completed jobs similar to your problem is *the* answer.

If the field of inquiry is unknown to you, consult someone who is likely to have experienced similar problems before or at least has reviewed some of the literature so that they can direct you to what may be the most appropriate sources. Developing an informal network of other professionals, architectural librarians and industry sources is an important part of finding good information. Trying to start from scratch on a literature search in an unknown field can waste your time and your client's money.

4. *Determine the sequence of source contact.* Once you have lined up the most likely sources, decide in what sequence to contact them so as to minimize unwanted redundancy and cost. Again, how you make this decision depends on the exact nature of your problem. Some of the possible ways to sequence contact may be:

Most general to the most specific.
Longest lead time first.
Sources most likely to have the information to the least likely sources.
Most reliable to the least reliable.
Unknown sources first (these may require the longest time to compile).
Tertiary sources first to define the field of inquiry, then secondary and
primary.

5. *Contact sources.* Be aware of the lead time required on various sources. In many cases, what may seem like a simple request for information by letter or telephone results in a four-week wait for something that is not as useful as expected.

	Reliability/Accuracy 1= Unreliable 5= Highly reliable		Completeness 1= Incomplete 5= Very complete		Bias 1= Very slanted 5= Independent		Timeliness 1= Dated quickly 5= Always timely		Accessibility 1= Difficult to access 5= Easy, quick access		Cost 1= Very high cost 5= Low cost		Total	
Professional associates	4		3		3		5		3		5			
Consultants/"Experts"	5		4		5		5		3		2			
Periodicals	4		3		3		4		4		4			
Books	4		4		3		3		4		3			
Manufacturers/Suppliers	4		5		1		5		4		5			
Trade associations	5		4		2		5		3		4			
Government agencies	4		3		4		3		2		4			
Information vendors	4		3		5		5		3		2			
Directories	3		3		5		3		4		3			
Indexes	4		4		5		5		4		3			

Figure 11-9
Evaluating Information Sources

6. *Analyze and compile into a useful form.* Identify similarities and differences in the collection of information you have on a particular topic. This will identify any gaps in what you have so that sources can be checked again or new sources contacted to confirm what you have. This phase should be considered as a continuing feedback process during the entire course of your research.

Reducing the information to a usable form is also a difficult part of the process. If you have defined this sufficiently in Step One of this procedure, the task will be much easier.

7. *Catalogue* and file for future use.

8. *Update* as new information becomes available.

Information Sources

Although a listing of the thousands of potential information sources is beyond the scope of this book, here are some starting points you will find useful. Many of these are available in larger public libraries and university libraries.

Professional Groups and Trade Associations

American Institute of Architects
Library
1735 New York Avenue N.W.
Washington, DC 20006
(202) 626-7493

National Trade and Professional Associations of the United States and Canada and Labor Unions
Columbia Books, Inc.
777 14th Street N.W.
Washington, DC 20005

Directory of Construction Associations
Professional Publications
Division of MetaData, Inc.
P.O. Box 319
Huntington, NY 11743

Encyclopedia of Associations
Gale Research Company
Book Tower
Detroit, MI 48226

Information Vendors

Visual Search Microfilm Files (VSMF)
Information Handling Services
15 Inverness Way East
P.O. Box 1154
Englewood, CO 80150
(303) 779-0600
>   Microfilmed product catalogue data, industry codes and standards, and military standards.

Microdex, Inc.
1028 Chestnut Street
Newton, MA 02164
(617) 969-2250
>   Interior contract furnishings catalogues on microfiche.

XETRON
Contract Furnishings Data Retrieval System
One IBM Plaza
Chicago, IL 60611
(313) 751-1104
>   Interior contract furnishings catalogues on microfiche.

Government Agencies

National Technical Information Service
U.S. Department of Commerce
5285 Port Royal Road
Springfield, VA 22161
(703) 487-4650
>   Responsible for dissemination of unclassified information resulting from government-sponsored research. Maintains computer data base, publishes newsletters announcing research reports, and supplies microfiche or paper copies of reports.

National Referral Center
Science and Technology Division
Library of Congress
Washington, DC 20540
(202) 426-5670
Reference service: (202) 287-5639
>   Provides suggested information sources based on specific questions. Service is free.

National Institute of Building Sciences
1015 15th Street N.W. Suite 700
Washington, DC 20005
(202) 347-5710

Periodicals

Ulrich's International Periodicals Directory
R. R. Bowker Company
1180 Avenue of the Americas
New York, NY 10036

The Standard Periodical Directory
Oxbridge Communications, Inc.
183 Madison Avenue
New York, NY 10016

Directories

Handbook of Construction Resources & Support Services
MetaData, Inc.
441 Lexington Avenue
New York, NY 10017
(212) 687-3836

Information Resources in the United States
Social Sciences volume
Physical Sciences volume
National Referral Center
Library of Congress
Washington, DC 20540
        Available through the Government Printing Office

National Source Directory
Resources Council
979 Third Avenue
New York, NY 10022
(212) 752-9040
        Directory of product sources for the interior furnishings industry.

Consultants and Consulting Organizations Directory
Gale Research Company
Book Tower
Detroit, MI 48226

Directory of Special Libraries and Information Centers
Gale Research Company
Book Tower
Detroit, MI 48226

Energy Information Referral Directory
U. S. Department of Energy
Office of Energy Information Services
Energy Information Administration
1726 M Street N.W. Mail Station 240
Washington, DC 20461
Available through the Government Printing Office

Indexes

Architectural Index
Box 1168
Boulder, CO 80306

The Design Index
820 Davis Street
Evanston, IL 60201

Art Index
H. W. Wilson Co.
950 University Avenue
Bronx, NY 10452

Geodex International, Inc.
P.O. Box 279
Sonoma, CA 95476

Engineering Index
United Engineering Center
345 E. 47th Street
New York, NY 10017

Architectural Periodicals Index
Royal Institute of British Architects
66 Portland Place
London, England W1N 4AD

Avery Index to Architectural Periodicals
G. K. Hall & Co.
70 Lincoln Street
Boston, MA 02111

TAPPING COMPUTER POTENTIAL

State of the Art

For the past ten to fifteen years computers have been used more and more in the information industry from cataloguing books to indexing and printing complex directories. Their most recent use has been in providing "data bases" for specialized fields of knowledge in which the pertinent information is collected, entered into the computer memory and made readily available through the use of various indexing and searching techniques.

An entire industry has grown up just within the last ten years or so by providing these types of data bases and the hardware and software needed to operate them. At this time, it is estimated that there are over 400 commercially available data bases, not including all the systems used internally by the private and government sectors. In large degree, however, the architectural profession and the building industry have not shared in this phenomenal growth.

There are a few scattered examples, but nothing on the scale of many of the data bases maintained for other professions and businesses. In France, for example, the ARIANE system has been in operation for about ten years. The data base and search system was created by the Center for Technical Assistance and Documentation (CATED) to manage the volume of technical material, regulations, and standards in the building and construction fields in France. It is updated weekly and at the time of this writing had about 600 million characters of information on line.

In Germany, the International Council for Building Research Studies and Documentation operates the CIBDOC system, a collection of computer data bases prepared by organizations in several countries. These data bases collectively provide literature and research information on the subjects of architecture, housing, civil engineering, and regional and town planning. Future plans include the integration of the files into one multilingual data base. Access is available through remote terminals connected by telephone lines or through the Euronet DIANE system.

In the United States, several similar systems have been tried, but on a smaller scale. The AIA Research Corporation, for example, operated the Research Information Retrieval Service for a time, but discontinued it. The system was based on a computerized index containing key words and bibliographic data and was accessed by mail or telephone inquiry.

Information Handling Services, a private company, offers one of the most sophisticated data bases available to the building industry. The actual data base (full text and illustrations) is on microfilm, but the index and cross-referencing procedure are computerized. Searching the online index, the user is directed to the proper microfilm cartridge and frame number for the information needed.

Specifically for the architectural profession, IHS, in collaboration with the Construction Specifications Institute, provides Spec-Data®/II building products information and Spec-Data®/II Product Selectors. This is essentially a microfilmed and cross-indexed "Sweet's-type" catalog, but is more comprehensive and is updated every sixty days. In addition, industry codes and standards, such as ASTM and ANSI, are filmed and indexed. For more information, contact Information Handling Services, 15 Inverness Way East, Englewood, Colorado 80150.

Another data base for the interior design and architectural professions is CompuSource, a computerized information service providing a national product directory including, among other data, product descriptions, costs, names and addresses of manufacturers and local representatives. Access is provided by terminals in the subscriber's office or at central locations where smaller firms can share a terminal on an as-needed basis. For more information, contact CompuSource, Inc., 2311 Fillmore Street, San Francisco, CA 94115.

Unfortunately, there are several problems hindering the development of computerized data bases in the building industry. The major one is that the practitioner's need for information covers a wide spectrum of knowledge. It crosses many disciplines and requires a diverse range of sources. Classifying and providing access to product information have been fairly well addressed by the Construction Specifications Institute and others, but this is only one type of needed data. The task of providing a reasonably comprehensive data bank would be a monumental one.

Additional problems include updating and the technical one of the computer memory required for storage of vast amounts of text as well as drawings and photographs that are essential to the architect's need for information. Although technically possible now, such storage implies greatly increased costs. Possibly, with improvements in computer memory technology this problem will become less of a stumbling block.

At the present time, the practicing architect *can* take advantage of computer use in research and information management in two ways: through the use of commercial data bases and with in-house micro or minicomputers to organize and store data unique to his or her office needs.

CASE IN POINT

Skidmore, Owings & Merrill, for example, uses the DIALOG service for gathering information for reports, presentations, and proposals, to track important issues and topics concerning a project, and for finding information on evaluation of products and services. They are able to locate abstracts and citations on subjects such as building technology, transportation, acoustical technology, mechanical and sanitary engineering, energy conservation, environmental pollution and control, urban planning, standards and specifications, modern art and business.

Their librarian reports that because they save time they save money; an online search can be performed in a fraction of the time required for a manual search. There are the additional advantages of the search's being more comprehensive and up-to-date, which aids them in producing the most advanced and efficient buildings possible. Overall costs are fairly low, too. There are no start-up costs or subscription fees and training costs are minimal.

Commercial Data Bases

Commercial data bases are files of information on a particular subject or subjects stored in computer memory and accessible in many different ways through particular kinds of search routines. Although the information stored may be statistical, the complete text of a document, or graphic (drawings, graphs, etc.) or a combination of all, most commercial data bases are "bibliographic." Enough information is provided in each record to enable the user to decide if the complete document should be consulted. Generally, this information includes the title and author of the reference, other bibliographic information such as publisher, date, document file number (location), an abstract of the information contained in the reference, and "descriptors," identifying terms that provide primary search access to all the records in the data base. An example of a typical printed citation is shown in Figure 11-10.

An important aspect of commercial data bases is that they are interactive. The user is online with the computer so that the search can be broadened, narrowed, or refined in such a way that the most relevant information possible can be retrieved. By using such Boolean logic terms as "and," "or," and "not" with a set of descriptors the searcher can describe very precisely the kind of information he or she wants and let the computer do the tedious searching (very fast, of course). With this approach you can search literally millions of references for precisely what you need, something that would be impossible through the use of the standard printed indexes, even though many of the computer data bases are simply electronic versions of these printed indexes.

```
     670316    ID NO.- EI761070316
FES DELTA FOCUSING SOLAR COLLECTOR.
Falbel, Gerald
Falbel Energy Syst Corp, Stamford, Conn
   SPIE Semin Proc   v 68 1975: Opt in Sol Energy Util,  for
Meet, San Diego, Calif, Aug 21-22 1975 p  112-119    CODEN:
SPIECJ
   Description   of   the   design   and   measured   performance
characteristics of a focusing solar  collector  that  requires
neither single nor dual axis tracking of the sun, but achieves
solar concentration  gains  exceeding 2:1 for both direct and
diffuse solar energy.  Both sides of a conventional flat plate
collector absorbing plate are used  to  collect  solar  energy
using   a   compound  cylindrical  reflector  and  no  thermal
insulation is required in the collector,  thus  effecting
significant  material  and  fabrication  cost  economies.   The
focusing   capability   allows   improved   high   temperature
performance  as compared to conventional flat plate collectors
without  requiring  a  selective  absorber  coating  on   the
collector   plate.   Measured   results   obtained   from   an
instrumented prototype collector operating since February 1975
are presented,   showing  that  a  single  collector  collects
approximately 50,000 Btus per average sunny day throughout the
year. Applications of the collector as a transparent window or
curtain-wall replacement in buildings are discussed, and large
production quantity cost estimates are presented.
   DESCRIPTORS: (*SOLAR RADIATION, *Collectors),
   CARD ALERT: 657
```

Figure 11-10
Data Base Citation

Access to these data bases can be through independent researchers who have terminals or through most large college or public libraries. If your need is infrequent, this is probably the best way to make use of them since you will not have the expense of leasing or owning a terminal. If your need is great enough, you can have a terminal in the office and connect by simply using the telephone. If you already have a microcomputer, chances are it can be used as a terminal with the purchase of a modem.

"Search services" provide the computer access to many different data bases. They buy data from other companies and make them accessible through the user's terminal. The three most widely used are DIALOG (Lockheed Information Systems), ORBIT (System Development Corporation), and BRS (Bibliographic Retrieval Services, Inc.).

For more information and for a current catalogue write to them at the following addresses.

DIALOG Information Services, Inc.
Marketing Department
3460 Hillview Avenue
Palo Alto, CA 94304

System Development Corporation
2500 Colorado Avenue
Santa Monica, CA 90406

Bibliographic Retrieval Services, Inc.
702 Corporation Park
Scotia, NY 12302

One major disadvantage of commercial data bases is that they tend to be specific to a particular field such as the AGRICOLA data base which provides indexing of the National Agricultural Library, covering literature on agriculture and related subjects. If the data base does cover a broad range of subject matter, the source material is often more general than a researcher may like. At present there is no single data base for the architectural profession in the United States. As a result, the practicing professional needs to pick and choose from among hundreds of available data bases.

The following list briefly outlines some that could be of use to architects and interior designers. However, the list does not include all engineering and planning resources and excludes most foreign data bases. Some are very specific while others may provide general information useful, for example, to develop marketing strategies. The matrix in Figure 11-11 suggests during what particular phase of the project delivery process each may be helpful and gives additional information, current at time of this writing, on availability.

For more information on available data bases, you can consult one of several directories.

	INFORMATION NEED															AVAILABILITY			
DATA BASE	General information	Management	Marketing	Programming	Regulations	Schematic design	Energy and environment	Post occupancy evaluation	Building system technology	Product information	Specifications	Building costs	Construction industry	Transportation design	Government affairs	Lockheed DIALOG	SDC ORBIT	BRS	Own company
ABI/INFORM		•	•												•	•	•	•	
API	•	•	•	•	•	•	•	•	•	•		•	•		•				•
ASI			•									•	•			•	•		
BUYLINE										•									•
CIS/INDEX					•		•						•			•	•	•	
COMPENDEX	•						•			•	•	•	•			•	•	•	
CDA	•	•	•			•	•	•	•				•			•	•	•	
CPI	•				•		•	•	•		•	•	•						
CIS							•					•							•
DMI			•																•
DODGE CP			•									•	•						•
DODGE/DRI			•									•	•						•
EIS			•										•			•			
EA	•															•			
ENERGYLINE						•	•	•		•	•		•			•	•	•	•
ENVIRONLINE						•	•	•	•							•	•	•	•
GPO						•		•		•			•			•	•	•	•
HUD USER	•			•	•	•	•			•			•			•			•
MASTERSPEC 2											•								•
NCJRS				•		•										•			
NNI	•															•			
NRC	•																		•
NI	•																•		
NYTIS	•																	•	•
NSHCIC					•	•	•		•	•	•		•						
NTIS							•	•	•			•	•	•		•	•	•	•
PTS F & S			•													•		•	
DOE/RECON							•												•
SCISEARCH	•						•		•							•			
SPECTEXT											•								•
SSIE	•						•	•	•							•	•	•	•
STANDARDSPEC											•								•
SCA							•	•								•			
TRIS														•		•			
WAA								•	•							•			
WT										•						•			

Figure 11-11
Data Bases for Architectural Use

Encyclopedia of Information Systems and Services
Latest edition
Gale Research Company
Book Tower
Detroit, MIl

Directory of On Line Information Resources, A Guide to Commercially Available Data Bases
Latest edition
Capitol Systems Group, Inc.

Computer-Readable Data Bases: A Directory and Data Source Book
Latest edition
American Society for Information Science

Directory of Online Data Bases
Latest edition
Cuandra Associates, Santa Monica, CA

DATA BASES USEFUL FOR THE DESIGN PROFESSIONS

ABI/INFORM

Covers all phases of business management and administration primarily oriented to the executive.

API

The data base version of the printed Architectural Periodicals Index of the British Architectural Library indexing about 300 journals.

ASI

The American Statistics Index covering all statistical publications of the U.S. Government.

BUYLINE

Telephone access to the McGraw-Hill Information Systems Company's Sweet's Division data base of building product sales representatives' names and locations based on manufacturer name or product tradename.

CIS/INDEX

The data base version of the Congressional Information Service's *Index to Publications of the United States Congress.* Provides access to all working papers, hearing transcripts, special publications, reports and other proceedings of Congress.

COMPENDEX

The data base version of *Engineering Index* providing international abstracted information coverage of approximately 3500 journals, conference proceedings, government reports and engineering society publications.

CDA (COMPREHENSIVE DISSERTATION ABSTRACTS)

Subject, title, and author guide to every American dissertation accepted at an accredited institution since 1861.

COMSPEC

Construction specifications including federal and military master specification, Navy, Corps of Engineers, FAA, Coast Guard, GSA/Public Building Service and others. Also includes Spectext. Available through Bowne Information Systems, Inc., 435 Hudson Street, New York, NY 10014.

CPI (CONFERENCE PAPERS INDEX)

Provides access to records of more than 100,000 scientific and technical papers presented at over 1,000 major meetings each year. Primary subject areas include engineering, geo-sciences, physical sciences, life sciences and chemistry.

CSI (COST INFORMATION SYSTEMS)

Provides access to the building cost data bases of McGraw-Hill Information System's Product Information Group offering 1) conceptual budget analysis, 2) energy requirement analysis, 3) preliminary design cost estimates and 4) detailed construction cost estimates.

DMI (DUN'S MARKET IDENTIFIERS)

Information from Dun & Bradstreet, Inc. data base including marketing information used to determine and classify markets among many other services.

DODGE CP (DODGE CONSTRUCTION POTENTIALS)

Customized reports of construction statistics based on various data bases of the F. W. Dodge Division of McGraw-Hill Information Systems Company.

DODGE/DRI CONSTRUCTION ANALYSIS SYSTEM

Provides access to national, regional, state and county construction and economic statistics.

EIS NON-MANUFACTURING ESTABLISHMENTS

Information on nearly 200,000 non-manufacturing establishments that employ twenty or more people. Provides data on location, headquarters name, percent of industry sales, employment size class, and other information.

EA (ENCYCLOPEDIA OF ASSOCIATIONS)

The data base version of the publication by the same name. Provides information on several thousand trade associations, professional societies, etc., consisting of voluntary members. Information includes address, phone, size of organization, abstract of scope and purpose, and publications by the association.

ENERGYLINE®

The data base version of *Energy Information Abstracts* containing information on the scientific, technical, socio-economic, political and current affairs aspects of energy.

ENVIRONLINE®

Provides access to primary and secondary source publications reporting on all aspects of the environment including management, technology, planning, law, political science, geology, biology, and chemistry as they relate to environmental issues.

GPO MONTHLY CATALOG

The data base version of the *Monthly Catalog of the United States Government Publications* containing all publications issued by U. S. government agencies including the U. S. Congress. Gives access to legislative reports, standards, statistics and state of the art summaries on major issues and technologies.

HUD USER

The computer data base developed by the U. S. Department of Housing and Urban Development containing information on HUD-sponsored research. Some of the topics indexed include housing for elderly and handicapped, residential safety, building technology, housing rehabilitation, and energy conservation.

MASTERSPEC 2

A master specification system for in-house use by architects. The computer data base version of the printed volume.

NCJRS (NATIONAL CRIMINAL JUSTICE REFERENCE SERVICE)

Covers literature related to law enforcement and criminal justice. One of the subject categories available is "architecture and design."

NNI (NATIONAL NEWSPAPER INDEX)

Indexes *The New York Times*, *The Wall Street Journal*, and *The Christian Science Monitor* including articles, news reports, editorials, letters to the editor, obituaries, etc.

NRC (NATIONAL REFERRAL CENTER MASTER FILE)

A subject-indexed file of over 13,000 organizations used by the staff of the National Referral Center at the Library of Congress to direct people with questions to sources that have the information and are willing to share it. Accessed by calling the National Referral Center. See listing previously mentioned in this chapter.

NI (NEWSPAPER INDEX)

Indexes *The San Francisco Chronicle, The Detroit News, The Chicago Tribune, The Los Angeles Times, The Houston Post, The New Orleans Times-Picayne,* and *The Washington Post.*

NYTIS (NEW YORK TIMES INFORMATION SERVICE)

Indexes *The New York Times* and sixty other publications of general interest.

NSHCIC DATA BASE

The combined data bases of the National Solar Heating and Cooling Information Center used internally by the staff to answer telephone or mail queries. It provides such information as listings of building and design professionals in the United States involved in passive or active solar building, selected commercial and residential buildings in the U. S., information on technology, laws, and solar equipment manufacturers.

NTIS

The data base of the National Technical Information Service operated by the Department of Commerce. The NTIS serves as a clearinghouse and disseminator of all government-conducted or government-sponsored, non-classified research. The data base includes the fields of building industry technology, energy, and materials technology among many others.

PTS F & S (FUNK & SCOTT)

Domestic and international company, product, and industry information including corporate acquisitions and mergers, new products, technological developments, socio-political factors, forecasts by company officers, and reports on factors influencing future sales and earnings.

DOE/RECON

Provides access to more than twenty data bases of the U. S. Department of Energy and the Oak Ridge National Laboratory. It is available only to DOE organizations, "contractors" working for the government and other federal agencies, but it can be accessed through other types of information requests.

SCISEARCH

Multidisciplinary index to the literature of science and technology corresponding to records in the printed *Science Citation Index* in addition to other records not in the printed version.

SPECTEXT

A master specification system for in-house use by architects. This is the computer data base version of the printed volumes produced by the Construction Sciences Research Foundation.

SSIE CURRENT RESEARCH

Data base of the Smithsonian Science Information Exchange containing reports of both government and privately funded research in progress or initiated and completed during the most recent two years. Research includes, among others, works in the behavioral sciences, materials sciences, and engineering.

STANDARDSPEC

A master specification system for in-house use by architects. The computer data base version of the printed volume.

SCA (SURFACE COATINGS ABSTRACTS)

Index to international research literature on all aspects of paints and surface coatings.

TRIS

Includes information of the Transportation Research Information Service (U. S. Department of Transportation) on subjects of regulation, energy, safety, environmental concerns, materials, design and construction technology. The data base consists of document abstracts or resumes of research projects.

WAA (WORLD ALUMINUM ABSTRACTS)

Provides coverage of the world's technical literature on aluminum from ore processing through end use.

WT (WORLD TEXTILES)

The data base version of *World Textile Abstracts* indexing the world literature on science and technology of textiles and related materials, the textile industry and international trade in textile materials and products.

CHAPTER 12
Using the Computer to Boost Profits

COMPUTERS: APPRENTICE AND MASTER

ONE OF THE FIRST EFFECTS OF THE TECHNOLOGY of the automobile was to improve on the horse and carriage system of transportation it replaced. Shortly after that happened, and continuing to this day, increased use of the new invention profoundly affected nearly every aspect of our society: economics, social structure, health, transportation, communication, urban planning, and politics to name just a few. The technology changed how we conducted our lives as much (or more!) as it helped perform an old task in a better way.

The same thing will happen with the use of computers in the architectural and interior design office. As computers become more widely used, design professionals will first look to the new technology to help perform old tasks. The computer can type faster, manipulate numbers better, can remember more, and can even draw better and faster than an entire drafting room of the best production people. All of these abilities are welcome additions to the professional's storehouse of tools and will improve his or her practice. By and large, however, computers will first be used under the same management as the people, equipment and processes they are replacing. In this sense they are the apprentices.

A technology as sophisticated as the computer, however, has a life of its own and makes certain demands on the people interacting with it. The first requirement of early generations of "electronic brains" was the exact environmental conditions necessary for proper functioning. Some of these still exist today: certain temperature ranges, power supplies and the like. Beyond these, computers require that humans interact with them in specific ways. Programming and input must be exact because that is the only way a computer will work. Input and output devices require a certain range of positioning of the human operator. Computers cost much more than traditional design tools and thus demand a different economic view of professional practice. The effects are far reaching and will cause fundamental changes in the way architecture is practiced. In this sense computers are part masters.

Some of the following comments are predictions; some are happening now. How will your office be affected in the years ahead? When your computer is finally spewing out design alternatives, working drawings, and specifications, then what?

Marketing

Computers will make it possible to track greater numbers of leads more accurately. More information will also be available on existing and potential markets by tying into large data bases. With word processing capabilities producing complete, comprehensive proposals is easy even today. Will you be using all of this simply to get more work of the same type you always have or will it encourage you to expand services? Will more leads mean a larger marketing *department*? Will you be selling your computer capabilities as much as your design expertise?

Promotional Tools

A greater range of possible promotional tools exists because of the computer. Automatic typesetting, computer-generated slides, and animation techniques are but a few examples. In the office it is possible to get out more printed material to more prospects much faster. Mailing lists are a simple work task for even the smallest microcomputer. How will you want to use these available tools? Whom will you mail to? How can the possibility of doing some of these things help you meet your goals? How will all of this affect the collective image of the profession of architecture in the minds of the public? What will your clients come to *expect*?

Day-to-Day Work

The new electronic marvels can easily maintain to-do lists, tickler files, help with correspondence, and assist with time management. How will teleconferencing and electronic mail affect your office communications? How will personal relations be helped or hurt? How will the "tone" of messages be affected when they move from spoken and written words to electric impulses?

Design and Production

It is in this area that most architects and designers see the greatest potential for computers to eliminate repetitive tasks and improve productivity and quality of service. Once most design professionals have graphic capability and have learned how to use it, will poor design and detailing decisions simply be digitized rather than committed to paper? Will the ability to generate more alternatives or make changes easier encourage unnecessary ones? Will drawings as we know them today be necessary? Drawings are simply one way of summarizing information to communicate it to someone else. Computers allow other choices. It may be possible for the structural engineer's calculations to directly drive automated steel fabricating equipment. The architect's site plan information might someday be able to direct a laser transit and layout system. In short, the design and production process as we know it today may be replaced due to the gentle nudgings of the computer.

Legal Considerations

You will never find a computer sitting in the witness chair in a courtroom. Although computers can make quality control much easier, calculations more accurate (usually) and generally improve service, humans still remain responsible for their output. There is a whole new area of professional liability developing for architects. Defects in both the hardware and software are the risks of the user, not the manufacturer or the designer of the program. In fact, most software agreements specifically state that there are no express or implied warranties concerning results obtained from using their products. Viewed from the opposite side of the fence, at some time in the future, *not* using computers in practice may be considered malpractice because using them will be the norm.

Human Resources

As computers are beginning to be used in the majority of offices the major people problems seem to be getting many of the old-timers to accept them, finding people to hire who are educated in their use, or setting up in-house training programs. As these initial hurdles are surpassed, however, there are more important questions. Ergonomics becomes a primary concern. The office's first computer (and often subsequent equipment) usually is dropped in a workroom designed for production procedures established a century ago in the profession. Lighting, workstation design, seating, length of work shifts and other items all need to be restudied for the new equipment and methods of working they imply.

Beyond this, the work and social structure of the office will change. Computers are too expensive and valuable to only work an eight-hour shift. Offices will have to run at least two shifts and possibly on a 24-hour basis. How will this affect your management and office routine? As with other businesses, too, the new technology makes it possible for many people to spend at least part of their time working at home. Writing specifcations, proposals, reports, manipulating data can all be done away from an office and may actually be done better when distractions and interruptions are not present. The power of the computer will also make it attractive to offer non-traditional services in order to make more efficient use of expensive hardware and software and to simply increase profit. Different people from different disciplines will be needed. How will their interaction with the design staff affect the office? How will staff members with differing computer skill levels be compensated? We know what the technology will do *for* us; what will it do *to* us?

Financial Management

The most wide-spread use of computers by architects and designers has been in the area of accounting. They have made record keeping and analysis of financial information much more accurate and useful as management tools. Additional considerations will be deciding how to make the most *financial* use of the purchased hardware and software and how to manage firms as they become more capital-intensive than in the past when they were entirely labor-intensive. In addition to working the equipment on double or round-the-clock shifts, design offices may find that they can even act as a service bureau to other firms. They may provide services not related to architecture, but that can be run profitably on the computer. This is happening already in a few firms. For professionals thinking of buying their first piece of equipment a fundamental decision-making attitude will also have to change. Rather than viewing the purchase of a very expensive piece of equipment in the same way as buying a parallel rule—that of an overhead cost item—architects and designers must view it as a revenue-producing investment. Economic analysis, including return-on-investment calculations, is necessary. Most architects are not used to thinking this way and for some the change will be difficult.

Project Management

It is here that computers will offer the most help with efficient project production. Job cost accounting, man-hour projection and monitoring, scheduling, and decision-tracking are easily implemented. For firms that do not already have good project management systems the change may be traumatic because the computer is very exact and methodical in its "thinking." Once a system is set up, to make it work will require adherence to the input and processes implied by the computer program. Fudging on schedules, claiming ignorance of fees left to complete a phase, or losing track of programming requirements or design decisions will be more difficult. For many staff members this kind of rigid, logical thinking process will be new to their established ways of working.

Research and Information Management

Computers are very good at remembering and manipulating great quantities of information. With the information "explosion" and the inherent difficulties of accessing the right kind of information at the right time (discussed in greater detail in Chapter 11) in the design professions, these machines will prove extremely useful. The challenge for the profession and for individual offices will be to set up *useful* systems, not just vast storehouses of data. The information will have to be organized and be the right kind of information to be useful. This capability will require architects and designers to be much more comprehensive in the application of available information to their designing. How will this affect time and fees for designing? Architects may even get into the information business as offices specializing in certain building types generate sellable data for other firms. Networking, that is, direct communication between offices using computers and sharing information will also be used. The AIA has already started such a system. Will architects and designers be inclined to share much of the very knowledge that may give them a competitive edge? If information is sold, how should it be priced?

COMPUTER USE IN THE DESIGN PROFESSIONS

As you develop your office's computer facilities you should keep the issues raised in the previous discussion in mind and plan for the long term as well as immediate needs. If you have not yet made the first step and are wondering what a computer can do for you, consider the following list of uses. Some are very simple while some, like three-dimensional graphics, are complex and require a sizable financial investment. Only you can analyze your particular practice to see where improvements can be made. Remember, though, that if sound management processes are not already in place, switching to computers will only automate your problems, not solve them.

Possible Uses of Computers in Design Practice
(not including engineering applications)

Calculations
> General ledger
> Project accounting
> Payroll
> Fee calculations
> Billing
> Cost estimating
> Scheduling
> Statistics
> Energy analysis
> Real estate analysis
> Site analysis
> Life cycle cost analysis

Word Processing

> Correspondence
> Proposals
> Contracts
> Report writing
> Marketing
> Commission list management
> Specifications
> Furniture specifications
> Project maintenance manuals
> Job history data

Data Management

> Programming
> Mailing lists
> Project management/Project decision coordination
> Filing indexes/Records management
> Directories
> Data base management
> Tickler files
> Finish schedules
> Door/Window schedules
> Furniture inventories
> Code checks
> Facilities management
> Shop drawing management
> Information management with microforms
> Product selection and evaluation

Graphics

> Simple graphs and charts
> Small size 2-dimensional drawings
> Working drawings
> 3-dimensional graphics, perspectives
> Simulation with motion

Communication

> Electronic mail
> Networking
> Access to commercial data bases

HOW TO GET STARTED AND GROW
WITH COMPUTERS

Getting Started—Basic Steps

Buying your first computer or upgrading to a more sophisticated model involves much more than just evaluating what hardware and software are available. A great deal of preliminary study is necessary to understand how automation can help the operation of your firm most effectively and what planning action you need to take. Purchasing a computer will not automatically solve fundamental operational problems within your firm—your management procedures and work flow methods must first be organized. The following discussion assumes that this is the case and that you have a clear view of your firm's future.

1. Review the goals and objectives of your firm. As with other aspects of firm management, this is always the first step. Computerization is only one of many tools you should be using to get you where you want to be. For example, a careful analysis at this point might reveal that you may not need the expensive computer-aided design and drafting (CADD) system everyone has been telling you should be in your office. If your goals are more along the lines of project feasibility and programming, you might need something else. Computers can do a lot of different jobs for professional design firms in different ways. You must know your priorities before deciding on any one direction.

2. Make a commitment. This must first come from top management. Without it, any computer purchase and use are doomed to failure. For small firms this is usually not a problem since the decision to start investigating automation begins with the principal. If, on the other hand, you are in a middle management position and are trying to convince a skeptical management board to buy, don't do anything until they are convinced it is the right action.

3. Analyze how you could make best use of a computer in your practice. This is a two-stage process. First, determine what work tasks are most appropriate for automation. Computers are best at doing simple, repetitive tasks very quickly, storing and manipulating large quantities of information, and dealing with many variables in many different ways in a short period of time. This is what makes them so useful for accounting, for instance. If you have a typical job task that is completed only twice or three times per year, it probably is not a candidate for automation unless it is *very* complicated and produces a great deal of revenue. A tedious record-keeping task performed every week is more likely to benefit from computer use. Second, consider what benefits you want from a computer. These generally include one or more of the following:

Improved service.
Better profitability.
Greater productivity.
A marketing edge or new markets.
Superior management.

4. Select one person to coordinate all the firm's efforts in the area of computerization. Even if a committee is appointed, one central control is necessary. All research, contact with top management, planning and evaluation should go through this person to minimize false starts, duplicated efforts, and general confusion.

5. Decide on implementing the following steps with in-house personnel or hiring a consultant. For a microcomputer or minicomputer purchase, you may be able to make a good decision with your own staff if you are willing to spend the time and money required for the selection. If you are considering a major mainframe purchase for interactive graphic capabilities or are simply confused about the whole matter or do not have the time to devote to it, hire a consultant for assistance. They are usually up-to-date on the latest software and hardware available and can help match your needs with what is available. Select a consultant carefully, however. Anyone can call himself a computer consultant to architectural firms without having many credentials. Selecting a consultant is discussed in more detail in a later section.

6. Study your software needs. After you have determined what aspects of your practice can be improved by using computers, translate this into programming needs. Exactly what do you need the computer to do? You need not know computer programming to establish this; simply define what kind of output you need—what you want to do with the information you give the computer. This will later be used to evaluate available software from vendors.

7. Decide on whether you want to buy your own in-house system, tap into a commercial on-line system with just a terminal in your office, or use a service bureau. There are many reasons for taking any one of these paths. For example, if you do not want to make a major financial commitment for a CAD system, you can subscribe to a service bureau to try it out. The bureau makes the hardware available, maintains it, and provides the programming. You pay an hourly or subscription charge for just the services you use. The advantages and disadvantages of service bureaus are discussed in a later section. You may find that your needs can best be met by owning an in-house computer for one set of functions, being on-line for another, and using a service bureau for yet a third.

8. Compile and review all the available information you can. This activity will actually be occurring simultaneously with the other steps and should never stop. The field changes so rapidly that you must keep constantly informed. The information sources listed at the end of this chapter will give you a good starting

point. In addition to reading the usual magazine articles, books and reports, you should subscribe to newsletters dealing with the subject and plan on attending seminars or conferences each year to stay current.

9. Some of the most valuable information can be obtained by talking with other professionals who have systems similar to the ones you are considering and who have been through the process. Get their honest opinions and, if possible, try a hands-on demonstration. One of the questions you should ask any software or hardware vendor who is trying to sell you something is for a list of the design professionals in your area who have already bought the vendor's product.

10. Begin detailed planning. This should include steps needed to:

> Analyze the cost and benefit implications.
> Finalize the selection process.
> Prepare the physical facilities of your office.
> Organize installation and start-up.
> Arrange for staff training.
> Establish a schedule for full implementation.

This planning step should be given careful consideration because the time from beginning evaluation of systems to the point at which the computer will be fully operational and working at top efficiency can be one or two years.

11. Prepare a Request for Proposal. This should be a formally written outline of all the requirements you desire in a software and/or hardware system and a format for vendors to submit their proposals. Simply listening to salespeople talk about what they can offer and accepting their terms and contracts will only confuse you. They will all be a little different and it will be impossible to make line-for-line comparisons. *You* determine what you want. If a vendor balks at providing the information, then he is probably not worth talking to. Evaluating vendors is discussed later in this chapter.

12. Buy the system and start implementing its use. This is a traumatic time for the office. Work habits will have to change, problems with the system will develop, learning will be slow at first and many will distrust the new "black box" in the office. Be prepared for these problems and for down time getting started. With a reasonable amount of perseverance, however, the problems will slowly be resolved and you will wonder how you ever managed without computer assistance.

13. Maintain records of the use of the computer. Time spent on it, work saved, problems, potentials, ideas from staff and similar information should be kept to feed back into future decisions on upgrading what you have or for purchasing a new computer. You then become your own best source of information.

Service Bureaus

Service bureaus offer a relatively "safe" way to become involved with computer use. There is no capital outlay, software is ready to use, maintenance is taken care of by someone else, and you can quit at almost anytime within the limits of your contract. You can find service bureaus that do anything from word processing to 3-D graphics. With the low-cost microcomputers available now for in-house use, however, outside services make most sense for the design firm in the area of graphics—design, drafting, structural analysis, space planning and similar tasks. These require the most sophisticated programs, the largest memory, and most expensive peripherals. For many firms, the expense simply cannot be justified for the amount of work they do.

Advantages of using a service bureau for graphics as well as other computing chores include:

1. The ability to try CAD without making a heavy financial commitment. Bureaus usually charge by the hour and most let you quit at any time.

2. You do not have to worry about maintenance problems. On a large system this can become a significant, and expensive, factor.

3. All the programming is worked out for you. The software is debugged and ready to go.

4. You can start small if you are not sure of the advantages of CAD for your office. You do not have to start worrying about generating enough work to make it pay for itself, going to double shifts, or any of the other concerns of having in-house equipment.

5. The cost of computer time is clearly indicated by the invoices from the bureau, so you know exactly what it is costing you. This is useful for billing clients, especially government clients who need exact accounting and justification of the costs.

6. You can try several different systems before buying your own and get direct experience impossible to glean from vendor reps or even associates who have the system. There is some built-in inefficiency with this approach, but it may be worth the trouble if you want to get the experience.

7. Service bureaus offer a "safety valve" if work becomes excessive. You can farm out the work without having to hire more staff temporarily. In order to make this work, however, you must have a bureau that you are confident in and which understands your needs and methods of operating so they can step in on an as-needed basis.

8. Start-up time is practically immediate. If you buy an in-house system it may be three months to nine months before it is up and operating the way you want.

Disadvantages of using a service bureau include:

1. Time delays in processing your data. The amount of time varies with the type of work, the particular service you have, and their workload from day to day. Some offices find even short delays to be unacceptable.
2. Service bureaus have many clients, some of whom may not be architectural or design firms. Their software must take this into account so it may not be exactly what you need. You may have to modify some of your operations to fit the software capabilities.
3. Output may also be limited to what the service offers and not exactly what you would like.
4. You may have to submit your data in "batch" form. This means that all the input must be given to the service at once, either by giving them information to be manually entered, transmitting over telephone lines or on some storage media. The interactive capacity of the computer may be lost to you. This is especially important to make full use of CAD systems. If you are interested in the design possibilities of service bureaus, try to find one that allows your staff to have "hands-on" access in the bureau's office.
5. Costs can mount up fast. If you start to do much work, the nominal hourly charge can become significant as a cash flow item every month even though most of the cost will be reimbursable.

Some of the disadvantages can be mitigated by subscribing to an on-line system. You have a terminal in your office and connect to a large mainframe computer. The expensive hardware and software are owned and maintained by someone else and you pay a connect charge along with whatever subscription cost is involved. This gives you immediate access anytime you want and fast processing of your information. Interactive capabilities are easier to provide this way as well. Unfortunately, being on-line for interactive graphics is very difficult. Not only are the costs of the terminals—CRT's, keyboards, digitizers, etc.—significant, but there is a technical problem in maintaining a "clean" transmission line between the user's office and the service bureau required for the vast amount of data that must travel back and forth instantaneously.

If you do decide to try a service bureau, investigate them thoroughly. Find those that do a large percentage of their work for architects, engineers, and designers. Use the following checklist to begin your evaluation.

Checklist for Service Bureau Evaluation

- How long have they been in business?
- What percentage of work is done for A/E type firms?
- Is the parent company of the bureau an A/E firm?

- Are there architects and designers using the service who can be called as references?
- Is there an architect on staff?
- What is the cost?
- Can terminals be placed in your office?
- Is training provided?
- What kind of support services are offered?
- Is software modification possible?
- Can output be tailored to your needs?
- What is the turn-around time?

Economics of Computer Ownership

Making the decision to buy an expensive piece of equipment for professional practice represents a relatively new challenge for many design firms. Architectural and interior design practice has traditionally been a labor-intensive business. The expense of having a person on staff is directly and immediately related to the amount of revenue he or she can produce for the firm. The "expense" item of an employee can be quickly added and revenue produced or just as quickly eliminated along with the overhead expenses of having that staff member.

Buying computers, especially the very expensive interactive graphic systems, forces the design professional's business to be more capital-intensive and requires a different kind of financial analysis to help make the decision of whether to buy or not. The decisions will generally have to be made on the basis of return on investment over a specified period of time, usually much longer than that used to evaluate the worth of an employee. A computer, no matter what kind or size, should create revenues, reduce other costs, or produce some tangible benefit. Reducing these benefits are the expenses of buying and maintaining the equipment.

Making a complete economic evaluation concerning the purchase of a computer for a design firm depends on many variables such as the size of the investment, the acceptable "payback period," the desired return on investment, the value you place on many of the intangible benefits, and the reasons for buying the computer in the first place. You should seek assistance from your accountant or other financial advisor if your commitment will be significant, such as the purchase of a CAD system. In addition to simple economic justification, there are many ways of financing the purchase or of leasing, some of which may be better than others for your particular business organization and tax situation.

The following comments will assist you in making a preliminary determination as to whether buying a computer system makes economic sense to you.

On the plus side are the economic benefits you can derive from automating some of your work. Assuming you are buying your system outright, these benefits include the following:

1. Direct income from billing computer time. Most firms charge on an hourly basis, either a lump sum or by splitting the charges into hardware time and operator time. These charges may vary anywhere from about $50 per hour to $100 per hour. Your charge should be determined by adding up all the expenses incurred in owning the systems for a year and dividing by the total number of hours per year you anticipate using it for billable work. Some people think that at least 50 percent of the cost of the system should be amortized through direct billing, with the remaining through tax benefits. Some firms try to recover the total cost from direct billing.

2. Reduction in costs of previous methods of working. If computerizing a function reduces the time (therefor cost) from twenty hours per week to five hours per week, you have saved the expense of fifteen hours to do the same task.

3. Tax benefits of the investment tax credit.

4. Tax benefits of depreciation of both the hardware and the software.

5. Depreciation of furniture and other items related to the installation of the computer.

6. Increase in business from either having or aggressively marketing the computer. You may offer services with the system that you could not without it, or some clients may select your firm over another simply because they think you can do the work more efficiently with a computer. This is especially true with government work where having computer graphic capabilities can be a prerequisite for even being considered.

7. Other "intangible" benefits that are difficult to put a price on such as accuracy, speed, quality control, image, and similar advantages.

The line item cost components you must consider include:

1. Research and selection of the system.
2. Hardware costs.
3. Software costs.
4. Software modifications or additions over the payback period.
5. Maintenance.
6. Interest on financing.
7. Training.
8. Operator costs.
9. Installation and start-up costs.
10. Rent for extra space.
11. Utilities and office modifications.
12. Research and development for new applications and improvement of operating methods.
13. Taxes on extra income from computer operations.

Compare expenses and income benefits over the anticipated payback period. Some experts think that the system should be amortized over a two-year period; others claim that for larger systems up to five years may be reasonable. It will generally depend on the size of the investment: the smaller systems should "payoff" quicker than the more expensive CAD systems.

EVALUATING AND SELECTING A SYSTEM

Making a final selection of a specific software and hardware system may well be the most difficult and frustrating experience you will have in your professional career. With so many different vendors getting into the business, dozens of programming languages and their variations, hundreds of proprietary trade products and the almost monthly changes in the industry, it is nearly impossible to compare every system that might meet your needs on an item-for-item basis. Chances are that you will find several that will work for you, and with all the critical parameters being equal, your selection will probably be based on the priorities you place on several selection factors.

After you have gone through the steps listed in the previous section on "Getting Started" you can begin final selection. The primary rule is to select software first, then the hardware to run it on. This applies to buying a $5,000 microcomputer or a $200,000 CAD system. The best hardware in the world is of no use to you if it does not do what you need. Of course, you can always have someone write custom programs, but that is *very* expensive and usually not necessary for the majority of uses.

Develop an evaluation matrix showing what features are important to you and the kind of system you are looking for—accounting, low-cost graphics, complete interactive graphics, or whatever. On the matrix you can list the various vendors you are considering and compare each item. Every office will have to tailor such a matrix to its particular needs, but the following checklist outlines some of the critical factors to consider. Although the list is more oriented toward micro- and minicomputer buyers, many of the same questions apply to mainframe interactive graphic systems as well. CAD evaluation becomes a more complex process with many of the checklist items. Refer to the sources at the end of the chapter for more information.

System/Vendor Evaluation Checklist

Software

1. Does the software do *everything* you want it to do? You may want to develop a separate checklist for software based on your office's specific requirements. Be skeptical if a salesman tells you that you "will get used" to doing something the program forces you to do. He may be right, but check it out first with someone who has the program.

2. Insist on a demonstration using your data. The canned demos most vendors provide, especially microcomputer stores, are designed to show the equipment and software at their best and always look great. Give them your desired application, some sample entry data and let them show you what it can do.

3. Where is the software coming from? Does the hardware manufacturer provide it, an independent software house or does the vendor propose to customize a program for your use?

4. Is the program part of a "family" of other programs? This can be very helpful for micro- and minicomputers. For example, a mailing list program may be designed to work with a related word processing program, or a statistical package may work with a data base management program so that reports can include statistical analysis. You do not have to buy all the programs at once, but the option is always there.

5. Is the software available immediately? Do not buy something that is promised for delivery "shortly." You do not have any guarantee it will be ready when the vendor says it will be and there may be bugs in the new program.

6. Determine how fast the program works with your application. Again, the vendor demonstrations usually work with small amounts of data so the response time is very fast. When you get the program and enter the normal amount of business data you may be surprised (and disappointed) at how "slow" the computer works. This is especially true with many data base management programs for microcomputers.

7. If you find a bug in the software, who is responsible for correcting it?

8. Does the vendor offer assistance in reviewing your business needs and recommending the best software available?

9. What are the *minimum* hardware requirements—CPU, storage, etc.—and what are the recommended requirements?

10. How many different users will the software support at one time? What operations can take place simultaneously? For example, can you be entering data at the terminal while the printer is producing a report?

11. Can the software be updated easily or does the software supplier offer updated disks when they are developed?

12. Can the software be transferred to other systems if you decide to upgrade your hardware?

13. Is the written documentation and instruction manual complete and easy to read? Insist on seeing one before you buy.

Hardware

1. What operating system does the hardware use? What languages are possible with the equipment? These are more technical questions, but can affect the amount of off-the-shelf software available, ease of mod-

ifying or writing your own programs, and the ability of the machine to communicate with other computers if you need that ability. Some computers use an operating system unique to one brand while others use more universal systems. In the future it is likely that more standardization will develop since the inability for one computer to "talk" to another is one of the major deficiencies in the industry. Selecting one with a common operating system may pay off in the years ahead.

2. What is the internal memory of the unit? This will affect speed and the ability to run some kinds of programs. A 64K random access memory (RAM) is considered minimum for most business applications. Find out how much of this is used for the various "housekeeping" functions such as keyboard control, disk control, and the like and how much is left over for actual processing of data.

3. What is the available peripheral memory capacity? This includes floppy disks, hard disks, and tape drives. Generally speaking, the more storage you can afford the better. While a great deal of storage is not necessarily required for word processing, accounting, and "electronic spread sheets," data base management programs with large amounts of information and, of course, graphics require much more storage. If you are buying a dual floppy disk unit, don't let the salesman convince you that the storage capacity is the sum of both disks. Typically, the program is on one disk and your data on another, so the amount of storage on one disk only is the best measure.

4. How easy is it to expand the system as you grow? Can internal memory be added? What is the maximum peripheral storage capacity? What is the maximum number of terminals that can run off one central processing unit (CPU)?

5. How long does it take to make backup disks? This is standard operating procedure for computer use. If the time required is excessive, daily backup can result in inefficient use of the operator's time and the computer's time.

6. How close do the terminals have to be to the central processing unit? On most multiple terminal installations there is a maximum distance allowable which might become important for larger offices.

7. Can different kinds of printers be connected to the same CPU so that you have a choice of printing speeds—dot-matrix for fast draft quality output and slower, letter quality for final reports?

8. Can the terminal(s) be used to connect with other terminals or with large, commercial data bases?

9. What are the electrical and environmental requirements of the system?

10. Does the vendor provide for all installation and setup, including a thorough check before you use it?

11. Are the ergonomic aspects of the hardware acceptable? Consider screen

size, color of image on the screen, separate keyboard from screen, adjustability, keyboard layout and similar concerns. Your staff will be spending a lot of time at the computer and poorly designed units will cause continuing problems and adversely affect productivity.

12. Are there other hardware systems close to your office that you could use in an emergency if something went wrong with yours? Finding other professionals close by with the same system is good insurance against this problem.

13. Can you change printers easily without extensive system modifications?

14. If you buy a letter-quality printer, can you get one with a keyboard on it to double as a typewriter when it is not being used as a printer?

15. If you are considering a letter-quality printer does it have a wide range of type styles available?

16. Will the printer accept different paper sizes, labels, etc.?

17. What is the speed of the printer—either for text or graphics? Selecting the best plotter for interactive graphics is a special process in itself. If you are buying a CAD system refer to the sources at the end of this chapter for more information on graphics plotters and selecting CAD systems.

Vendor's Company

1. Are you talking to a hardware manufacturer that also provides software, a distributor for several brands of hardware, or an independent third party that will suggest the best system for your use?

2. How long has the vendor been in business?

3. Is the vendor a subsidiary of a parent company? If so, is the parent company in the computer business?

4. Verify the financial status of the vendor and the manufacturer it may represent.

5. How many people are currently using the vendor's systems? How many design professionals?

6. Is there a users' group for the hardware you are considering? For the first-time buyer of smaller systems, user groups can be a great asset in helping you understand the finer points of your computer and assisting with applications and software availability.

7. Does the vendor provide peripherals, supplies, and other support?

8. Does the vendor provide maintenance or is this contracted with a separate maintenance company?

9. Does the vendor provide analysis services of your firm's needs, training, installation, and follow-up?

10. Does the vendor's company have programmers or technical people on staff to assist with problems that may develop in either the hardware or software or are you on your own?

Maintenance/Support

1. Who will provide maintenance if the vendor does not? What is the cost? If you have an independent maintenance company provide this service, get price quotes before you decide. There may be a great difference for the same service.
2. How fast can the maintenance company respond when you have a problem? If the system goes down the day before you have a big project due, you need immediate service.
3. What is being planned by the manufacturer in the way of upgrading? Most manufacturers come out with new equipment every year, usually in the summer. Will you be able to upgrade if desired? How significant will the change be?
4. Will the vendor take parts of your system in on trade if you decide to upgrade?
5. Where do replacement parts come from? How long would it take to repair your equipment if new parts are needed?
6. Does the vendor provide backup facilities if your system does go down at a critical time? Could you take a disk to the vendor and run a last-minute report?
7. Does the vendor have a preventive maintenance program as part of his service contract?

Contractual and Legal

1. Are all of the items you agreed to verbally with the vendor in writing?
2. Do you have delivery dates guaranteed for all of the equipment?
3. Are you protected against the software's or hardware's possible infringement on copyrights or patents of others?
4. Have some kind of warranty that the equipment and programs are fit for the particular use you agreed to with the vendor. Your attorney will be able to help you in this area to tailor the agreement to be consistent with your state's laws. Normally, software and hardware suppliers specifically exclude any such warranty and it may be difficult to include such a clause in your contract. Remember, though, that if the program has a bug in it, you may be liable for the consequences.
5. Check carefully for any limitations the vendor may try to place on his responsibility for defective equipment, delivery dates, and liability.
6. Review the entire purchase and contract with your attorney. Do not take the vendor's contract at face value.

Preparing a Request for Proposal

When you have narrowed your search of computer vendors to those you think can fulfill your needs, you are ready to ask for specific proposals. Each vendor will present its product in a slightly different way and it is usually up to you to ask the same questions of all vendors so that an accurate evaluation can be made. The formal request for proposal (RFP) is one way to do this. Not only does it indicate to the vendors that you are serious, but also forces them to respond to *your* needs instead of just pushing the most desirable features of their wares.

Preparing an RFP assumes that you have completed all of the other steps mentioned above: establishing your goals, specific computer needs, software criteria, educated yourself in the available software and hardware, and worked out financing and preliminary implementation procedures. The exact format and level of detail of the RFP will depend on your needs and the complexity of the system type you are considering, but as a general guide, include the following sections.

1. A cover letter indicating your request, the date of submission required and the basis for selection of a vendor. You might also request that the vendor visit your office to understand your operating procedures and specific needs just as you would call for a pre-bid conference on a construction project.
2. State your firm's goals and objectives for the system. List specific tasks and the output you require from the computer system.
3. Make a specific list of the software and hardware attributes you require. These will be developed from the evaluation checklist outlined above and from your own investigations. You will soon become familiar with what attributes you absolutely need, those that are desirable but not critical, and those that are not needed. The RFP should provide a space for the vendor to fill in his response.
4. Specify the installation dates you need and ask for the vendor's installation requirements.
5. Specify the maintenance, training, and support you require.
6. Price quote and financing (if applicable).

Computer-Aided Design and Drafting Vendors

The following list includes a majority of the turnkey CAD vendors offering systems for architectural, interiors and engineering applications including some low-cost applications. The list is current at the time of this writing, but since the field is changing so rapidly you should check the current companies and their addresses with some of the updating services listed at the end of this chapter. These companies have proved to offer good services and can be a starting point in your search for a CAD system.

AMBruning
Department AR 9
1800 Bruning Drive West
Itasca, IL 60143
(312) 397-2900

Applicon Incorporated
32 Second Avenue
Burlington, MA 01803
(617) 272-7070

Arrigoni Computer Graphics
231 O'Conner Drive
San Jose, CA 95128
(408) 286-2350

Automated Planning Technologies
1600 West 38th Street
Austin, TX 78731
(512) 454-2504
    Low-cost graphics

Auto-trol Technology Corporation
12500 North Washington Street
Denver, CO 80253
(303) 452-4919

Aydin Controls, CAD/CAM Division
401 Commerce Drive
Fort Washington, PA 19034
(215) 542-7800

Bausch & Lomb, Inc.
Instruments & Systems Division
42 East Avenue
Rochester, NY 14604
(800) 828-6967

Boeing Computer Services
P.O. Box 24346
Seattle, WA 98124
(206) 763-5098

CAD, Inc.
1325 Fourth Avenue
Seattle, WA 98101
(206) 625-0229

CADCOM Division of Mantech International
7800 West Park Drive
McLean, VA 22102
(703) 827-3291

Calcomp, Inc.
3320 East LaPalma Avenue
Anaheim, CA 92806
(714) 632-5108

Calcomp/Sanders, Inc.
Graphic Display Division
P.O. Box 868
Daniel Webster Highway South
Nashua, NH 03061
(603) 885-5280

Calma Company
5155 Old Ironside Drive
Santa Clara, CA 95050
(408) 727-0121

Cascade Graphics Development
1000 South Grand
Santa Ana, CA 92705
(714) 558-3316
    Low-cost graphics

Computervision Corporation
201 Burlington Road
Bedford, MA 01730
(617) 275-1800

Control Data Corporation
8100 34th Avenue South
Minneapolis, MN 55440
(612) 853-4656

Design Dynamics, Inc.
P.O. Box 88
Solana Beach, CA 92075
(714) 481-5549

Design Systems Corporation
2100 Chestnut Street
Philadelphia, PA 19103
(215) 564-4026
    Low-cost graphics

DFI Systems, Inc.
11801 South Apopka-Vineland Road
Orlando, FL 32811
(305) 876-2157

ECOM Associates
8634 West Brown Deer Road
Milwaukee, WI 53224
(414) 354-0243
    Low-cost graphics

Engineering Design Concepts
160 Old Derby Street
Hingham, MA 02043
(617) 749-1794
    Low-cost graphics

Gerber Systems Technology, Inc.
P.O. Box 905
South Windsor, CT 06074
(203) 644-2581

Grafcon Corporation
P.O. Box 54909
Tulsa, OK 74155
(918) 663-5291

Graphic Horizons, Inc.
Box 312
Cambridge MA 02238
(617) 396-0075

GTCO Corporation
1055 First Street
Rockville, MD 20850
(301) 279-9550
   Low-cost graphics

Herman Miller, Inc.
8500 Byron Road
Zeeland, MI 49464
(616) 531-8860
   Low-cost graphics

Holguin and Associates
5822 Cromo Drive
El Paso, TX 79912
(915) 581-1170

IBM Corporation
ISG Division
1133 Westchester Avenue
White Plains, NY 10604
(914) 934-4488

Information Displays, Inc.
28 Kaysal Court
Armonk, NY 10504
(914) 273-5755

Interactive Computer Systems, Inc.
13541 Tiger Bend Road
Baton Rouge, LA 70816
(504) 292-7570

Intergraph Corporation
One Madison Industrial Park
Huntsville, AL 35807
(205) 772-2000

Keuffel & Esser Company
20 Whippany Road
Morristown, NJ 07960
(201) 285-5000
   Low-cost graphics

McDonnell Douglas Automation
Department K 052
P.O. Box 516
St. Louis, MO 63166
(314) 232-5047

Nicolet CAD Corporation
2450 Whitman Road
Concord, CA 94518
(415) 827-1020

Sigma Design West, Ltd.
7306 South Alton Way
Englewood, CO 80112
(303) 773-0666

J. S. Staedtler, Inc./MARS CAD Division
21034 Osborne Street
Canoga Park, CA 91304
(213) 882-6000

Summagraphics Corporation
35 Brentwood Avenue
Fairfield, CT 06430
(203) 384-1344

Synercom Technology, Inc.
500 Corporate Drive
Sugarland, TX 77478
(713) 491-5000

Sys Comp Corporation
2042 Broadway
Santa Monica, CA 90404
(213) 892-9707

System House, Inc.
8600 West Bryn Mawr
Suite 82
Chicago, IL 60631
(312) 693-0250

Tektronix, Inc.
P.O. Box 4828
Portland, OR 97208
(503) 627-7111

Trans Micro Systems
2233 Bailey Avenue
San Jose, CA 95128
(408) 998-7118
   Low-cost graphics

T & W Systems   VL Systems, Inc.
18437 MT Langley   17801 Cartwright
Fountain Valley, CA 92708   Irvine, CA 92714
(714) 963-3913   (714) 966-1113
   Low-cost graphics

SOURCES FOR MORE INFORMATION

The field of computer use in architectural and interior design practice is changing so rapidly that it is difficult to keep up. New software and hardware packages are introduced almost monthly and improvements in technology will continue to offer new possibilities. This chapter is intended to help you get started with computers if you are a first-time user, or continue to grow if you have had some experience in the area. In order to stay up-to-date and explore certain aspects of design firm automation in more detail you should investigate at least some of the following sources. At a minimum, I would recommend subscribing to at least two newsletters and attending one or more conferences and workshops each year. Send away for sample copies of the various newsletters before you decide which ones may be best for you. Maintaining contact with people who specialize in the field is really the only way to stay current. Even some of the journal articles are out of date from the time they are written to the time they are published.

Newsletters

A-E-C Automation Newsletter
7209 Wisteria Way
Carlsbad, CA 92008

A/E Computerization Bulletin
Guidelines
18 Evergreen Drive
P.O. Box 456
Orinda, CA 94563
   Offers a "Special Edition" for medium and large firms and a "Digest Edition" for small firms.

A/E Systems Report
P.O. Box 11316
Newington, CT 06111

The Anderson Report
4505 East Industrial Street
Suite 2J
Simi Valley, CA 93063

CAD/CAM Alert
Reservoir Executive Park
824 Boylston Street
Chestnut Hill, MA 02167

CEPA Newsletter
Society for Computer Applications in Engineering, Planning and Architecture, Inc.
358 Hungerford Drive
Rockville, MD 20850

Computers for Design & Construction
MetaData
441 Lexington Avenue
New York, NY 10017

ECAN-Engineering Computer Applications Newsletter
P.O. Box 3109
Englewood, CO 80111

The S. Klein Newsletter on Computer Graphics
P.O. Box 392
Sudbury, MA 01776

Directories

Auerbach Reports
Auerbach Publishers, Inc.
6560 North Park Drive
Pennsauken, NJ 08109

CAD/CAM Computer Graphics, Survey and Buyers Guide, U.S. Directory of Vendors
Daratech Associates
P.O. Box 410
Cambridge, MA 02238

Construction Computer Applications Directory
Construction Industry Press
1105-F Spring Street
Silver Spring, MD 20910

Datapro
Datapro Research Corporation
1805 Underwood Boulevard
Delran, NJ 08075
Offers various short reports as well as complete, multi-volume directories on all aspects of office automation. Send for their listing of available information.

Design Compudata (annual)
45 Van Brunt Avenue
Dedham MA 02026

> Directory of computer usage in professional design firms including listings of hardware, software, service bureaus, consultants, "how-tos," and a glossary.

Design Professionals Computer Users Directory
45 Van Brunt Avenue
Dedham, MA 02026

> Includes listings of several thousand design firms that are using computers with a description of the hardware and software used.

The S. Klein Directory of Computer Graphics Suppliers
Technology and Business Communications, Inc.
730 Boston Post Road
Suite 27
Sudbury, MA 01776

Conferences/Seminars/Workshops Contact each for current topics, schedules and prices.

> International Conference on Automation and Reprographics in Design Firms. Annual. Best known as "Systems 84" (or current year).
> P.O. Box 11316
> Newington, CT 06111.

> > This exhibit and seminar program has developed into the largest show for professional design firms and is one of the best.

A/E Systems Report Seminars
45 Van Brunt Avenue
Dedham, MA 02026.

> Offers such topics as "Breakthroughs in Design Firm Automation," "How to Finance your Computer," "Computer Graphics in Architecture & Engineering," "How to Select Word Processing Systems," and "Using Microcomputers in the Professional Design Firm." Some are co-sponsored with the *Professional Services Management Journal* and Design Compudata Exchange.

EMA Management Associates, Inc.
1145 Gaskins Road
Richmond, VA 23233

GSB Associates, Inc.
P.O. Box 11316
Newington, CT 06111

Sweet's Seminars.
1805 Underwood Boulevard
Delran, NJ 08075

Professional Services Management Association.
1770 East Dyer Road
Suite 165
Santa Ana, CA 92705

University of Wisconsin, Extension.
Department of Engineering and Applied Science
432 North Lake Street
Madison, WI 53706

Don Thompson Associates.
3247 Embry Hills Drive
Atlanta, GA 30341

Society for Computer Applications in Engineering, Planning, and Architecture, Inc.
358 Hungerford Drive
Rockville, MD 20850

World Computer Graphics Association.
2033 M Street N.W.
Washington, DC 20036

Associations

Association of Computer Users.
P.O. Box 9003
Boulder, CO 80301

Independent Computer Consultants Association.
P.O. Box 27412
St. Louis, MO 63141

Society for Computer Applications in Engineering, Planning, and Architecture, Inc. (CEPA)
358 Hungerford Drive
Rockville, MD 20850

World Computer Graphics Association.
2033 M Street N.W.
Washington, DC 20036

Books/Reports These list only a few of the hundreds of available books and reports available. Consult your library for others if you want to go into any topic in more detail.

Business System Buyer's Guide.
Adam Osborne & Steven Cook. Osborne/McGraw-Hill
630 Bancroft Way
Berkeley, CA 94710.

Buying a Small Computer, ECAN Application Reports, Inexpensive Small Computer Hardware, Software Guide for Small Computers
ECAN
P.O. Box 3109
Englewood, CO 80111

Computer Graphics and Applications: Selecting and Implementing a Turnkey Graphics System
American Institute of Architects
Washington, DC.

How to Select Data Processing Systems.
Frank A. Stasiowski
45 Van Brunt Avenue
Dedham, MA 02026.
Practice Management Associates, 1981.

How to Select Your Small Computer . . . Without Frustration
Association of Computer Users
P.O. Box 9003
Boulder, CO 80301

Implementing an Interactive Computer Graphics System: Some Initial Thoughts
G. Anthony DesRosier
GSB Associates, Inc.
3400 Edge Lane
Thorndale, PA 19372

Planning and Organizing for Computer-Aided Design and Drafting
A/E Systems Report
P.O. Box 11316
Newington, CT 06111

Index